Articulatory Phonetics
Tools for Analyzing the World's Languages

Fourth Edition

Anita C. Bickford and Rick Floyd

SIL International
Dallas, Texas

© by SIL International
First edition 1981
Second edition 1986
Third edition 2003
Fourth edition 2006
Library of Congress Catalog No.: 2005937534
ISBN10: 1-55671-165-4
ISBN13: 978-1-55671-165-7

Printed in the United States of America

Copies of this and other publications of SIL International may be obtained from

International Academic Bookstore
7500 West Camp Wisdom Road
Dallas, TX 75236-5699

Voice: 972-708-7404
Fax: 972-708-7363
E-mail: academic_books@sil.org
Internet: http://www.ethnologue.com

Articulatory Phonetics

Tools for Analyzing the World's Languages

Fourth Edition

Senior Editor

Mary Ruth Wise

Editor

Rhonda Hartell Jones

Production Staff

Rhonda Hartell Jones, Compositor
Kirby O'Brien, Graphic Artist
John Edwards and Ted Goller, Fonts

Contents

Preface

Our primary goals for you as a phonetics student are threefold:

⌘ that you gain confidence as a linguist, capable of transcribing data accurately as a basis for good analysis of a language;

⌘ that you gain confidence as a language learner whose spoken language will sound virtually identical to that of native speakers because you can mimic all the aspects of the language accurately and readily; and

⌘ that you gain facility in using other linguists' written materials, especially their phonetic transcription, from which you can derive data, ideas, and information for further research in your own language(s) of interest.

This textbook is a revision of an earlier book, *A Manual for Articulatory Phonetics*, compiled by Rick Floyd in 1981; a second edition was published in 1986 and a third in 2003. All three versions include many other people's materials and derive their basic organization from articulatory phonetics courses as taught for over sixty years in the training schools of SIL International. We also include much information from sources outside of SIL. However, much of the content is original work by Rick Floyd and reflects techniques and ideas that he used during several years of teaching phonetics. He also did extensive research to provide most of the language data included in the book, some of which is his own field data and some of which he found in published sources. The third edition, besides retaining portions of Floyd's book verbatim and others reworded and amplified but still essentially his, also contains many ideas original to me which have evolved during my years as a phonetics teacher; it also reflects extensive research that I have done in phonetics publications since 1990. This fourth edition is essentially the same as the third except for the chapters on vowels and palatography; many corrections and minor rewordings have been incorporated.

This book is oriented primarily towards native speakers of American English, particularly with reference to examples used to guide pronunciation of new sounds. However, most of the information included should be profitable to students regardless of their native language.

Articulatory phonetics is only one of several disciplines dealing with the production, perception, identification, and categorization of speech sounds. The study of the other disciplines serves to complement, clarify, and explain many areas not covered in an articulatory phonetics course. Rather than attempting to be exhaustive, this manual is meant to introduce you, a beginning linguistics student, to principles that will enable you to approach any language and begin to describe and mimic its sounds with accuracy and confidence.

We have three main purposes for revising Floyd's earlier editions: (1) to update some of the linguistic terminology to match what is in current use, (2) to replace the Americanist transcription system with the symbols approved by the International Phonetic Association (IPA), since those symbols are used more commonly throughout the linguistics world, and (3) to make some pedagogical adjustments, in particular to expand on some of the explanations so that class hours for a course utilizing the book can be spent more on production, mimicry, and transcription practice and less on lecture and explanation of phonetic theory and terminology. We are also including some commonly used symbols from non-IPA transcription systems in the hope that seeing alternative symbols side-by-side with IPA symbols will facilitate your becoming somewhat familiar with the one while focusing on learning the other. This contributes to our third goal above, that of equipping you to use other linguists' materials, regardless of which system they use to transcribe their data.

Besides agreeing wholeheartedly with the credits and acknowledgments that Rick Floyd listed in his 1986 version (Eunice Pike for contributing valuable suggestions and skill as a linguist and phonetician, Norris and

Carol McKinney for guiding him to many of the sources mentioned, and Lil Howland for providing continual enthusiastic encouragement), we would like to express appreciation to Ruth Mary Alexander for her input and comments on the lesson plans and early drafts, to Albert Bickford for his comments and generous contribution of time in helping with computer aspects of the manuscript, to Norris McKinney for his numerous and invaluable suggestions on almost every page, and to Kathryn Keller for her early lesson plans around which these chapters are organized. Our editors, Mary Ruth Wise and Rhonda Hartell Jones have done marvelous, careful editorial work on many drafts of this book and provided gracious encouragement and wisdom. Credit is also due to the SIL graphic artists for providing the face diagrams. Others who gave input and comments on early drafts of the 2003 edition were Dave Whisler, Barbara Allen, Paul Kroeger, and William Sischo. Marvel Bascom also gave input on the lessons plans; Beth Merrill, Gene Burnham, and Joyce Kiester helped with verifying the language data included herein and determined how to credit its sources; Lloyd Milligan and Gene Burnham gave input and corrections from a teacher's perspective, and Sue Montag spent hours proofreading. Others including Ken Olson, Velma Pickett, Kathryn Keller, Kari Ranta, Keren Everett, and Mike Cahill offered very helpful discussions of various issues—they all greatly improved this book. All remaining errors are mine. Finally, we offer thanks and praise to the Lord for including such fascinating stuff in language as he was creating it. What fun it is to work with sound systems and see the wide variety of sounds and combinations that he has built into them, yet all neatly arranged into comprehensible patterns!

Anita C. Bickford, March 2006

1

Sound Identification

Goals

⌘ You will be able to define each of the terms listed at the end of this chapter. They are fundamental to your understanding of the rest of the book.

⌘ You will be able to identify each part of the vocal apparatus by name and to find it on a diagram and in your own mouth.

⌘ You will be able to explain the difference between *articulators* and *places of articulation* and to state which *active articulator* and *passive articulator* is involved in each place of articulation.

Speech sounds are produced by a moving and vibrating stream of air that is shaped and altered in various ways by the vocal tract. There are many parameters by which speech sounds can be identified and classified. These parameters specify where the stream of air comes from, in what direction it is moving, how the vibrations are initiated, what specifically happens to change it as it moves and resonates, and what part or parts of the vocal apparatus interact to cause the change. Six such parameters, sometimes called PHONETIC CHARACTERISTICS,[1] form the basis for the sound identification used in this book. The list is incomplete—there are other parameters that can also be used to identify and classify sounds, but these six are the most basic ones.

State of the vocal folds

The VOCAL FOLDS, which are in the larynx (sometimes called the voice box, and located in the throat), function differently for different sounds. The main differences involve whether they are together or apart and whether or not they are vibrating. At this point, we will consider only two different states of the vocal folds: for VOICED sounds, the vocal folds are close together and vibrating; for VOICELESS sounds, the vocal folds are usually apart and stationary.[2] Examples of voiced sounds include *b*, *d*, and *z*. Examples of voiceless sounds include *p*, *t*, and *s*. We can group these six sounds into pairs whose sounds are identical in all ways except for voicing: *b* and *p; d* and *t; z* and *s*. In each pair, the first sound is voiced and the second is voiceless.

There are several other terms for the vocal folds that you may encounter in linguistic writings: VOCAL LIPS, VOCAL BANDS, VOCAL CORDS. They all mean the same thing.

---

[1]We have chosen not to use the term "phonetic feature" in this text so as to minimize confusion for beginning linguistics students who are also learning to deal with phonological features. Phonological features and phonetic features do not always coincide exactly.

[2]There are other states of the vocal folds and other terms which represent them that will be introduced in chapter 27 "States of the Glottis."

Airstream mechanism and direction of airstream

A stream of air can be set in motion and provide the energy needed for a speech sound by what we refer to as an AIRSTREAM MECHANISM. Each airstream mechanism (of which there are three different possibilities) involves a CAVITY in the vocal apparatus which changes size due to a complex muscle movement or contraction, thus initiating the motion of the air. Table 1.1 shows the three airstream mechanisms, and the cavity and INITIATING MOTION pertinent to each. The INITIATOR(S) of the airstream mechanism, the specific part or parts of the body which move to create the airstream, are listed in the third column. The final column describes the motion of each initiator. The labels in table 1.2 should help identify parts of the vocal apparatus whose names are initially unfamiliar.

Table 1.1. Airstream mechanisms

Airstream mechanism	Cavity	Initiators	Initiating motion
pulmonic	pulmonary	muscles of the rib cage	downward and inward movement
		diaphragm	upward movement
glottalic	pharyngeal	larynx with closed glottis	movement up or down
		walls of the pharynx	contraction or expansion
velaric	oral	back of tongue	closure against back of roof of mouth (velum)
		tongue body	downward movement

Note: "Closed glottis" means that the vocal folds are tightly together, eliminating any space between them.

The airstream for every speech sound moves either inward or outward. An outward airstream, which is normally used in all English speech sounds, is called EGRESSIVE. An inward airstream is called INGRESSIVE. The distinction is crucial only for glottalic air, which may be either ingressive or egressive. Pulmonic air as used in speech sounds is always egressive, and velaric air is always ingressive.[3]

Velic closure and the cavities in which the sound resonates

A crude analogy to the vocal apparatus is a set of tiny rooms (CAVITIES) in which sounds resonate. The two rooms most commonly utilized to distinguish speech sounds are in the mouth (ORAL CAVITY) and the nose (NASAL CAVITY). The third room (the PHARYNGEAL CAVITY) is in the throat above the larynx. There is sometimes also a LABIAL CAVITY between the front teeth and the lips.[4] For now, you can ignore the pharyngeal and labial cavities; they will be discussed more fully in later chapters.

Unlike the rooms in a house, most of these cavities change shape and size freely and often, because their walls are mostly very flexible muscles. (Because the walls of the nasal cavity are bone and cartilage, the shape and volume of this one cavity are fixed.) The size and shape of a cavity in which the airstream moves and vibrates affect the sound.

Different speech sounds are produced by varying the size and shape of the cavities, thus changing the RESONANCES (sound frequencies at which the air vibrates most freely) of the vocal tract, in the same way that rooms of different sizes and shapes in a building have different echoes.

---

[3]For a few sounds, ingressive glottalic or velaric air and egressive pulmonic air may be used simultaneously. They will be introduced in chapters 28 "Implosives" and 36 "Clicks."

[4]Projection and rounding of the lips creates a small cavity between the front teeth and the lips, which modifies the acoustic effect of the oral cavity. Speech sounds involving such lip positions resonate in the labial cavity as well as some combination of the other three cavities.

When the passageway between the nasal and oral "rooms" or cavities is open, there is said to be VELIC OPENING.[5] The upper part of the soft palate (the VELUM), which faces the pharyngeal wall, functions as a door to close off that passageway. When there is VELIC CLOSURE (that is, the velum is raised against the pharyngeal wall, closing the opening to the nasal cavity), air cannot enter the nasal cavity but instead enters only the oral cavity. Figure 1.1 offers side views of the head, tongue, etc., illustrating these two velic positions. Diagrams such as these, called "face diagrams," will be explained more fully in chapter 2.

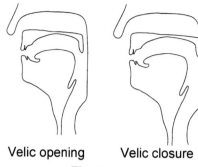

Velic opening   Velic closure

Figure 1.1.

Sounds produced with sound waves resonating in the oral cavity are called ORAL sounds. Sounds produced with sound waves resonating in the nasal cavity (for which there is velic opening) are called NASAL sounds. Some sounds have sound waves resonating in both the oral and nasal cavities, with an air passageway through both the nose and mouth simultaneously. Such sounds (for which there is velic opening) are called NASALIZED sounds.[6]

A somewhat more realistic analogy to the way in which the vocal tract actually functions is that of a tube whose width varies along the length of the tube. As was true for the rooms analogy, variation in the shape of the tube for different speech sounds results in the sounds having different resonances. If there is velic opening, then the nasal branch on the tube is participating in production of the sound; if there is velic closure, the nasal branch is not participating in production of the sound.

Consider the following pairs of sounds: *b* and *m; d* and *n*. In each pair, the vocal tract is shaped the same for the two sounds except for velic closure. For *b* and *d*, which are oral sounds, there is velic closure; for *m* and *n*, which are nasal sounds, there is velic opening.

Manner of articulation

Speech sounds involve a moving and vibrating stream of air that has something happen to it as it moves along. One thing that can happen is for the airstream to be IMPEDED (blocked) to some degree by some part or parts of the vocal mechanism. This alters the shape and size of the resonance cavities also. The MANNER OF ARTICULATION of a sound describes the DEGREE OF IMPEDANCE of the airstream and the type of closure that produces that impedance.

If the airstream is blocked altogether for a given sound, it is said to be COMPLETELY IMPEDED. Such sounds, all of which are consonants, are called STOPS (or occasionally PLOSIVES), for example, *p, t,* and *k*.

If the airstream is blocked quite a bit but not completely, audible turbulence is introduced into the airstream. The airstream for a sound characterized by audible turbulence is said to be GREATLY IMPEDED, and the sound is called a FRICATIVE. (The term fricative resembles the word "friction," and we can think of a fricative as a sound with audible friction.) Examples of fricatives include *s, f,* and *z*. All fricatives are consonants as well.

If the airstream is hardly blocked at all, instead being merely shaped or directed by some part of the tongue and perhaps the lips, then the airstream is said to be SLIGHTLY IMPEDED. Examples of such sounds include vowels like *a, i,* and *o* and approximants like *l* and *w* (to be defined in chapters 13 and 18).[7]

For the three sounds, *d, z,* and *l,* the vocal apparatus is the same in all ways except for how much the tip and sides of the tongue are turned up to impede the airstream, which determines the manner of articulation for these sounds: for *d* (a stop, according to its manner of articulation), the airstream is completely impeded by complete

---

[5]Some linguists call the backside of the uvula the VELIC, saying that "the velic is closed" when the velum is raised to close off passage of the airstream into the nasal cavity and that "the velic is open" when the velum is lowered to permit passage of the airstream into the nasal cavity.

[6]The distinction between sounds labeled *nasal* and *nasalized* is frequently not relevant. In phonological theories that use formal features, a *positive value* on the feature *nasal* is assigned to all sounds made with velic opening, whether or not there is unobstructed airflow through the mouth as well.

[7]For trills, which will be introduced in chapter 26, the airstream is said to be INTERMITTENTLY IMPEDED.

closure of both the tip and the sides of the tongue against the roof of the mouth; for *z* (a fricative), it is greatly impeded by complete closure of the tongue sides but only partial closure of the tongue tip against the roof of the mouth; and for *l* (a lateral approximant), the airstream is slightly impeded since, although the tongue tip is raised in complete closure against the roof of the mouth to shape and direct the airstream, the tongue sides are only slightly raised, resulting in neither closure nor friction between them and the roof of the mouth.

Articulators

The vocal apparatus contains many distinct parts. Carefully study figure 1.2, "Parts of the vocal apparatus," and learn the names of all the parts.[8]

There are two types of articulators. The term ACTIVE ARTICULATOR refers to a movable part of the vocal apparatus (Crystal 2003:33) that impedes or directs the air stream. We have already described sounds according to how much the airstream is impeded during their production. An active articulator is one that moves to cause an impedance. It may be the lower lip, some part of the tongue, or something else in the vocal apparatus.[9]

The other type of articulator is the PASSIVE ARTICULATOR. This is the more fixed part of the mouth that the active articulator touches or gets very close to as it articulates the sound, such as the upper lip, the front teeth, and various parts of the roof of the mouth.[10]

Since there are no clear boundaries drawn on the tongue to indicate where one region ends and the next begins, it is not surprising that there is confusion as to what the "blade" and "front" of the

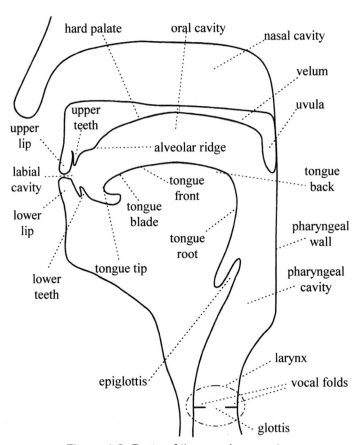

Figure 1.2. Parts of the vocal apparatus.

tongue are and what they do. According to Ladefoged (1993:4), "Behind the blade is what is technically called the front of the tongue; it is actually the forward part of the body of the tongue and lies underneath the hard palate when the tongue is at rest." On p. 7, he then lists the tongue blade as the active articulator of palato-alveolar sounds, and the front of the tongue as the active articulator for palatal sounds. In contrast, Crystal (1997:391) lists the tongue blade and front as equivalent terms but distinguishes between them in his discussion of palato-alveolar sounds on p. 276: "the BLADE of the tongue...makes contact with the alveolar ridge, while the FRONT of the tongue is raised in the direction of the hard palate." On p. 275 he lists the front of the tongue as the articulator of palatal sounds. The first sound in the English word "she" is palato-alveolar, articulated with the tongue blade; the first sound in the English word "key" is palatal, articulated with the tongue front. Ladefoged and Crystal treat palatal sounds as being articulated by the tongue front (which is sometimes called the "top").

---

[8]You will learn in later chapters that some parts of the vocal apparatus function as articulators of speech sounds and others as nonarticulators and, in fact, that some can function as articulators for some sounds and as nonarticulators for others. For now it is sufficient to learn the names of all the labeled parts in figure 1.2.

[9]See table 1.2 for a partial list of the active articulators.

[10]Table 1.2 also gives a partial list of the passive articulators.

Figure 1.3 shows in which directions the various active articulators move and thus which passive articulators they interact with. Experiment with some speech sounds, paying close attention to what part of your mouth is moving to make the sound and where that part is moving to. For example, compare the different tongue movements involved in *d* and *g* and the differences in the actions of your lips and teeth for *m* and *v*.

Since most passive articulators are located along the upper surface of the oral cavity, they are sometimes called UPPER ARTICULATORS. In contrast, most active articulators are located relatively lower in the vocal tract than the corresponding passive ones; active articulators are thus sometimes called LOWER ARTICULATORS. Whenever you see the term ARTICULATOR without specification as to whether it is an active or passive articulator being discussed, you can usually assume it is an active articulator.

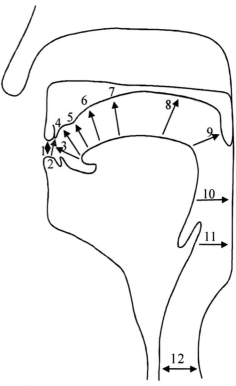

Figure 1.3. Articulator movement.

Place of articulation

Sounds are also described according to their PLACE OF ARTICULATION.[11] To understand the term "place of articulation," you need to consider first what it does *not* refer to. The place of articulation is *not* the place where the active articulator comes in contact with some other part of the vocal apparatus (for example, alveolar ridge or velum); such a place is called the PASSIVE ARTICULATOR. Rather, the "place of articulation" is actually the RELATIONSHIP (or "mapping" or "pairing") between the active and passive articulators as they shape or impede the airstream. Table 1.2 on the next page contains a partial list of the places of articulation and the articulators for each.[12]

The only difference between the pronunciations of the words *lip, lit,* and *lick* is the place of articulation of the final sound: *p* is bilabial, *t* is alveolar, and *k* is velar.

Table 1.3 shows what active articulators are used for each of the most basic places of articulation. Note that some of the active articulators can have a relationship with more than one passive articulator. For example, the tongue tip can articulate a sound between the teeth (the English *th* sound), right behind the top teeth and touching them (Spanish *t, n, l*), or slightly further back along the alveolar ridge, that is, the hard part of the roof of the mouth (English *t, n, l*). These three relationships are called INTERDENTAL, DENTAL, and ALVEOLAR, respectively.

---

[11]Place of articulation is also often called POINT OF ARTICULATION. We choose to refer to a *place* rather than a *point*, since a point has no area and articulations involve areas on the articulators.

[12]The term "place of articulation" may be misleading since it implies that terms specifying the places of articulation will be nouns. Instead, they are adjectives. For example, an articulation made by the tongue tip touching the alveolar ridge is said to be "alveolar" because it is made with the alveolar place of articulation, that is, with the tongue tip and the alveolar ridge. Perhaps it will help you avoid confusion in this matter if you focus on the word *relationship* in the definition and draw a parallel with kinship relationships, such as maternal or filial, which are also labeled with adjectives. In any case, when you give the place of articulation of a sound, it should be an adjectival term such as those listed in the "Place of articulation" column of table 1.2, not a noun.

Table 1.2. Partial list of places of articulation and articulators

	Place of articulation	Active articulator	Passive articulator
1.	bilabial	lower lip	upper lip
2.	labiodental	lower lip	upper teeth
3.	interdental	tongue tip	teeth
4.	dental	tongue tip	behind top teeth
5.	alveolar	tongue tip	alveolar ridge
6.	palato-alveolar	tongue blade	behind alveolar ridge
7.	palatal	tongue front	hard palate
8.	velar	tongue back	front of soft palate; velum
9.	uvular	tongue back	back of soft palate; uvula
10.	pharyngeal	tongue root	back of
11.	glottal	vocal folds	(none)

Table 1.3. Articulation

Active articulator	Place of articulation
lips	bilabial
	labiodental
tongue tip / apex	interdental
	dental
	alveolar
tongue blade	palato-alveolar
tongue front	palatal
tongue back	velar
	uvular
tongue root	pharyngeal
vocal folds	glottal

Note: The IPA usually uses "postalveolar" instead of "palato-alveolar."

Key concepts

Each chapter in this book contains a list of key concepts and terms to serve as a summary of the new material introduced in the chapter.

phonetic parameters / characteristics
state of the vocal folds
> voiced: together and vibrating

> voiceless: apart (usually) and not vibrating

airstream mechanism
initiating motion
initiator
> pulmonic air: pulmonary; diaphragm and/or muscles of ribcage, etc.

> glottalic air: pharyngeal; larynx with closed glottis, etc.

> velaric air: oral; back of tongue against velum, etc.

direction of the airstream
> egressive: pulmonic and glottalic airstreams

> ingressive: glottalic and velaric airstreams

cavity
    oral cavity
    nasal cavity
    (pharyngeal cavity)
    (labial cavity)
resonance
    velic closure / velic opening / velum
    oral, nasal, and nasalized sounds
manner of articulation
    completely impeded (for stops)
    greatly impeded (for fricatives)
    slightly impeded (for vowels, etc.)
articulator: everything in columns two and three of table 1.2 and in figure 1.2
    active (lower, moves)
    passive (upper, remains relatively stationary)
place of articulation: everything in table 1.2 (first column)

Exercises

1.   List the three major airstream mechanisms and their initiators.

Airstream mechanism	Initiators
Pulmonic egressive	muscles of rib cage
	diaphram
glottalic ingressive & egressive	larynx & closed glottis
	walls of the pharynx
Velaric ingressive	back of tongue
	tongue body

2. Study and memorize the terms in figure 1.2.
    Notice especially the velum and parts of the
    tongue. From memory, fill in the list of parts of
    the vocal apparatus numbered on the large facial
    diagram below. Check your answers against figure
    1.2; with a contrasting pen or pencil, fill in any
    labels you missed.

Resonating cavities

1. oral
2. nasal
3. pharyngeal
4. labial

Parts of the tongue

5. tip
6. blade
7. front
8. back
9. root

Other parts of the vocal apparatus

10. lower teeth
11. lower lip
12. upper lip
13. upper teeth
14. alveolar ridge
15. hard palate
16. soft palate (velum)
17. uvula
18. pharyngeal wall
19. larynx
20. vocal cords
21. glottis
22. epiglottis

3. Study and memorize the terms in table 1.2 and table 1.3. From memory, fill in the list of places of articulation numbered on the following facial diagram. Check your answers against table 1.2 and table 1.3; with a contrasting pen or pencil, fill in any labels you missed.

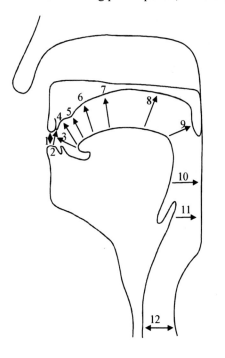

1. bilabial
2. labio dental
3. interdental
4. dental
5. alveolar
6. palatal - alveolar
7. palatal
8. velar
9. uvular
10. pharyngeal
11. epi glottal
12. glottal

4. Describe the first sound in the word "baby," using the six phonetic characteristics explained in this chapter.

State of the vocal folds	voiced
Airstream mechanism and direction of the airstream	pulmonic - outward
Velic opening or closure	closure
Manner of articulation	stop
Articulators	active - upper lip, lower lip
Place of articulation	bilabial

2

Face Diagrams

Goals

⌘ You will be able to explain the purpose of *face diagrams* and a few of their limitations.

⌘ You will be able to use *face diagrams* in a standard way to depict the state of the vocal folds, airstream mechanism and direction of the airstream, velic opening or closure, manner of articulation, and passive and active articulators for a given sound.

The list of phonetic characteristics for identifying speech sounds outlined in chapter 1 may be overwhelming at first. A device called a FACE DIAGRAM[13] is helpful for visualizing what is going on in the vocal apparatus during an individual speech sound. A face diagram, which depicts a side view of the head, jaw, tongue, etc., is a static representation of the six identifying characteristics of a particular speech sound.

Face diagrams have some limitations, being unable to represent the true nature of a stream of speech as a continuum of sounds that almost always slur together without definite boundaries. Nevertheless, a face diagram functions usefully as a cross-sectional representation of the vocal apparatus, frozen at one point in time during the articulation of a speech sound, as, perhaps, one "frame" in a videotape of a spoken word, frozen on "pause" during the utterance of one single speech sound in the word.

A face diagram should include information about each of the six characteristics of sound identification. Instead of using verbal labels, we depict each characteristic of the sound in a standardized pictorial fashion.

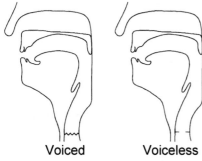

Voiced   Voiceless

Figure 2.1.

1. *State of the vocal folds* is indicated in the larynx, where the vocal folds are located. To show that a sound is voiced, that is, that the vocal folds are vibrating, a wavy line is drawn across the area depicting the larynx. To show that a sound is voiceless, that is, that the vocal folds are apart and not vibrating, a short straight line is drawn on either side of the larynx, with a space between them. (See figure 2.1.)

---

[13]Face diagrams are sometimes called "sagittal sections."

2. *Airstream mechanism* is represented by an arrow near the initiator of the airstream. In the case of a pulmonic airstream, the arrow is drawn just below the glottis (nearly at the bottom of the diagram), not way down by the actual initiators (the diaphragm and muscles of the rib cage), because the face diagram only includes the head and neck, not the chest. Ways to represent the other two mechanisms will be described later.

Direction of the airstream is indicated by the direction in which the arrow is pointing. For egressive pulmonic air (by far the most common situation in speech), the arrow points upward toward the glottis, symbolizing air being pushed up out of the lungs. (See figure 2.2.)

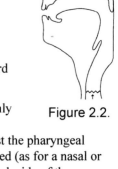

Figure 2.2.

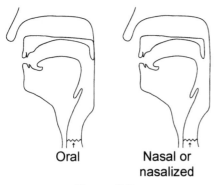

| Oral | Nasal or nasalized |

Figure 2.3.

3. *Velic opening or closure.* To indicate that only the oral resonating cavity is used for a sound, draw the back side of the velum pressed against the pharyngeal wall. To indicate that the nasal cavity is involved (as for a nasal or nasalized sound), allow a space between the back side of the velum and the pharyngeal wall. Think of there being a door to the nasal passage. Remember that for nasal and nasalized sounds that door is open, but for purely oral sounds it is closed. (See figure 2.3.)

4. The *manner of articulation* for a sound is reflected in how close the active articulator is drawn to the passive articulator. We portray a fricative by allowing a bit of space between the articulators, as shown for [f] in figure 2.4. Note that this deviates somewhat from reality, since, for example, your lower lip (active articulator) definitely touches your upper teeth (passive articulator) when you pronounce the fricatives *f* and *v*.

Leaving a small space between the articulators is just a convenient way to symbolize that the airstream is not completely impeded for fricatives. For a stop, the active and passive articulators should actually touch in the drawing, as for [t] in figure 2.5. This symbolizes the complete impedance of the airstream for stops.

5. *Active and passive articulators.* Drawing ARTICULATORS into a face diagram provides information concerning not only the articulators themselves but also the place and manner of articulation for the sound depicted. Carefully draw the active articulator interacting with the pertinent passive articulator.

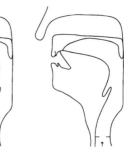

Figure 2.4. [f]   Figure 2.5. [t]

6. *Place of articulation.* If the articulators are correctly portrayed, a face diagram can be read to determine what *place of articulation* is symbolized. Look at figure 2.4. Since the active articulator is the lower lip and the passive articulator is the upper teeth, you know that the sound depicted in the diagram is labiodental. In figure 2.5, the tongue tip drawn to touch the alveolar ridge tells you that the sound depicted is alveolar.

One more thing to note about the preceding completed face diagrams is that they include all the articulators, not merely the ones that are directly involved in production of the sound depicted. For example, the tongue and lower teeth are drawn into the depiction of [f], even though they are neither active nor passive articulators of that sound. The less pertinent organs of the vocal tract are not removed from the diagram simply because they are not actively involved in producing a certain sound; even the neutral (relaxed) position they assume during production of a sound affects its acoustical properties. Consider how different the pronunciation of a person without teeth is, even on those segments that do not directly involve the teeth as active or passive articulators. Thus, it is common practice in face diagrams to include all articulators, not just the ones directly involved in the production of the sound being depicted.

Limitations of face diagrams

Before we leave this introduction to face diagrams, a few limitations need to be noted as to what can be shown in a face diagram. It is difficult to draw vowels on face diagrams since their articulators' positions are much less easily defined and described than those of consonants; indeed, analysts do not usually even try to specify places of articulation for vowels. Certain lip positions and some things that the sides of the tongue do in certain sounds cannot easily be shown because of the side view nature of a face diagram. You will also learn about other modifications to the consonants that cannot as easily be drawn on face diagrams because this would necessitate showing transition and change rather than a static representation of a frozen moment. However, for a large number of the sounds that are covered in this book, face diagrams can be very useful for presenting the basic facts about their production.

Key concepts and symbols

face diagram
lines in vocal fold area: wavy to show voicing, straight and broken to show voicelessness
arrow: placement of arrow indicates which airstream mechanism is used, direction of arrow indicates direction
    of airstream
velum: as an open or closed door to the nasal cavity
articulators: both active and passive ones drawn in to show how the sound is made; touching each other to
    depict a stop, slightly separated to depict a fricative

Exercises

1. Identify the six characteristics of each sound depicted in the two face diagrams shown below.

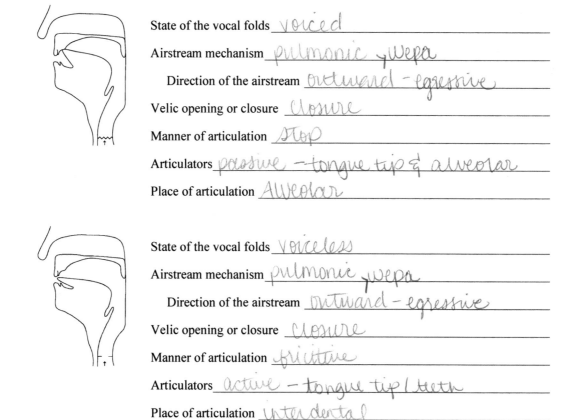

State of the vocal folds _voiced_

Airstream mechanism _pulmonic, wepa_

    Direction of the airstream _outward - egressive_

Velic opening or closure _closure_

Manner of articulation _stop_

Articulators _passive — tongue tip & alveolar_

Place of articulation _Alveolar_

State of the vocal folds _voiceless_

Airstream mechanism _pulmonic, wepa_

    Direction of the airstream _outward - egressive_

Velic opening or closure _closure_

Manner of articulation _fricative_

Articulators _active — tongue tip / teeth_

Place of articulation _interdental_

2. Complete a face diagram for the first sound in the word "baby." In chapter 1, you thought through the six characteristics of the sound; now you just need to draw their representations.

3

Fricatives

Goals

⌘ You will be able to define a *fricative* as a speech sound made with great impedance of the airstream, causing sufficient turbulence between the articulators to result in audible noise.

⌘ You will *control* the eight fricative sounds given in table 3.1. (By *controlling* sounds, we mean being able to recognize and mimic them, read them when presented in written form, and represent them in writing yourself, using the symbols taught in the chapter. Most chapters will have the goal of controlling the sounds presented there.)

⌘ You will be able to define a *segment* as a speech sound.

⌘ You will be able to explain the use of brackets [ ] around *phonetic representations.*

⌘ You will be able to explain the concepts of *stress* and *stressed syllable,* and will be able to read and write the *stress mark* (') preceding the syllable to which it pertains.

⌘ You will be able to explain the concept of *technical names* for sounds and be able to state the technical name for each of the eight fricatives in the table.

⌘ You will be able to construct and use various *frame drills* with *consistent frames* to help you learn the production of new or difficult sounds.

⌘ You will be able to recognize and explain various positions in which a segment can occur relative to a word: *word-initial, word-medial,* and *word-final,* relative to other segments: *intervocalic,* or standing alone: *in isolation.*

⌘ You will be able to draw and read a face diagram of each of the eight fricatives in the table.

A FRICATIVE, already mentioned in previous chapters, is a SEGMENT (speech sound) in which the airstream is greatly but not completely impeded. Turbulence in the airstream at the point where the articulators meet produces audible noise—a "hissing" or "buzzing" sound that may sound like "friction," hence the term fricative.

Table 3.1 introduces the symbols for eight fricative sounds. They are organized in columns according to their places of articulation and in two rows according to their voicing.

Table 3.1. Fricatives

	Bilabial	**Labiodental**	**Interdental**	**Velar**	
voiceless	ɸ	f	θ	x	fricative
voiced	β	v	ð	ɣ	(with egressive pulmonic air)
passive articulator	upper lip	upper teeth	teeth	velum	
active articulator	lower lip	lower lip	tongue tip	tongue back	

Technical names

Every speech sound has a unique label called its TECHNICAL NAME, in which the terms specifying its articulatory features are arranged in a standard order. All the pertinent information to be included in a sound's technical name can usually be found by reading clockwise around a table of sounds, starting from the left.

The technical name for [β], for example, is "voiced bilabial fricative with egressive pulmonic air." The first column on the far left of a sound symbol table deals with the state of the vocal folds. In the case of [β], that is "voiced." The next set of labels in the table, reading clockwise, is the row of terms indicating place of articulation, which for [β] is "bilabial."

At the far right of the table, you find a label describing the manner of articulation ("fricative"), then direction of the airstream ("egressive"), and finally the airstream mechanism that initiates the airstream ("pulmonic air"). "With egressive pulmonic air" is rather long to write out for sound after sound, so you may wish to abbreviate that to "wepa" once you are sure that you will remember what the abbreviation stands for. Since egressive pulmonic air is by far the most common air mechanism for speech sounds, you may eventually omit mention of it in the technical name. Naturally if some other airstream mechanism is involved, that must be explicitly mentioned.

Note: Explicit mention of specific articulators is excluded from technical names, being redundant since information as to which passive and active articulators interact to produce a sound is implicit in the place of articulation term, which follows the term for state of the vocal folds in each technical name. For example, for the sound [β], the place of articulation term "bilabial" in the technical name identifies that sound's articulators as the two lips. We have included the two articulator rows in table 3.1 simply as a reminder, since these places of articulation are new to many students using this book. Such information is not usually included in tables of this type and will not appear in most tables in future chapters of this book.

Technical names do not mention resonating cavities at all. No fricatives produced with nasal resonance have been found in languages, so the feature "oral" is inherent in the term "fricative" and as such need not be mentioned explicitly. ([h] is a marginal case.) In fact, no technical name needs to include the word "oral," since that is considered to be the default characteristic for a sound unless it is explicitly labeled as "nasal" or "nasalized." However, there will be sounds for which you will need to specify the characteristic "nasal" or "nasalized," to differentiate them from their more common oral counterparts, for example, the sounds introduced in chapters 6 "Nasals" and 12 "Nasalized Vowels."

Use of brackets

Brackets [ ] around phonetic symbols indicate that everything between them is a PHONETIC REPRESENTATION or PHONETIC TRANSCRIPTION. In this book, you may ignore brackets for the most part, because most of the transcriptions are phonetic representations. However, in other contexts linguists often need to differentiate between phonetic and other kinds of representations (for example, phonemic data or practical writing systems), which are usually marked in other ways.

Production hints

In each chapter introducing new sounds throughout this book, we will provide production hints, in an attempt to facilitate your correct production of the new sounds presented in the chapter. For sounds which occur in English, we will include English words as examples. For sounds which do not occur in English, we will try to provide example words from other languages commonly learned in school by English speakers. If you do not speak the language from which an example is drawn, simply ignore that example, as it might be misleading to you.

[f] lower lip against upper teeth; voiceless; as in English "fife."

[v] lower lip against upper teeth; voiced; as in English "valve."

[θ] tongue tip between the upper and lower front teeth or just behind the upper front teeth; voiceless; as in English "thigh."

[ð] same tongue position as for [θ], but voiced; as in English "thy."

[β] lips brought together gently, kept relaxed and flat, neither pressed together tightly nor pursed; blow through your lips very gently, as if to blow out a small birthday candle; voiced; as in the last syllable of many Spanish verbs like "estaba;" try saying the English phrase "a bubble above Bobby" with very lazy lips and you should approximate the sound [β].

[ɸ] same lip configuration as for [β] above, but voiceless; try saying the English phrase "apple pie" with very lazy lips, and you should approximate the sound [ɸ].

[x] tongue in the same position as for the first sound in English "cool" but slightly dropped, so there is a small space between it and the roof of the mouth and articulating lazily; pass air through this space gently; voiceless; as in German "ach" and similar to Spanish "ajo."

[ɣ] same tongue position as for [x] above, but voiced; similar to the consonant in the middle of Spanish "hago."

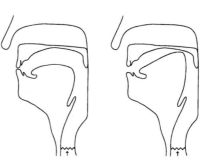

Face diagrams of fricatives

Figures 3.1 and 3.2 show face diagrams for the [β] and [ɣ] sounds, which depict all the features described previously. Notice especially the small separation between the articulators, indicating great but not complete impedance of the airstream.

Figure 3.1. [β]   Figure 3.2. [ɣ]

Frame drills

FRAME DRILLS provide useful practice for learning to produce new sounds. To construct a frame drill, choose an invariant context into which to insert new consonant sounds, perhaps two identical vowels, one on either side of the new consonant. Then practice each new consonant systematically in this CONSISTENT FRAME. Since we have not taught you any vowels yet, let us start with a simple one, [a], pronounced like the "ah" you are supposed to say when the doctor looks into your throat (but do not stick out your tongue!). Put each of these eight fricatives between two [a]s and say those eight "words" aloud in sequence. As you say them, focus your attention on what your tongue and lips are doing differently for each fricative.

aˈɸa

aˈfa

aˈθa

aˈxa

aˈβa

aˈva

aˈða

aˈɣa

The tiny raised vertical line preceding each fricative in the frame drill above is a STRESS MARK, indicating that the syllable following it should receive STRESS. For now, just make that STRESSED SYLLABLE a little bit louder. You will find a fuller discussion of stress in chapter 11. In linguistic writings in which careful phonetic transcription is not the focus, you will very often find stress indicated with an acute accent mark over the vowel in the stressed syllable, for example, [afá] rather than [aˈfa]. However, in this book we will consistently use the raised vertical line, the stress symbol officially recognized by the International Phonetic Association.[17]

It is useful to vary the way in which you group the "words" of a frame drill. For example, as the words are listed above, the first four fricatives are all voiceless, the last four all voiced. (All of the [a]s in the consistent frame are voiced.) Try flowing the first four "words" together into one long "word" [aɸafaθaxa], placing stress on whichever syllable you please, and notice that the voicing is "on-again-off-again," interrupted once for each fricative, showing that each of those first four fricatives is voiceless. Now flow the last four words together, [aβavaðaɣa], and notice that the voicing never stops throughout the whole "word," a sure indication that those fricatives are voiced.

Another good way to arrange the "words" in a frame drill is in pairs according to like places of articulation. For example, [v] and [f] are both labiodental. Say them together as a pair: [aˈva], [aˈfa], being sure that nothing changes anywhere in your vocal apparatus except for the state of the vocal folds (vibrating for voiced [v], not vibrating for voiceless [f]). [x] is easier for most people to say than is [ɣ], so pairing these two this way can be helpful in learning the harder one by analogy with the easier one: [aˈxa], [aˈɣa].

In general, a given frame drill will be most beneficial to your production of the segments that you repeat the most as you practice that frame drill, that is, the segments in the consistent frame. The part that varies from word to word in a frame drill will be repeated less, and your production of that varying portion will consequently be facilitated less by that particular drill. Therefore, to take advantage of frequent repetition, once you have mastered the basic frame drill, you should sometimes include in the consistent frame sounds that are really hard for you. For example, if you have trouble with the [ɣ] sound, try tacking it onto the beginning of each word in the original frame drill (as shown in the left column in the following set of drills) or onto the end of each word (as shown in the middle column), or place a varying consonant at the beginning of each word and [ɣ] in the middle (as shown in the right column).

ɣaˈɸa	aˈɸaɣ	ˈɸaɣa
ɣaˈfa	aˈfaɣ	ˈfaɣa
ɣaˈθa	aˈθaɣ	ˈθaɣa
ɣaˈxa	aˈxaɣ	ˈxaɣa
ɣaˈβa	aˈβaɣ	ˈβaɣa
ɣaˈva	aˈvaɣ	ˈvaɣa
ɣaˈða	aˈðaɣ	ˈðaɣa
ɣaˈɣa	aˈɣaɣ	ˈɣaɣa

Placing an especially difficult sound in a different position in each of several frame drills, as we did in these three related drills, has the added advantage of drilling your production of that difficult sound in several different positions in a word. The difficult [ɣ] sound is WORD-INITIAL (at the beginning of the word) in

---

[17]Pullum and Ladusaw (1996:208) call it a "vertical stroke (superior)." (Editor's note: The IPA "stroke" is slightly thinner than the font used for stress in this book.)

the left-hand drill, WORD-FINAL (at the end of the word) in the middle drill, and both WORD-MEDIAL (in the middle of the word) and INTERVOCALIC (between vowels) in the right-hand drill. You may find it very easy to produce a certain sound intervocalically but have great difficulty with it word initially or word finally.

You should include at least one vowel in your consistent frame, as it is not particularly beneficial to practice pronouncing consonants IN ISOLATION (all by themselves, out of any context). Sometimes it is best to use easy vowels so you can focus your attention on the harder consonant sounds as you say the words. But if there is a vowel that is particularly difficult for you (chapter 7 provides some possibilities), try including it in the consistent frame context, so you repeat it frequently as you practice the drill.

Common alternative symbols

There are two primary systems for transcribing speech sounds, one which is defined by the International Phonetic Association (IPA), and the other which represents traditional usage by linguists studying languages in the Americas.[18] We feature the IPA system in this book. However, when an Americanist symbol, or perhaps another symbol from some other less major system, is used quite commonly in the linguistic literature, we include it in a special section like this, called "Common alternative symbols." We recommend that you focus on learning the IPA system. It would be ideal, however, if you could learn to recognize other commonly used symbols, so you can read data in linguistic articles regardless of what system the author(s) used.

Each of the alternative symbols given in table 3.2 is from the Americanist transcription system. The symbols are often called "barred p," "barred b," "barred d," and "barred g."

Table 3.2. Fricative symbols

IPA symbol	Common alternative symbol
ɸ	₱
β	ƀ
ð	đ
ɣ	ǥ

Key concepts and symbols

fricative
segment
technical name
all the symbols in table 3.1, and the technical name describing each one
phonetic representation / phonetic transcription
frame drill / consistent frame
word-initial / word-medial / word-final / intervocalic / in isolation

---

[18]The Americanist system is also used widely throughout the world by linguists who received their transcription training at the SIL schools, since their teachers also used the Americanist tradition. However, the Americanist system is by no means peculiar to SIL. Many other linguists use a hybrid of the two systems and perhaps other individual symbols not included in either of these two main systems.

Oral exercises

1.   Practice each frame drill in the chapter aloud at least three times, varying the order of the "words" to suit your needs. If you have a fricative other than the [ɣ] sound that causes you trouble, insert it in various positions in the repeated frames.

2.   Practice saying the following words aloud.

Seri of Mexico (Stephen Marlett, personal communication)

ɸaɸa   '(said to the moon, equivalent of "when I wish upon a star")'

German (Bickford, field notes)

ax   '(exclamation similar to "wow")'

Spanish (various dialects; Bickford, field notes)

aθ   'do, make (impeartive)'
'aɣa   'do, does (subjunctive)'
a'xa   'aha'
βa   'he/she/it goes'
'βaxa   'under, lower (feminine)'
'ðaβa   'he/she/it gave (imperfect)'
'ðaða   'given (feminine)'
'faxa   'sash'

Written exercises

1.   Give phonetic symbols (IPA) for the sounds depicted in the following face diagrams.

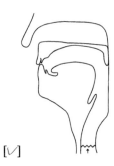

[ʌ]

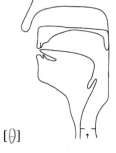

[θ]

2.   Complete face diagrams and write the technical names of [x], [ɸ], and [ð].

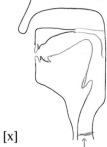

[x]

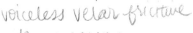

voiceless velar fricative with egressive pulmonic air

[ɸ]

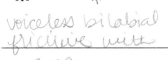

voiceless bilabial fricative with epa

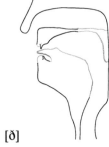

[ð]

voiceless interdental fricative with epa

3. Write the place of articulation for each of the following sounds.

    [f] _labiodental_

    [ɣ] _velar_

    [ð] _interdental_

    [β] _bilabial_

4. Write the active articulator for each of the following sounds.

    [f] _lower lip_

    [ɣ] _tongue back_

    [ð] _tongue tip_

    [β] _lips_

Transcription conversion exercises

1. Convert the following words from IPA symbols to Americanist symbols.

    [aˈβa] _aˈƀa_

    [aˈɸa] _aˈpa_

    [aˈða] _aˈđa_

    [aˈɣa] _aˈga_

2. Write the IPA equivalents of the following Americanist symbols.

    [đ] _ð_

    [ƀ] _β_

    [g̶] _ɣ_

    [ƥ] _ɸ_

3. List the fricative symbols from this chapter that are the same in both major transcription systems.

    f

    v

    x

4

Stops

Goals

⌘ You will be able to define a *stop* as a sound in which the airstream is completely impeded.

⌘ You will control the ten stops in table 4.1.

⌘ You will be able to give technical names for the ten stops in table 4.1.

⌘ You will be able to state the difference between *voiced, voiceless,* and *voiceless aspirated* stops, as well as the concepts of *aspiration* and *voice-onset time.*

⌘ You will be able to read and draw face diagrams for the ten stops in the table.

STOPS[16] are sounds in which the airstream is completely impeded ("stopped"). Table 4.1 organizes ten stop symbols for you. Three of the stops are bilabial, three alveolar, three velar, and one glottal. There are three voiced stops symbolized, four voiceless ones and three voiceless ones with ASPIRATED RELEASE. The IPA symbols are the only ones in common use for these ten sounds.

Table 4.1. Stops

	Bilabial	Alveolar	Velar	Glottal		
voiceless	p^h	t^h	k^h		aspirated	
voiceless	p	t	k	ʔ		stop
voiced	b	d	g			(wepa)
passive articulator	upper lip	alveolar ridge	front of velum			
active articulator	lower lip	tongue tip	tongue back	vocal folds		

Aspirated release of stops

An ASPIRATED sound is one that is released with an audible puff of air called ASPIRATION, a period of voicelessness following the release of the articulation. You can feel the aspiration if you hold your hand close to

---

[16]Occasionally you will encounter the term *plosive* rather than *stop*. Some linguists use the two terms interchangeably. Others consider plosives to be a subset of stops; some say that plosives are stops made with egressive pulmonic airstream, while others define plosives as released stops. Because of the inconsistent usage of the term, we have chosen not to use it, instead referring to all these terms simply as stops.

your mouth as you say the English words "pool," "tool," and "cool." The stops that begin those three words are all aspirated. Aspirated release of voiceless sounds is symbolized by a small superscript "h" following the basic symbol for the sound itself, for example, [pʰ] for the first sound in "pool."

Technical names of stops

Like fricatives, stops have technical names that can be derived by reading the labels on the symbol table clockwise. For example, [b] is a "voiced bilabial stop (wepa)," and [tʰ] is a "voiceless alveolar aspirated stop (wepa)." Again there is some information that is not stated explicitly because it is the default situation. You never have to include the word "unaspirated" in a technical name, as that is assumed to be the default case. From here on we will also omit the specification "wepa." Unless some other is specified, we will assume this to be the default airstream mechanism and direction.

Face diagrams of stops

Compare the two face diagrams in figures 4.1 and 4.2. Notice that the place of articulation for both sounds is the same (velar), as are the state of the vocal folds (vibrating, for voiced sounds), airstream mechanism and direction of airstream (wepa), and velic closure (for oral sounds).

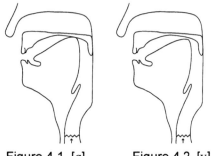

The only difference between these two face diagrams is the degree of closure depicted between the articulators. There is complete closure depicted in the left-hand face diagram of the stop [g], that is, the back of the tongue actually touches the velum in the drawing. By contrast, less impedance is depicted in the diagram of the fricative [ɣ], by means of a small gap drawn between the back of the tongue and the velum. In face diagrams for stops, complete impedance of the airstream should always be depicted by drawing the active articulator touching the passive articulator.

Figure 4.1. [g]   Figure 4.2. [ɣ]

Note: Aspiration cannot conveniently be shown on a face diagram, since it involves relative timing and coordination of movements, not just a frozen moment in time. Thus, a face diagram of [pʰ] will look just like that for [p].

Glottal stop

The GLOTTAL STOP at the far right of table 4.1 deserves special discussion. This is a sound that occurs frequently in English but is seldom included in the spelling of English words. Consequently, many English speakers are not even aware that they have been articulating glottal stops all their lives! Say the word "awe" several times with a brief pause between repetitions. Did you notice the slight catch in your throat just before the vowel each time? That is a glottal stop. There is a glottal stop at the beginning of most English words that begin with a vowel.[17] There is a glottal stop in the middle of the English expression "uh-oh!" (an interjection used when something goes wrong). There is also a glottal stop in the middle of the negative expressions "huh-uh" and "hmm-mm." Glottal stops are very common in English, but we rarely notice them because their presence or absence never determines the meanings of words, so they are not included in the English writing system.

However, in some languages they are very important since two words with different meanings can be exactly alike except that one contains a glottal stop and the other does not. For example, in the Sui language of China,[18] [da]

---

[17]Indeed, presence or absence of a glottal stop before an English word that is spelled with an initial vowel can be an indicator of whether or not that vowel is truly phonetically word initial. If you say the English word "use," which is spelled with an initial "u" vowel, you will not insert a glottal stop before it because there is actually a "y" sound (functioning as a consonant) preceding the "u" vowel. "Use" is not truly a vowel-initial word, so it is not subject to the rule that inserts glottal stop before a word-initial vowel in English.

[18]E. Pike 1978:73.

means 'eye' and [ʔda] means 'to erect'. In chapter 17, "Glottal Consonants," you will encounter many more examples, as well as hints to facilitate hearing such contrasts. (It is important to become aware of them.)

There is no such thing as a voiced glottal stop—it is physically impossible to produce one. That means that "voiceless" is inherent in the term "glottal stop" and need not be included in the technical name of this sound. As for aspirated glottal stops, they do occur but not with the same frequency and distribution[19] as other aspirated stops. Consequently, we will not deal with aspirated glottal stops until chapter 22, which specifically treats the type of context in which they do occur.

Figure 4.3 shows one possible face diagram for the glottal stop. Besides the arrow indicating egressive pulmonic airstream, the only pertinent part of the diagram is the straight line drawn across the larynx, indicating closure of the vocal folds, the articulators of this sound. The positions of other parts of the vocal apparatus are irrelevant for this sound because the airstream is completely impeded before it even reaches them. Notice the differences in your lips, jaw position, and velic opening for the glottals in "hmm-mm," "huh-uh," and "uh-oh." This diagram depicts the vocal tract during the glottal stop in "uh-oh."

Figure 4.3. [ʔ]

Production hints

[ʔ] It is often more difficult to avoid inserting a glottal stop where it is not wanted than to make one where it is appropriate. See the foregoing discussion. Try saying "uh-oh!" which has a glottal stop at the beginning and between the two vowels. Now try saying it without the glottal stop in the middle. Try this with various pairs of vowels with glottal stops between and then without such that the vowels flow smoothly from one to the next. Then try real words like "Laos," "chaos," "oasis," "owing," "per diem," etc., first as they are normally pronounced, then with glottal stops interrupting the flow from one vowel to the next.

[pʰ], [tʰ], and [kʰ] occur as the first sounds in the English words "pool," "tool," and "cool."

[p], [t], and [k] occur as the second sounds in the English words "spool," "stool," and "school." The phonological system of English calls for unaspirated stops following the "s" sound. Hold your hand or a slip of paper up to your lips and note the difference between the stops in "pool / spool," "tool / stool," and "cool / school."

It is often difficult for English speakers to produce voiceless unaspirated stops without an "s" preceding them. To isolate these sounds, pronounce those three English words again but make the initial "s" at first very long and then progressively shorter:

ssssspool...ssspool…spool...pool

ssssstool....ssstool…stool...tool

sssssschool…ssschool…school...cool

Now try saying those three words again, but this time just think the long "s" and then say the rest of the word aloud. Check your aspiration level by holding your hand in front of your mouth. You should not feel any little puff of air following [p], [t], or [k].

Since all Spanish stops are unaspirated, you might be able to achieve these sounds by simply imitating a Spanish speaker's pronunciation of such English phrases as "Peter Piper picked a peck of pickled peppers," "two times ten is twenty," or "Coca Cola is cool."

It may seem that [b], [d], and [g] should be easy to produce since all of those letters occur in the English alphabet.[20] In fact, however, very few English speakers put much voicing on their voiced stops, especially in certain specific environments such as utterance initially. Thus, the English sounds written with the letters "b," "d," and "g" are often actually phonetically closer to [p], [t], and [k] than to [b], [d], and [g]. As such, it is often hard to pronounce or hear the difference between voiced and voiceless stops. To train yourself to voice stops fully, as speakers of many languages do, practice saying sequences such as [aba], [ada], [aga] while holding one

---

[19]For example, no known language uses an aspirated glottal stop word initially.

[20]Note, however, the difference in shape between the IPA character [g] and the "g" typical of fonts used for ordinary typeset materials.

hand on your throat to feel the vibration of your vocal folds.[21] As you say the words, they should never stop vibrating. Gradually shorten the first vowel until you are saying just [ba], [da], [ga], with strong voicing on each stop. If you are not sure whether or not you are really voicing those stops, say [apa], [ata], [aka], again with your hand on your throat, and note what the cessation of vibrations feels like during the stops. Now go back to saying [aba], [ada], [aga] and start the above practice cycle again.

It may seem at times that phonetics is more of a physical education course than a linguistics course. Make use of your hands, a mirror, and anything else that helps you produce these sounds and assess the correctness of your production.

Voice-onset time

VOICE-ONSET TIME (VOT) refers to the point in time at which the vocal folds begin vibrating relative to the release of the articulator that has been impeding the airstream (Ladefoged 1993). VOT helps us to understand the differences between voicing, voicelessness, and aspiration more precisely. Consider the following three sequences of sounds:

[pa] The voicing for the vowel begins *at virtually the same moment* that the articulators for the consonant are released (that is, at the moment when the lips open).

[pʰa] Here the voicing does not begin until *after* the lips open and typically a puff of air has escaped from the lungs. This tiny bit of lag time is the aspirated release of the stop, and how long it lasts will vary from language to language.

[ba] In this case the voicing starts *before* the lips open for the vowel. In some languages, voicing on a voiced stop begins simultaneously with the closure of the articulators for the stop. In other languages, there may be a brief delay between when the articulators close and when voicing begins. In this book, a word-initial stop will be considered voiced only if vibration of the vocal folds precedes release of the airstream.

This presentation of stops has shown three separate voice-onset times: (1) voicing beginning simultaneously with release of articulators, (2) voicing beginning after release of articulators, and (3) voicing beginning before release of articulators. These three possibilities allow for a whole continuum of voice-onset times, and indeed acoustic analysis of speech in various languages reveals that a whole continuum of voice-onset times occurs from language to language. Figure 4.4 illustrates some of the possibilities:

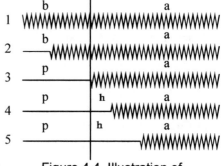

The first two stops are considered to be voiced [b], even though the second has voicing for a shorter time before release of the articulators.

The third is a voiceless stop, [p], with release of the lips and start of voicing occurring simultaneously.

The fourth and fifth stops are considered to be voiceless aspirated [pʰ], although delay between release of the articulators and start of voicing on the fourth is much shorter than on the fifth.

Figure 4.4. Illustration of voice onset times.

A note about handwriting phonetic symbols

Individual people's handwriting styles vary greatly, and that variation is perfectly acceptable when the handwriting is used nontechnically. However, it is important to write phonetic symbols carefully with as standard a style as possible, not indulging in tendencies to be unique and creative simply for the sake of convenience or nonconformity. On the other hand, there are significant differences between how some phonetic

---

[21]It requires more care to maintain voicing throughout velar stops than throughout stops made at places further forward in the mouth, because there is less available space in which air coming through the glottis can accumulate between the velum and the glottis than between the alveolar ridge or the lips and the glottis. Thus, it should not be too surprising that many languages have sound units [b] and [d] but not [g].

symbols will look depending on whether they are handwritten, typed on a typewriter, or printed on a computer. One example is [g], which when handwritten should be "g," plain and clear and without embellishments, as opposed to the typewritten symbol "g." (This is true of the Americanist fricative symbol [ɣ] as well.) The glottal stop symbol, [ʔ], can be handwritten without the serif at the bottom: [ʔ]. Other examples will arise in later chapters.

The symbol [t], when handwritten, needs to have a curved tail on it, not just a straight vertical line. This is to differentiate it from [l] (which will sometimes have a slash through it, [ɫ]) and from some other phonetic symbols with which it can be confused.

Key concepts

stop / plosive
symbols and technical names for all sounds in table 4.1.
aspiration / aspirated / unaspirated
voice-onset time (VOT)

Oral exercises

1. Practice saying aloud the following frame drills three times each.

ˈpʰaba	gaˈpʰa	ˈtapʰa
ˈpaba	gaˈpa	ˈtapa
ˈbaba	gaˈba	ˈtaba
ˈtʰaba	gaˈtʰa	ˈtatʰa
ˈtaba	gaˈta	ˈtata
ˈdaba	gaˈda	ˈtada
ˈkʰaba	gaˈkʰa	ˈtakʰa
ˈkaba	gaˈka	ˈtaka
ˈgaba	gaˈga	ˈtaga
ˈʔaba	gaˈʔa	ˈtaʔa

2. Practice saying aloud the following words three times each.
    American English

ˈpʰapa	'papa'
tʰatʰ	'tot'
kʰab	'cob'
datʰ	'dot'
gad	'God'
ʔad	'odd'

Sui of China (E. Pike 1978:12; Fang-Kuei Li; tone omitted)

pa   'parent's elder sister'
pʰa   'blue'
ba   'to add'
ɸa   'cloth'
ta   'to pass'
tʰa   'to lose'
da   'eye'
ka   'hard'

Written exercises

1. Determine what sound is depicted in this face diagram. Write its symbol, technical name, and enough prose to explain what you saw in the diagram to lead you to your answer, for example, "vocal folds vibrating."

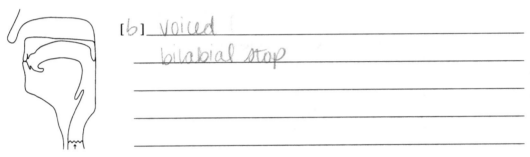

[b] voiced
bilabial stop

2. Draw face diagrams of [d] and [t]. How do they differ?

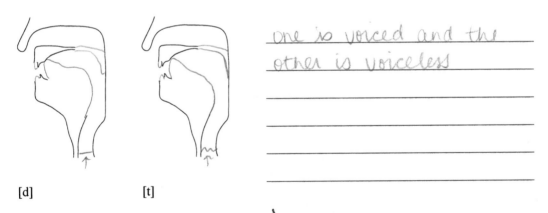

[d]   [t]

one is voiced and the
other is voiceless

3. Arrange the following strings of sounds according to the voice-onset times for the stops involved, from earliest to latest onset of voicing: [atʰa], [ada], [ata]   [ata] [ada] [atʰa]

4. List all the differences you can think of between the sounds [β] and [pʰ]. What phonetic characteristics do the two sounds have in common?

voiced/voiceless, fricative/stop

bilabial,

5.   Write technical names for the following stops.

[p] voiceless bilabial stop

[d] voiced alveolar stop

[kʰ] voiceless velar stop

[ʔ] glottal stop

5

Vowels

Goals

⌘ You will be able to explain the difference between *vowels* and *consonants* and to define the phonetic term *vowel* concisely as a *"central oral sonorant."*

⌘ You will learn that the phonological boundaries between vowels and consonants are somewhat fuzzy and that in some languages a few segments that are phonetically vowels will function phonologically as consonants and vice versa.

⌘ You will be able to control all the vowels presented in the chapter using IPA symbols, and, by referring to tables in this book, you will be able to convert transcriptions of vowels from Americanist into IPA.

⌘ You will be able to give the technical name for each vowel in the IPA system.

⌘ You will be able to explain, recognize auditorily, mimic, and read from a transcription the difference between *glided* and *unglided* vowels and will be able to pronounce consistently all the vowels in the figures in this chapter as unglided vowels.

Articulatory characteristics of vowels

We have been looking at all the sounds presented so far with a number of questions in mind: What parts of the vocal apparatus move? Where do they move to? How? In what sequence do the various movements take place? By answering ARTICULATORY questions like these, we are able to explain why one speech sound is distinct from another.

What, then, are the articulatory parameters for vowels? It should be stated straightaway that describing vowels in terms of the places of articulation used for consonant description is not very helpful since the "location" of a vowel articulation is much less clear-cut. For one thing, vowels form a continuum of sounds rather than being neatly divisible into separate pinpointable units. In addition, the degree of impedance of the airstream is so minimal that places of articulation and articulators are not easily determined. Also, x-ray photography studies have shown that consonant sounds adjacent to vowels affect the tongue positions used on the vowels (the reverse is somewhat true as well); thus, two vowels perceived as being identical may in fact be produced with different tongue shapes owing to the articulatory characteristics of the surrounding sounds.[22]

---

[22]Phoneticians who view vowels as having specific articulators would consider the articulator for front and central vowels to be the tongue front, articulating more or less in the region of the palate, and the articulator of back vowels to be the tongue back, articulating more or less in the region of the velum. We might say that the active articulator for vowels is the part of the tongue that is probably highest in the mouth.

If we cannot neatly characterize vowels in terms of places of articulation, what parameters *are* relevant?

First of all, vowel qualities are affected by different positions of the tongue in the mouth, both front-to-back and up-and-down. The vowel in the English word "bee" (symbolized [i]) is produced with the tongue farther forward in the mouth than for the vowel in the word "boo" (symbolized [u]). The face diagram in figure 5.1 shows approximate relative positions of the tongue on these two vowels. (We will not be using face diagrams of vowels, since the articulatory gestures for vowels are more fluid and variable than they are for consonants. The two face diagrams in this chapter are only included to illustrate a point.)

Likewise, the vowel in the American English word "bat" (symbolized [æ]) is produced with the jaw farther open and thus the tongue at a lower height in the mouth than for the vowel in the word "beat" (symbolized [i]). The face diagram in figure 5.2 gives approximate relative tongue heights of these two vowels.

Clearly, tongue height and frontness-and-backness contribute to the distinguishing of vowel sounds.

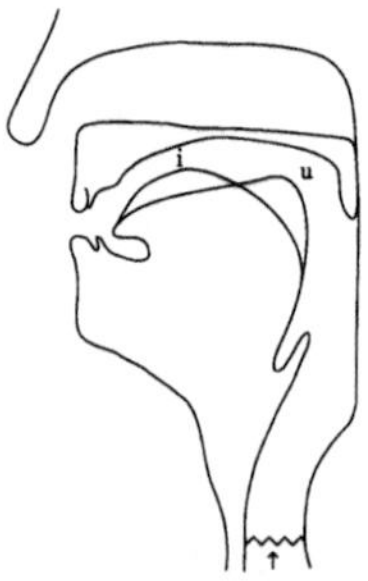

Figure 5.1. [i] and [u].

Figure 5.2. [æ] and [i].

Try saying the vowels [i] and [u] several times in an alternating sequence: [iuiuiu], etc., paying attention to what else about your mouth, besides tongue position, changes as you switch back and forth between the two vowels. Notice that your lips were moving, being quite rounded on the [u] and either relaxed or actively spread into a smile on the [i]. Lip rounding, or lack of it, is another important articulatory characteristic of vowels. When the lips are rounded, they also project forward slightly, creating the small resonating cavity between the lips and the front teeth called the *labial cavity;* its presence affects the resonances in the oral cavity. It happens that for all the English vowels produced with the tongue relatively forward in the mouth, the lips are unrounded, and for almost all the English vowels produced with the tongue relatively far back in the mouth, the lips are rounded.

Another subtle difference between [i] and [u] that we are generally less aware of, is the position of the tongue root: the tongue root is quite a bit further forward for the [i] than it is for the [u]. These two vowels also differ as to which part of the tongue is raised highest as they articulate. For [i], the highest part is probably the tongue front. For [u], the highest part is probably the tongue back. Say the two vowels again in the alternating sequence [iuiuiuiu].

The principle point to remember is that with vowels, much more so than with consonants, we are endeavoring to reproduce an auditory signal. In order to match a vowel that we hear, our own mouths may do something quite different from what the other speaker's mouth did to produce that "same" vowel. By describing various vowels in articulatory terms, we can get an idea of the muscular movements and positions used to produce them. But it must be emphasized that, while articulatory description may be practical as a technique for labeling vowels, ultimately it is the sound that counts.

Defining the term "vowel"

We can arrive at a workable definition of "vowel" by considering how speech sounds in general can be grouped in terms of factors like sonority (the degree to which a sound resonates), orality (whether or not the air flows through the mouth), and centrality (whether or not the air flows over the center of the tongue).

- Speech sounds that are characterized by a relatively unimpeded flow of air "resonate" and are thus referred to as *sonorants*. This classifies stops, such as [b], [tʰ], and [ʔ], and fricatives, such as [β] and [x], as *non*sonorants[23] because of the high degree to which the airflow is impeded.

---

[23]In phonology, nonsonorants are often called "obstruents."

- Sonorants in turn may be grouped into those which are *oral* (i.e., have airflow through the mouth), and those which are *nasal* (have airflow exclusively through the nose, *not* through the mouth). In this latter category we find sounds such as [m] and [n].[24]

- Finally, oral sonorants are either *central* or *lateral* depending on whether the air flows over the center of the tongue or over its sides. Laterals will be introduced in chapter 13.

This general classification scheme can be summarized as follows:

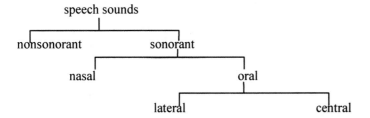

- We can consider a vowel to be any speech sound that is a central oral sonorant. All other speech sounds are consonants.

The function of vowels in syllables

Another way to look at the difference between vowels and consonants, more of a phonological approach than phonetic, is to focus on the way that they function in syllables. A vowel prototypically forms the NUCLEUS of a syllable, that is, the most prominent, acoustically resonant peak of the syllable. A consonant prototypically constitutes the periphery of a syllable, either preceding or following the nucleus. For example, in the syllable [buθ], the vowel in the middle forms the syllable nucleus while the two consonants are non-nuclear elements.

As you study the sound systems of more and more languages, you will notice that occasionally what may occupy the resonant peak of a syllable may not necessarily be a vowel. Indeed, within the structure of a syllable, some vowels may act like consonants and some consonants may act like vowels. For example, in the English word "with," the "w" is essentially a very short [u] vowel, but it is acting like a consonant since it does not occupy the resonant peak of the syllable. Likewise, in the word "puddle," the lateral [l], though a consonant, is the most sonorant element in the second syllable and thus occupies its nucleus, a role that vowels usually take. Determining the role of such segments within the sound system of a particular language is more properly the domain of phonology and not phonetics. Simply be aware that defining a vowel in articulatory terms as a "central oral sonorant," may not always precisely capture the phonological function of that segment within a given word in a particular language.[25]

---

[24]Some linguists use the term "oral" to mean "involving airflow through the mouth only, not through the nose" and others use the term oral to mean "involving airflow through the mouth, whether or not there is also airflow through the nose." We use the second definition in this book.

[25]Kenneth Pike in *Phonetics* (1943) coined the phonetic terms "vocoid" and "contoid," as distinct from the phonemic or phonological terms vowel and consonant, to try to clear up this problem. His term vocoid is defined as a "central resonant oral continuant," which is a slightly more complex way of stating the three characteristics outlined in this book. His term contoid refers to any segment that does not meet *all four* of those qualifications. This frees the terms "vowel" and "consonant" to refer to the language-specific function of a sound in relation to other sounds in a particular language, that is, in relation to the "sound system" of that language.

The problem of diagramming and symbolizing the vowels

Traditionally, "vowel space" or the array of vowel sounds has been conceptualized in terms of a grid within the mouth that represents degrees of tongue height and frontness or backness. These positions on the vowel diagram have been said to portray the positions of the highest point on the tongue for the respective vowels. We now know that the vowel diagram is a better picture of how vowel sounds are *perceived* than of how they are *produced*. Thus, when we talk about a vowel being close, open, front, or back, we are talking about the sound of the vowel and only approximately about tongue position.[26]

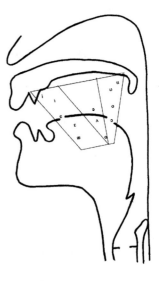

Figure 5.3. Grid of vowel sounds.

The cardinal vowels

The cardinal vowel system, devised by the British phonetician Daniel Jones (1881–1967), consists of theoretical vowel qualities against which the actual vowels of a language are to be compared (Crystal 2003:62). It consists of four levels, with the [i] position being defined as the highest front position that the tongue can assume without resulting in a fricative, the [a] position being the lowest position the tongue can assume in the mouth, and the two in-between levels evenly dividing the intervening distance. Such vowel systems rarely occur in actual languages; Jones's intent was simply to provide a scheme for phoneticians to plot a graph of how the actual vowels in a language compare with these idealized cardinal positions. For example, the eight primary cardinal vowels are plotted on a graph as in figure 5.4.

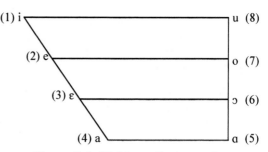

Figure 5.4. Eight cardinal vowels.

Figure 5.5, adapted from Ladefoged (1993:224), shows how the five Spanish vowels compare with the cardinal grid. It should be noted that the positions of the vowels here reflect how similar the analyst perceives the vowels to be with respect to the extreme targets represented by the cardinal vowels.

The cardinal vowel scheme provides the basis for the system used by the IPA.

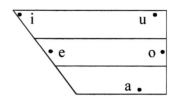

Figure 5.5. Five Spanish vowels.

---

[26]Acoustic measurements show that the location of a vowel on a vowel chart more closely reflect what are referred to as its "formant frequencies", that is, the intensity peaks in a sound wave produced during the articulation of a vowel. Plotting the two lowest formant frequencies of the vowels yields a diagram that is much more similar to the traditional vowel diagram than is a diagram of the actual positions of the tongue as it articulates the various vowels. A study of acoustic phonetics is beyond the scope of this book, but you can find a detailed description of the acoustic nature of speech sounds in Ladefoged (1993, 1996). (Norris McKinney, Keren Everett, and Mark Karan contributed to the authors' understanding of acoustic phonetics, especially regarding the acoustic nature of vowels as reflected in these diagrams.)

The International Phonetic Association vowel system

Figure 5.6 illustrates the IPA arrangement of the more English-like vowels. (Several other vowels will be added in chapter 7 and later lessons.) Notice that there are seven degrees of openness of the vocal tract (in rows) and three degrees of tongue frontness and backness (along the diagram's vertical lines).

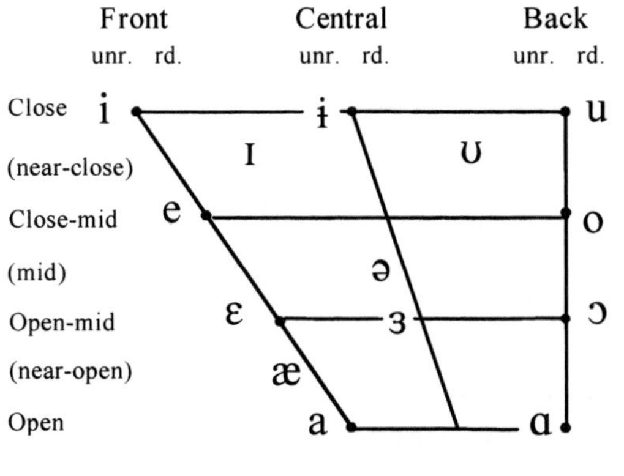

Figure 5.6. English vowels (adapted from IPA).

A note about [a] and [ɑ]

The official IPA vowel chart does not include a symbol in the open central unrounded position, because no language has yet been found that contrasts open vowels in all three positions: front, central, and back. However, the open central unrounded vowel is probably the most common vowel to occur in languages, so we feel it necessary to suggest two means to transcribe this very common vowel. Strict adherents to the IPA vowel system would probably use the symbol [a] or [ɑ], explaining that the vowel being described is shifted forward from the open back position or back from the open front position. Alternatively, some linguists choose to adapt the IPA vowel chart by inserting an alpha symbol [ɑ] in the open central unrounded slot. In this book, for convenience we will use [a] as representing an open central vowel rather than an open front vowel, unless otherwise specified.

Technical names for most of these vowels can be found by reading the labels in the diagram clockwise starting from the left-hand side of the grid. For example, [i] is a "close front unrounded vowel," [ə] is a "mid central unrounded vowel," and [ɔ] is an "open-mid back rounded vowel." Two vowels' technical names are not obvious from the diagram: [ɪ] is a "near-close near-front unrounded vowel"; [ʊ] is a "near-close near-back rounded vowel."[27]

All the vowels taught in this chapter are voiced. Indeed, vowels are much more frequently voiced than voiceless in most languages. Consequently, the characteristic value "voiced" does not need to be part of the technical name, being the assumed default value on all vowels until some conflicting value is specified.

The Americanist vowel system

There are two main systems for transcribing the vowel sounds that occur in languages. The IPA system outlined in the previous section began in Europe in the latter part of the 1800s and is currently defined and distributed by the International Phonetic Association. The Americanist system was developed early in the twentieth century as Americanist linguists strove to transcribe vowel sounds in the unwritten languages they studied. The two systems differ somewhat in terms of some of the symbols and in terms of some of the qualities represented as well.

Figure 5.7 is a table of the English-like vowels arranged according to the Americanist system. Notice that many of the symbols are the same as those used by the IPA, but that several of them are placed in columns and rows differently from the IPA system. The Americanist system has three degrees of tongue frontness-and-backness and three primary levels of tongue height, and each primary level of tongue height is divided into "close" and

---

[27]Note that the labels "near-close," "mid," and "near-open" are in parentheses in figure 5.6. They are not official IPA labels, but they greatly facilitate discussion of several vowels using precise, if not official, technical names. Some linguists (including Ladefoged) have suggested that [ɪ] and [ʊ], which are somewhere between close and close-mid, be called "near-close," and that [æ], which is between open-mid and open, be called "near-open." We may infer from the official IPA chart of symbols that "mid" is the term for vowels between close-mid and open-mid. Similarly, [ɪ] and [ʊ] do not fall neatly into the front-central-back columns. [ɪ] can be called "near-front" and [ʊ] "near-back." They could also be called "centralized." Check with the instructor of your phonetics course to see if (s)he has a preference for how you name these vowels. Note that column labels for rounding have been inserted into the official IPA vowel diagram.

"open" sublevels, [28] for a total of six tongue height levels. To name the height level for a vowel in this system, you must always specify either "high," "mid," or "low," *and* either "close" or "open." For example, [i] is a "high close front unrounded vowel" and [a] is a "low open front unrounded vowel."

			Front		Central		Back	
			unr.	rd.	unr.	rd.	unr.	rd.
vd.	high	close	i		ɨ		u	
		open	ɪ				ʊ	
	mid	close	e		ə		o	
		open	ɛ		ʌ			
	low	close	æ				ɔ	
		open	a		ɑ		ɒ	

(vowel (wepa) appears at right spanning)

Figure 5.7. English vowels (Americanist system).

Again, technical names are derived by reading the labels in the diagram clockwise, starting at the left. This time, [ɪ] is a "high open front unrounded vowel" and [ɔ] is a "low close back rounded vowel." And again, the default characteristic "voiced" need not be specified in the technical names.

Vowel symbols used in this book

This book uses IPA symbols. However, you should strive for facility in reading data transcribed in either system, since published and unpublished data exist in both systems and will be valuable to you in your future linguistic research only if you know how to read the symbols used. As we have done for the consonants, we will continue to provide transcription conversion exercises to facilitate your learning how to convert Americanist transcriptions into IPA. However, note that the conversions of vowels will be much more complicated and consequently perhaps less accurate than the conversion of the consonant symbols, which have a much closer one-to-one correspondence between the IPA symbols and alternate symbols in common use.

When working with a specific language, you will find it useful to plot a chart showing how the vowels of that language compare to the cardinal vowels, in the style of Ladefoged's plotting of Spanish vowels in figure 5.5.

Some preliminary comments on glided vowels

As we mentioned earlier, the tables in this chapter introduce symbols representing vowels that are quite similar to the English vowels. However, they differ from several English vowels in one very important way: all of the symbols given in these tables represent UNGLIDED vowels, that is, vowels that remain fairly constant in quality throughout their articulation. Many English vowels are GLIDED (that is, the tongue position changes significantly during the pronunciation of the vowel), such that what may seem to a speaker of English to be one vowel is actually a continuous movement through two or more vowel qualities in rapid succession. During the articulation of a glided vowel in English the body of the tongue usually moves upward or toward the center of the mouth. Two of the most obvious English glides occur on the vowels "o" (which glides toward [u] in most dialects) and "e" (which glides toward [i]), resulting in what is phonetically written [oṷ] and [eị] or sometimes as [oᵘ] and [eⁱ]. Either a subscript arch or superscription is used to indicate which element in a vowel combination is perceived as less prominent. A number of other English vowels are in fact glides as well.

Do not worry about symbolizing vowel glides yet; that is not the point of mentioning them here. The main thing is to pronounce phonetic vowels *without* glides unless the glides are specifically called for. (We will deal more fully with glides in chapters 18 and 32.)

---

[28]Sometimes these sublevels are talked about as 'tense' and 'lax' (referring to differing tensions of the tongue root) rather than in terms of miniscule subdivisions of tongue height. However, Americanist vowel charts usually utilize the terms 'close' and 'open'.

What follows are some American English words that contain the designated vowel sound (or glided versions thereof, so be careful) and some hints on how to get rid of the habitual glides if you are a native speaker of American English. Individual speakers' dialects vary considerably on the vowels, so some of these example words may not work for you if your dialect is different from the "broadcast English" dialect described here. (Here is where you must have a teacher or a tape to hear the sounds represented by the symbols.)

[i] "ski," "beet"

[ɪ] "bit"

[e] "bait," "bay," "day" (*if* you can do it without the glide!), or the French word "été." Many people of Scandinavian descent in Minnesota, North Dakota, and Iowa make this vowel without a glide.

[ɛ] "bet"

[æ] "bat," but this time, watch out not to glide toward [ə].

[a] *"park* your *car* in *Harvard Yard"* (New England dialect); *"I'm tired because I typed all night"* or *"595-9955"* (some southeastern US dialects).

[ɨ] In English, this vowel occurs mainly in unstressed syllables, such as the second syllable in the word "roses" said quickly and carelessly; if you say the second vowel carefully in such a word, you will probably put in an [ɪ] or [ɛ] vowel instead of [ɨ]. The vowel [ɨ] is sometimes used alone, greatly prolonged, to mean "yuck" (as, for example, in the old sitcom "I Love Lucy").

[ə] In English, this vowel occurs frequently in unstressed syllables, for example, in the word "the" in a phrase like "It's time to walk the dog." The IPA system uses the [ɜ] symbol to show the open-mid central vowel which occurs in stressed syllables, such as the word "cup." To practice differentiating between unstressed [ə] and stressed [ɜ], say "the cup" several times in succession, being careful not to stress "the."

[u] "blue," "boot" (but be careful not to precede the [u] with a front unrounded vowel such as [i] or [ɪ])

[ʊ] "push," "foot," "book"

[o] The words "no" and "como," in some dialects of Spanish. This vowel is virtually never said unglided in English, except by those Midwesterners of Scandinavian descent mentioned in the discussion of [e].

[ɔ] "awl," "call" in most dialects. Many English dialects do not differentiate between [ɔ] and [a]. Some merge both sounds into [ɔ], while others merge them both into [a]. This makes it harder for students who speak these dialects to hear or produce the difference between the two vowels. To test yourself to find out if you speak one of these merging dialects, say the words "cot" and "caught." If your dialect differentiates between these two vowels, you will probably say the first word as [kʰat] and the second as [kʰɔt]. If you merge the two vowels, you will say both words with the same vowel. In that case, simply treat the other vowel as a "foreign" sound and learn it along with the other non-English vowels in this course.

[a] "ah" (what you say when the doctor looks into your throat) in most dialects, but see the note regarding the merger of [ɔ] with [a] in some dialects.

Hints for producing unglided vowels

Now for a few hints on how to get rid of the glides that you almost certainly have on many of your vowels if your mother tongue is English. Just becoming aware of them is half the battle! Say a word like "hoe" or "Oh!" several times in succession, focusing your attention on any movement of your tongue, lips, or jaw during the vowel. It would be helpful to use a mirror as you do this, so you can really see what changes are taking place. Now try it with the word "ate." The changes that you see in your jaw and feel in your tongue are what cause the vowel to glide upward, [e] becoming [eɪ̯] and [o] becoming [oʊ̯]. So how can you get rid of those glides? Try these techniques:

1. Say [ʔoʔoʔoʔoʔoʔoʔoʔo] without allowing any part of your mouth to move. Again, stand in front of a mirror so you will catch yourself if you move your lips into tighter rounding for the [oʊ̯] glide. Now do the same thing with [ʔeʔeʔeʔeʔeʔeʔeʔeʔe], again not letting your lips or tongue position change. This time look in

the mirror for jaw movement upward and feel upward movement of your tongue, both of which would indicate that you are gliding toward [ei̯].

2. If you speak a dialect that has an [i̯u] on-glide, it will show up immediately if you say [ʔuʔuʔuʔuʔuʔuʔuʔu], again watching in the mirror for lip and jaw movement.

3. Try saying a very long [ooooooooh] or [eeeeeeeh], ending by blowing an [h] instead of gliding.

These techniques should work for almost any glide. A few more to watch out for include [æə̯], [ɛi̯] and [ɛṷ]. Your dialect may not have these, but you may have others instead. Just use a mirror and your eyes and ears very faithfully as you begin to fight the battle against glides.

Key concepts

lip position
  rounded
  unrounded
vowel / consonant
  central / lateral
  oral / nasal
  sonorant / nonsonorant (stop or fricative)
nucleus
syllable / nucleus / periphery
cardinal vowel / ideal / extreme position / basis of comparison
minimal impedance of the airstream
tongue positions
  frontness / backness
  front / central / back
  four primary degrees of openness of the vocal tract and three intermediate ones (IPA system)
  six degrees of tongue height (Americanist system)
glided / unglided vowel
symbols and technical names for all vowels in the chapter

Oral exercises

1. Practice saying aloud the following frame drills three times each.

ˈkiɸɛ	ˈdiɣɔ
ˈkɪɸɛ	ˈdɪɣɔ
ˈkeɸɛ	ˈdeɣɔ
ˈkɛɸɛ	ˈdɛɣɔ
ˈkæɸɛ	ˈdæɣɔ
ˈkaɸɛ	ˈdaɣɔ
ˈkɨɸɛ	ˈdɨɣɔ
ˈkəɸɛ	ˈdəɣɔ
ˈkuɸɛ	ˈduɣɔ
ˈkʊɸɛ	ˈdʊɣɔ
ˈkoɸɛ	ˈdoɣɔ
ˈkɔɸɛ	ˈdɔɣɔ

2.   Practice saying aloud the following words.

Ewe of Ghana (Westermann and Ward 1933:84; stress omitted)

xɔ	'house'
gaxɔ	'prison'
xe	'bird'
ɣe	'sun'
aɣe	'poverty'

Kikuyu of Kenya (Westermann and Ward 1933:84; stress omitted)

ɣekɔ	'dirt'
ɣete	'stool'

Lao of Laos (E. Pike 1978:17)

kak	'skin disease'
kʰop	'bite'
tɔt	'to strike'
kat	'gnaw'
bap	'sin'

Spanish, various dialects (simplified, E. Pike 1978:7; Bickford, field notes)

aˈxi	'chili pepper'
ˈoxa	'leaf'
ˈixo	'son'
ˈiɣo	'fig'
ˈoxo	'eye'
ˈaβe	'bird'
ˈxefe	'boss'
aˈɣaβe	'century plant'
ˈθexa	'sharp'
oˈβexa	'sheep'
aˈɣuxa	'needle'
eˈðað	'age'
kaˈfe	'coffee'
ˈaɣo	'I make / do'
ˈiθe	'I made / did'
ˈaxo	'garlic'
ˈuβo	'there was'
ˈtoðo	'all'

Culina of Peru (E. Pike 1978:11; stress omitted)

poβi	'hammock'
aβi	'tapir'
abi	'father'
kokoba	'hammer'

American English

kʰæf	'calf'
fɪtʰ	'fit'
pʰɪtʰ	'pit'
θɔtʰ	'thought'
bɜf	'buff'
vɛtʰ	'vet'
ʔɔtʰ	'ought'

Written exercises

1. Write the technical names of these segments.

    [kʰ] _voiceless velar aspirated stop_

    [ɪ] _near-close near-front unrounded vowel_

    [u] _close back rounded vowel_

    [ɛ] _open-mid front unrounded vowel_

    [θ] _voiceless interdental fricative_

    [ə] _mid-central unrounded vowel_

2. For the following sounds, state whether or not they meet the phonetic definition of vowels. If you answer "no" for a given segment, explain how that segment fails to meet the definition.

    [e] _yes_

    [f] _no, touches articulators_

    [pʰ] _no, touches articulators_

    [n] _no, touches articulators_

    [o] _yes_

    [θ] _no, touches articulators_

    [l] _no, touches articulators_

3. Write the following American English words using phonetic transcription. Compare your answers with those of someone else in the class. Each of you say the words aloud. If you find differences in your written lists, they could reflect either transcription mistakes or simply differences in how you pronounce the words. Work out the differences as well as you can. Check with someone who knows the words well if you have questions.

    path _pʰæθ_

    feet _fitʰ_

    fed _fɛd_

    pig _pʰɪg_

took ˈtʊkʰ _____

the (unstressed) ˌðə _____

4. Make up and transcribe ten two-syllable words, using the sounds and symbols presented so far in the book. Dictate them to another student, who will transcribe them phonetically and then show you his/her written list. Compare your transcription with his/hers. They should be identical! Then trade places.

1 ʊgon	6 ækʰæ	1. ɹæ̆ven
2 flʌl	7 togɔ	2. tæ̆kɛn
3 dImt	8 kaka	
4 ðumɛ	9 ɔpʰa	
5 ʃɛpʰn	10 ɛθbo	

Transcription conversion exercises

In the two lists of words given here, convert the left-hand list from IPA to Americanist symbols, and the right-hand list from Americanist symbols to IPA symbols.

βɪˈdu _____   kʰæˈɟɪ _____

ˈbɛvɔ _____   ˈɓuʔa _____

ðeˈɣu _____   ˈɖʊθæ _____

ˈɸɨpʰə _____   xiˈƥʌ _____

6

Nasals

Goals

⌘ You will be able to define a *nasal* as a consonant in which the sound resonates in the nasal cavity due to velic opening, but complete closure at some place in the mouth prevents the airstream from flowing out of the mouth.

⌘ You will control[29] the nine nasal consonants presented in this chapter.

⌘ You will be able to give the technical name, place of articulation, and articulators for each of these nasals.

⌘ You will be able to read and draw face diagrams of these nasal sounds, focusing especially on the velic opening that distinguishes them from oral stops.

NASALS are consonant sounds in which the velum is lowered, allowing the sound to resonate in the nasal cavity, while closure between articulators in the mouth prevents the airstream from passing out of the mouth. Thus, they are consonants, not vowels, because although they are sonorants they are not oral sonorants. Some linguists define the nasal consonants as stops since the airstream is completely impeded through the mouth;[30] others define them as continuants because there is unobstructed air flow through the nose.

Table 6.1 on the next page shows seven of the nasal sounds to be presented in this chapter. Two more are presented in the "Common alternative analyses and symbols" section later in the chapter.

Note that an under-ring [̥] is used underneath a nasal symbol to indicate that the nasal is voiceless, unless the nasal symbol involves a descender, in which case an over-ring [˚] is used above the symbol instead. Notice also that there is no symbol given for a voiceless labiodental nasal. That is because, although it is a theoretically possible sound, that sound is not known to occur in any language of the world.

---

[29]Recall that the term "control" is used in this book to indicate that you can recognize and produce the sound in context and read and write its symbol.

[30]However, nasals are never called "plosives" along with oral stops.

Table 6.1. Nasals

	Bilabial	**Labiodental**	**Alveolar**	**Velar**	
voiceless	m̥		n̥	ŋ̊	nasal
voiced	m	ɱ	n	ŋ	
passive articulator	upper lip	upper teeth	alveolar ridge	front of soft palate; velum	
active articulator	lower lip	lower lip	tongue tip	tongue back	

As with the other sounds taught so far, the technical names for nasals are derived by reading the chart clockwise. For example, [m] is a "voiced bilabial nasal" and [ŋ̊] is a "voiceless velar nasal."

Figures 6.1 and 6.2 display face diagrams for the sounds [b] and [m]. Note that the only difference between the two diagrams (and indeed, between production of the two sounds) is the position of the velum. For the oral stop, it is raised, thus preventing the sound from resonating in the nasal cavity; for the nasal, it is lowered, thus allowing resonance of the sound in the nasal cavity.

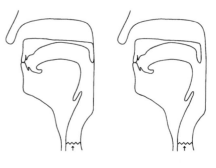

Figure 6.1. [b] Figure 6.2. [m]

Common alternative analyses and symbols

There are differences in the way that some places of articulation are analyzed in the IPA and the Americanist systems. The two systems do not agree as to the existence of unique nasals produced at a palato-alveolar place of articulation.[31] Most Americanist linguists and many others do attest to the existence of such nasals,[32] for which the tongue blade as the active articulator touches just behind the alveolar ridge, the passive articulator. The Americanist system thus includes the symbol [ñ] for which the technical name is "voiced palato-alveolar nasal." The IPA does not acknowledge such a nasal and there is thus no base symbol for it in the official IPA alphabet. In transcribing this sound we and many other linguists use the Americanist symbol, [ñ]. Others use [n̠] or [ɲ] (although beware, this last symbol is the IPA symbol for a nasal at another place of articulation, to be introduced in chapter 20). Possible options for symbolizing a voiceless palato-alveolar nasal include [ñ̥], [n̠̥], and [n̠̊] (creating unofficial "IPA-like" characters with the IPA under-ring or over-ring) or the normal Americanist symbol, [Ñ].

Table 6.2. Common symbols for nasals

IPA symbol	**Common alternative symbol(s)**
m̥	M
n̥	N
ŋ̊	Ŋ
ɲ	ñ / n̠
none	ñ̥ / Ñ / n̠̥ / ɲ̥

Note: Even though it necessitates introducing controversial analyses and symbols that are not accepted by the IPA, we recommend enlarging the table of nasal sounds to include a palato-alveolar place of articulation, as in table 6.3.

---

[31]The terms "alveopalatal" and "postalveolar" are considered equivalent to palato-alveolar in this text. All three terms are commonly used in the linguistic literature.

[32]For example, in Amuzgo (Amy Bauernschmidt) and Highland Mazatec (Eunice Pike) of Mexico and Gunwinggu (William and Lynette Oates) and Pitjantjara (W. H. Douglas) of Australia, as cited in E. Pike 1978.

Table 6.3. Nasals including palato-alveolars

	Bilabial	Labio-dental	Alveolar	Palato-alveolar	Velar	
voiceless	m̥		n̥	ñ̥ / n̥̠	ŋ̊	nasal
voiced	m	ɱ	n	ñ / n̠	ŋ	
passive articulator	upper lip	upper teeth	alveolar ridge	behind alveolar ridge	front of soft palate; velum	
active articulator	lower lip	lower lip	tongue tip	tongue blade	tongue back	

Production hints

[ɱ] Put your upper teeth and lower lip in position to say [v], but then say "mama." For some English speakers, this sound occurs in such words as "emphasis."

[ñ / n̠ / n] and [ñ̥ / n̥̠ / n̥] To keep your tongue tip from jumping in and articulating this sound, hook the tongue tip behind your lower teeth and form the closure on the roof of your mouth with the tongue blade. Be careful not to produce this sound with a little "y" following it.

[ŋ] is an easy, common sound in English in the middle or at the ends of words, but it never occurs word-initially in English. To train yourself to make this sound at the beginning of a word, say "a song" over and over again, gradually shifting the [ŋ] onto the beginning of the next word "a" (that is, [ə sɔŋ ə sɔ ŋə sɔ ŋə sɔ ŋə sɔ ŋə ...]). For some people, it helps to think of humming a "g" through your nose.

You can produce the voiceless counterpart of any voiced nasal simply by not activating the vocal folds. It helps some people to think of saying the nasal and an [h] *simultaneously;* however, avoid simply saying the [h] first and then the nasal (for example, [hm], [hn]) because such sequences are *not* the same as voiceless nasals.

Voiceless nasals in combination with other consonants

One final thing about nasals bears discussion at this point, and that is the use of voiceless nasals in sequence with other consonants. It is very common in languages for a voiceless nasal to be either preceded or followed by a voiced nasal at the same place of articulation, for example, [m̥ma], [n̥na], or [amm̥], [ann̥], etc. However, voiceless nasals do sometimes occur without those voiced partners, for example, [m̥a], [n̥a], [am̥], [an̥], etc. And voiced nasals can occur in combination with an [h], for example, [hma], [hna]. Thus, you need to be able to hear, produce, and transcribe all of these combinations as phonetically distinct. One thing you will not have to worry about is a sequence of voiced and voiceless nasals in the same syllable at *different* places of articulation, as this rarely if ever occurs.

Key concept and symbols

nasal
technical names and all the symbols in table 6.3

Oral exercises

1.   Practice saying these words aloud.

   Kikuyu of Kenya (Pat Bennett, personal communication; tone omitted)

ŋanɔ	'stories'
ŋanɔŋanɔ	'a variety of stories'
ŋima	'complete'
ŋɛni	'strange'
ŋumɔ	'wild fig'
ŋondo	'estate'
ŋɔmbɛ	'cow'

   Ewe of Ghana (Westermann and Ward 1933:63; tone omitted)

ɲe	'to break'
ɲu	'outside'
ɲɔti	'nose'
ɲɔ	'to perforate'

   Gunwinggu of Australia (E. Pike 1978:21; William and Lynette Oates)

guɲ	'kangaroo'
ŋaˈɲunɛŋ	'I sat'
ŋaˈgiɲɛ	'I cook'
ŋaˈbuɲma	'I kiss'

2.   Practice saying aloud these words with voiceless nasals that are *not* preceded or followed by voiced nasals at the same place of articulation.

   Kuanyama of Angola and Namibia (Westermann and Ward 1933:65)

na	'with'
n̥a	'quite (straight)'
n̥ano	'five'
omunue	'finger'
omun̥u	'man'
om̥ito	'escape'
om̥epo	'wind'

Written exercises

1.   For each of the following nasals, give a symbol for an oral stop that corresponds to the nasal in *all* articulatory characteristics except velic closure.

   [n]_____ d _____

   [ŋ̊]_____ k _____

   [m] _____ b _____

   [m̥] _____ p _____

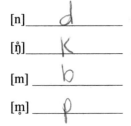

2. What are the active and passive articulators for the following sounds?

[m̥] *lower lip, upper lip*

[ŋ] *tongue back, front of soft palate / velum*

[n] *tongue tip, alveolar ridge*

[ɱ] *lower lip, upper teeth*

[ñ] *tongue blade, behind (palatal) alveolar ridge*

3. Identify the sounds depicted in the following face diagrams and give their technical names.

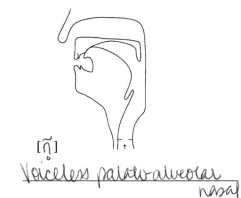

[ñ̥]

Voiceless palato-alveolar nasal

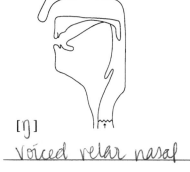

[ŋ]

Voiced velar nasal

4. Draw face diagrams of [n] and [ŋ̊] and give the technical names for the two sounds.

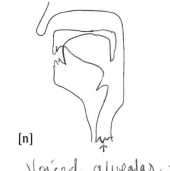

[n]

Voiced alveolar nasal

[ŋ̊]

Voiceless velar nasal

Transcription conversion exercises

Retranscribe each of the following, using only IPA symbols.

o'Mepo   *oˈm̥epo*

Ni   *n̥i*

θιŋN   *θɪŋŋ̊*

7

More Vowels

Goals

⌘ You will control all the vowel sounds and symbols represented in the vowel diagram and be able to give the technical name for each.

⌘ You will be able to explain that the primary difference between most of the vowels introduced in this chapter and the ones presented in chapter 5 is in the interaction of lip rounding and front-back tongue position, which is reversed from what you are probably used to in English.

⌘ You will overcome common English habits of lip rounding, so that you can produce rounded front vowels and unrounded back vowels.

⌘ You will learn to use the techniques of *slurring* and *bracketing* to help you identify and control unfamiliar vowel sounds.

⌘ You will be able to explain why some phonetic detail can sometimes be omitted in good transcription.

In English, front and central vowels are made with unrounded lips, while back vowels are made with rounded lips.[33] However, the vowels conform to a different pattern in many languages of the world. In this chapter, we present rounded front and central vowels, unrounded back vowels, and a few other non-English vowels to increase your repertoire of vowel sounds.

As in chapter 5, we present the vowels in two different diagrams, one for the IPA and one for the Americanist system. The vowels that are new in this chapter have now been added to the tables of the previous vowel chapter, completing the inventory of basic vowel symbols available in the two systems.

---

[33]Vowels in many other languages conform to this pattern. This coordination of lip rounding with tongue position increases the acoustic and auditory contrast between vowels produced with tongue front positions and those produced with tongue back positions.

The IPA vowel diagram

Figure 7.1 contains IPA symbols representing a more complete inventory of the world's vowel sounds.[34]

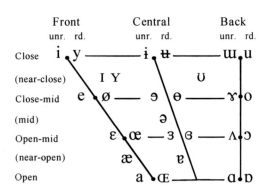

Figure 7.1. IPA vowel diagram.

The Americanist vowel diagram

		Front		Central		Back	
		unr.	rd.	unr.	rd.	unr.	rd.
vd.	high close	i	ü	ɨ	ʉ	ï	u
	open	ι	Ü			ï	ʊ
	mid close	e	ö	ə		ë	o
	open	ε		ʌ			
	low close	æ	ö̈			ä	ɔ
	open	a		a			ɒ

vowel (wepa)

Figure 7.2. Americanist vowel diagram.

There is a pattern that may help you to remember some of the Americanist symbols introduced in figure 7.2. Each front rounded vowel in the Americanist system has the symbol for the back rounded vowel of the same height (u, ʊ, o, or ɔ) as its base character, and each back unrounded vowel has the symbol for the front unrounded vowel of the same height (i, ι, e, ε, or æ) as its base character. An umlaut (¨) is placed over one of those symbols, as in [ü] or [ï], to indicate an extreme shift of tongue position, either front-to-back or back-to-front, from what the base character indicates, while the lip position remains unchanged. Thus, Americanist symbols for all unrounded vowels utilize base characters of unrounded English vowels, while Americanist symbols for all rounded vowels utilize base characters of rounded English vowels. A bar through the vowel symbol, as in [ɨ] and [ʉ], indicates central vowels with the same rounding that their basic symbols denote. The charts in figure 7.3 summarize these rules.

---

[34]Again, column labels for rounding have been inserted into the official IPA vowel diagram.

Table 7.1. Americanist vowel symbols

Rounded vowels				Unrounded vowels		
front	central	back		front	central	back
ü	ʉ	u		i	ɨ	ï
ö		o		e	ə	ë
ö̈		ɔ		æ		ä̈

Symbolizing vowels that fall in the cracks on the diagrams

You may encounter some other vowels, ones that fall in the cracks between those symbolized in the diagrams, because the sounds found in languages include the whole continuum of vowel sounds, not just those vowels for which we have convenient symbols. Any such "new" vowels that you find will be just a little higher or a little lower or a little further toward the front or back than some vowel represented by a symbol in the diagram. For example, the Spanish sound that is spelled with the letter "e" is about halfway between [e] and [ɛ], lower than [e] but higher than [ɛ].

To symbolize such a vowel, write the symbol of the vowel in the diagram that it seems to be closest to, and use a diacritic from table 7.2 to indicate the difference between the vowel represented in the diagram and the vowel you wish to symbolize. IPA diacritics go directly beneath the base character; the Americanist diacritics are superscripts immediately following the base character.

Table 7.2. Diacritics indicating shifted
tongue position on vowels,
using "e" and "o" as examples

	IPA symbol	Americanist symbol
Advanced (fronted)	o̟	o<
Retracted (backed)	e̠	e>
Raised	o̝	o^
Lowered	e̞	e^v

As an example, the Spanish vowel mentioned above can be symbolized as [e̞] in IPA or [e^v] in the Americanist system, indicating that it is lower than [e]. Alternatively, this Spanish vowel can be represented as [ɛ̝] in IPA or [ɛ^] in Americanist, indicating that it is higher than [ɛ]. Note that in the Americanist system, the direction of the arrows correlates with a face diagram—left indicates fronted and right indicates backed.

Note: It is very unlikely that the only phonetic difference between two words with different meanings will be as slight as the difference between, for example, [e] and [e̞]. It is much more likely that some vowels in a language will consistently be pronounced a bit further front than the ones in the phonetic vowel diagram, or a bit higher, while the ones nearest them in the chart would not be used at all. That is, minor variations in tongue position on vowels are not likely to be *phonologically contrastive*. Therefore, after you have discovered, for example, that /e/ is always pronounced a bit higher in the language you are studying than your own norm, you may decide to stop writing [e̞] and simply write "e." However, you will need to remain aware that that vowel is pronounced higher than your own auditory norm for that vowel, so that you will not have a foreign accent when you use that vowel as you speak the language, and you will also need to make a note of that phonetic difference in any papers that you write about the language.[35] It is inadvisable to ignore such phonetic detail too early in your language study or to omit it entirely, because your initial hypotheses about what is phonologically contrastive may turn out to be wrong, and you do not want your data to lock you into a skewed understanding of the language!

---

[35]This can be done easily by means of a vowel graph as described in chapter 5.

Production hints for vowels

Accurate pronunciation of the vowels introduced in this chapter requires as much care not to glide the vowels as was the case in chapter 5. English speakers are just as likely to let their tongues drift upward on "foreign" vowels as they are on the ones that more closely resemble their own English ones. Apply the same techniques that were suggested in chapter 5 to eliminate glides.

An easy way to learn to make these vowels with non-English lip rounding is to make up English sentences containing their normal-rounding counterparts and then to do the opposite with your lips from what you are used to. For example:

[y] Say "He sees me," or another sentence with several instances of [i]. Then say it again with your tongue in the same position as for [i] but your lips rounded as for [u]. Now just say [y] a few times in isolation.

[ø] Say "Kate bakes eight cakes" slowly *without gliding*. Then say it again with your tongue in position for [e] but with your lips rounded as for [o]. Now say [ø] in isolation a few times.

[œ] Say "Ted, get fresh bread." Then say it again with your tongue in position for [ɛ] as before but lips rounded as for [ɔ]. Now say just the vowel in isolation.

[ɯ] Say "Whom do you choose to shoot?" Again position your tongue as for [u] but with your lips spread in a gentle smile throughout as for [i]. You will be tempted to let your tongue shift forward toward the [i] position as well, but do not let it. Now say the back unrounded vowel in isolation.

[ɤ] Say "Joe, go hoe snow!" slowly *without gliding*. Say it again with your tongue consciously held back in the [o] position and your lips gently smiling as for [e]. Now say the back unrounded vowel in isolation.

[ʌ] Say "Call Paul, y'all!" Say it again with your tongue kept back in the position for [ɔ] but with your lips gently smiling, as for [ɛ]. Now say the back unrounded vowel [ʌ] in isolation.

If you find that your tongue and lips seem to work together as an "English set" and insist on making only unrounded front vowels and rounded back ones, the techniques of *slurring* and *bracketing* might help you. Slurring involves sliding your tongue back and forth or up and down through a whole range of vowel qualities while maintaining a constant lip position. For example, keeping your lips in a gentle smile and your voicing continuous in a monotone, slide your tongue slowly back and forth between [i] and [ɯ].

      i ———————— ɯ

Keeping your lips rounded and your voicing going, slide your tongue slowly back and forth between [y] and [u].

      y ———————— u

Slurring in this way should help you become aware of what your tongue is doing, independently of what your lips are doing. Notice, too, that as you slur between the extremes, you are moving through the whole continuum of possible vowel sounds at a given tongue height.

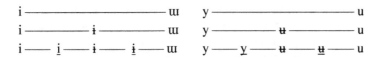

Bracketing is similar to slurring, except that you concentrate more on the extremes of your tongue position, moving fairly quickly from, for example, [i] to [ɯ]. Then consciously place your tongue at a point intermediate between the extremes, for example, [ɨ]. This is a good way to locate in-between vowels that are often difficult to produce in the right place.

The examples of slurring and bracketing given thus far have shown tongue movement along the front-central-back dimension. It is also possible and can be useful to slur and bracket up and down, from open to close or close to open.

In this case, you are keeping your lip position and tongue frontness-or-backness constant while moving your tongue up and down through the full range of possible vowel heights.

ɨ

ə

a

Key concepts and symbols

slurring / bracketing
phonologically contrastive
all symbols and technical names for the vowels in the chart

Oral exercises

1. Practice slurring and bracketing with any vowels that you have difficulty producing.

2. Practice the following drills aloud three times each. Note that in the left-hand column your lip position is to remain constant on the two vowels within a word while your tongue position shifts forward or backward. In the right-hand column, the tongue position is to remain constant on the two vowels within a word while your lip position changes. In both drills, the tongue height is to remain constant on the two vowels within a word.

'tuty	'tity
'tʊtʏ	'tɪtʏ
'totø	'tetø
'tɔtœ	'tɛtœ
'titɯ	'tutɯ
'tetɤ	'totɤ
'tɛtʌ	'tɔtʌ
	'titʉ

3. Practice saying aloud the following words.
   French (E. Pike 1978:17; Barbara E. Hollenbach)

ty	'you, familiar'
tu	'all'
to	'soon'
poto	'post'
puf	'plump'
pyf	'exaggerated statement'

   Norwegian (E. Pike 1978:18; Eva Sivertsen; length omitted)

by	'town'
bʉ	'shack'
bu	'to live'

4. Create a frame drill to practice whatever vowels are difficult for you. Practice it aloud three times. It may be most helpful to do this exercise with a friend.

Written exercises

1. For each vowel symbol given, write a symbol for a vowel that corresponds with the given one in all ways except lip rounding or unrounding.

    [i] _____y_____

    [o] _____ɤ_____

    [ɨ] _____ʉ_____

    [u] _____ɯ_____

    [œ] _____ɛ_____

2. For each vowel symbol given, write a symbol for a vowel that corresponds with the given one in all ways except tongue frontness-or-backness.

    [ʊ] _____ɪ_____

    [y] _____ʉ_____

    [e] _____ɤ_____

    [ø] _____o_____

    [ɔ] _____œ_____

3. Write the technical name for each of these sounds.

    [y] _close front rounded vowel_

    [ø] _close-mid front rounded vowel_

    [ɯ] _close back unrounded vowel_

    [œ] ~~near-open~~ open-mid front ~~un~~rounded vowel

Transcription conversion exercises

Rewrite each of the following, using only IPA symbols.

xeʔʊˈbʉ _____

ˈtʰædö_____

ˈgëtʰi _____

tʉˈkʰɨ _____

8

Tracking

Goals

⌘ You will be able to use the technique of *tracking* to help you incorporate the *prosodic features* of the language into your own pronunciation.

Every language has unique features that you will want to reproduce as closely as possible as you speak the language yourself. These features—including such things as relative pitch of the voice, rate of speed, relative lengths of various segments, and certain voice qualities—are called PROSODIC FEATURES. TRACKING is a technique to help you copy the prosodic features that mother-tongue speakers use when they speak their language. It will be invaluable to you as you seek to eliminate your own foreign accent and sound as much as possible like a native speaker.

You have no doubt heard of mimicking, in which you echo what is said in a sample of speech you have heard just after you have finished hearing it. Tracking is different; it involves *speaking right along with your sample as nearly simultaneously as possible.*

The language sample used for tracking should be recorded[36] rather than live, primarily for two reasons: (1) Tracking live speech in the presence of the speaker can drive that person crazy. It is difficult to concentrate on your train of thought if someone is speaking back every word that you say, the very second that it comes out of your mouth! (2) You should listen to the sample several times before you even begin tracking it. Then you will need to track the same sample several times. It is very unlikely that a speaker will be happy to repeat the sample for you as many times as you will need to hear it and track with it.

It usually works best at first to track a fairly short sample, maybe a sentence containing just four or five words. Listen to it several times; then begin tracking it, tracking only as far as you feel comfortable. Rewind, listen, rewind, track, rewind, etc. Each time you track, focus your attention carefully on just one prosodic feature of the language. Tracking can be used to help in the mastery of troublesome individual segments as well.

It can be extremely helpful to use two tape recorders while tracking. Play the sample tape on one recorder, and use the second one to record your tracking and the original sample playing simultaneously. When you play back what you recorded on the second machine, you can hear clearly where you have deviated from the sample in some way. Go back and track with the sample again, focusing on whatever weaknesses the tape reveals. Again, record your tracking. You should be encouraged as you find improvement from one tracking session to the next.

---

[36]Any record-playback system of suitable quality will serve the purpose, such as a cassette tape recorder, a video camcorder, or a computer with sound recording capability. This discussion of tracking will assume, for simplicity of description, that cassette tapes are being used.

Tracking involves a lot of rewinding of the tape. It will be much easier for you to use the valuable technique of tracking if your tape recorder has a memory rewind function. You set it at the beginning of the passage that you want to work with, and it will automatically rewind to that same spot on the tape each time you rewind. If you have a computer equipped with hardware and software that can record sound and play it back,[37] it may serve very well for tracking.

The amount of rewinding necessary for tracking can cause wear and tear on your tape recorder. This can be minimized by using *tape loops*, very short tape cassettes allowing for a recording to be played over and over in a loop without rewinding. They are available in varying lengths of from seven seconds to approximately one minute. Shorter loops are most useful for tracking. You copy the phrase you want to track from a regular master cassette onto the tape loop, using two tape recorders. When you finish tracking that phrase, you can record another phrase over it from your master tape.

Note: When you are doing actual linguistic fieldwork, you will probably come to regard tape recorders as almost disposable field equipment; you should expect to wear out several of them during a career of language learning and linguistic research. Even if tape loops are not available, we suggest that you not skip tracking simply to prolong the life of your tape recorder; that would waste time more valuable than the tape equipment by depriving you of the benefit of an efficient language learning tool.

As you gain proficiency in the technique of tracking, you will be able to track somewhat longer utterances, which will greatly boost your facility in pronunciation of the language. If you use material that you have memorized, you can even track whole paragraphs and stories. However, it is best to avoid tracking unfamiliar material of great length, as you will be tempted to lapse into mimicking after a slight pause rather than tracking, thus losing the benefit of the simultaneity of tracking.

From now on, use tracking as a tool in learning to produce any difficult words or phrases you encounter in a new language of study.

Key concepts

prosodic features
tracking / simultaneity

Exercises

1. Choose a partner, preferably someone whose mother tongue is the same as yours. Have your partner tape a very short paragraph, in your mother tongue, for you to use as a tracking sample. Listen to it repeatedly, until it becomes very familiar. Then begin tracking along with it, one sentence at a time, dropping out and going back to just listening if it becomes confusing. Keep working at it until you can successfully track the whole paragraph. Then track it several more times, each time focusing on just one aspect of the language, for example, pitch variation, speed, rhythm, etc. If possible, use a second tape recorder to record your tracking practice; it will reveal things on which you need to focus more as you track.

2. If exercise 1 was quite easy for you, as a more challenging exercise try the same procedure again, but this time with a sample of a language that is *not* your own. Be sure to find a mother-tongue speaker of that language to make the tape for you. Perhaps your phonetics instructor can provide you with such a tape if there are no mother-tongue speakers of languages other than your own available to you.

---

[37]The basic hardware requirements as of this writing are a sound card and microphone, both of music quality and adequate hard-disk space for storing the recordings; sound files tend to be quite large. Sound cards usually come with software that allows you to record and play back sound, usually using controls similar to a tape recorder. Waveform editors and specialized linguistic software (for example, Praat or SIL's Speech Analyzer) can provide additional useful capabilities, such as limiting the playback to one section of a recording, automatic repeats, and varying speed without altering the pitch.

9

Sibilants

Goals

⌘   You will be able to define *sibilants* or *grooved fricatives* as a class of fricatives produced by a narrow, groove-like stricture between the tip or blade portion of the tongue and the passive articulator and characterized by a high-frequency hiss.

⌘   You will be able to explain the difference between sibilants and the *flat fricatives* presented in earlier chapters (those having *flat articulators*).

⌘   You will control each sibilant represented in table 9.1, and be able to give a technical name for each symbol in the chart.

The fricatives that have already been presented have FLAT ARTICULATORS, that is, there is air flow across the entire width of the articulators. Such fricatives are sometimes called FLAT FRICATIVES.

For the fricatives in focus in this chapter, however, the sides of the tongue are closed against the roof of the mouth, creating a narrow groove-like stricture over the tip and blade portions of the tongue along the alveolar ridge (especially the back part of the alveolar ridge). When air flows through this channel for a speech sound, the sound is characterized by a high-frequency hiss. Such speech sounds are called SIBILANTS or GROOVED FRICATIVES. Alveolar sibilants have a higher pitched hiss than palato-alveolar ones, because the cavity in front of the noise source is smaller in volume, and thus resonates at a higher frequency.

The two diagrams shown in figures 9.1 and 9.2 are front views of the front portion of the tongue as it looks for [θ] and [s].

Figure 9.1. [θ] flat   Figure 9.2. [s] grooved

Table 9.1 shows symbols representing the four most common sibilants. As before, the technical names are derived by reading the labels clockwise. For example, [s] is a "voiceless alveolar grooved fricative," and [ʒ] is a "voiced palato-alveolar grooved fricative." You may freely substitute the word "sibilant" for "grooved fricative."

Table 9.1. Common sibilants

	Alveolar	Palato-alveolar	
voiceless	s	ʃ	grooved fricative /
voiced	z	ʒ	sibilant
active articulator	tongue tip	tongue blade	

Prototypical alveolar sounds are articulated with the tongue tip (apex), and prototypical palato-alveolar sounds are articulated with the tongue blade. However, there is some variation from speaker to speaker in the production of these sibilants, particularly with regard to the tongue tip. Some speakers produce some or all sibilants with the tongue tip up; others place the tongue tip behind the lower front teeth.[40] We consider sibilants made with the tongue tip *up* to be the norms. After you have practiced producing these sounds in both ways, you will be prepared to observe this difference in other people's articulation of sibilants.

Since we have defined face diagrams to represent only a side view of what the speech mechanism is doing, they are not very useful in depicting sibilants, whose salient characteristic is the length-wise grooved shape of the tongue during articulation of these sounds. It is unlikely that you will encounter face diagrams of sibilants or be required to draw any.

Production hints

[s], [z], and [ʃ] are common English sounds and pose no problem for most native English speakers. Some words to demonstrate contrast of these three sounds at the beginning of a word are "seal" [s], "zeal" [z], and "she'll" [ʃ]. Two other similar sets of words are "so," "Zoe," and "show" and "sip," "zip," and "ship."

[ʒ] occurs in the middle of English words such as "pleasure," "vision," "azure," "excursion," etc., but it never occurs word initially in English. Thus English speakers, when trying to pronounce a word with initial [ʒ], may inadvertently begin with a [d] stop before the [ʒ], as they would in pronouncing the English word "Joe." As practice in pronouncing initial [ʒ], say the first name of the actress ZaZa Gabor, which is phonetically [ʒaʒa]. Alternatively, say a word like "pleasure" slowly, pausing between the syllables, until you can correctly produce just the second syllable alone.

One final caution: Most English speakers pronounce both initial [ʃ] and [ʒ] with rounded lips. Such is not the case in every language. Say a few words with these sounds and unrounded vowels, for example, "shake," "sheet," "ZaZa," and observe whether or not your natural inclination is to round your lips to some extent. If so, practice controlling this feature of your pronunciation of sibilants by not allowing your lips to round at all throughout the word.

Alternate transcription symbols

The two new symbols in table 9.2 are commonly used to represent the palato-alveolar sibilants. They are called "s-wedge" and "z-wedge."

Table 9.2. Alternative symbols for sibilants

IPA symbol	Alternative symbol
ʃ	š
ʒ	ž

---

[40]When the tongue tip is placed behind the lower front teeth, the upper articulator tends to be a place further forward in the mouth than when the tongue tip is up, and the lower articulator tends to be a place further back along the tongue. Despite these articulatory differences, the sounds made by producing sibilants with the two different tongue positions may be quite similar to each other and quite different from nonsibilant sounds. Thus Ladefoged (1993:168) asserts that "We can divide fricatives into sibilant and non-sibilant sounds only by reference to auditory properties," that is, according to how they sound.

Key concepts

flat fricative / flat articulator
grooved fricative / grooved articulator
sibilant

Oral exercises

1. Practice saying this frame drill aloud three times, noticing whether or not your lips are rounded during the palato-alveolar sibilants and being careful not to round your lips during at least two of your times through the drill.

    ˈʒasa
    ˈʒaza
    ˈʒaʃa
    ˈʒaʒa

2. Practice saying aloud the following words.

    Yoruba of Southern Nigeria (Westermann and Ward 1933:81)

oʃo	'he is obstinate'
oʃe	'he does'
iʃu	'yam'

    Gã of Ghana (Westermann and Ward 1933:81)

ʃɛ	'to reach'
ʃika	'money'
ʃa	'to rot'

    Chuana of South Africa (Westermann and Ward 1933:81)

ʃome	'ten'
seʃoba	'bundle'
diʒɔ	'food'
ʒa	'to eat'

    English

ˈfɪʃɪŋ	'fishing'
ʃuz	'shoes'
zum	'zoom'
ˈməstæʃ	'mustache'
ˈkʰæʃu	'cashew'

Written exercises

1. Write the four sibilant symbols from this chapter and give the technical name and active articulator for each.

    [s] voiceless alveolar grooved fricative / sibilant   tongue tip
    [z] voiced alveolar grooved fricative / sibilant   tongue tip

[ʃ] *voiceless palato-alveolar grooved fricative / sibilant* — tongue blade

[ʒ] *voiced palato-alveolar grooved fricative / sibilant* — tongue blade

2.   For each of the following fricatives, state whether it is made with a flat articulator or a grooved articulator.

[s] *grooved*

[θ] *flat*

[f] *flat*

[ʒ] *grooved*

[β] *flat*

[z] *grooved*

[ʃ] *grooved*

[ɣ] *flat*

3.   For each pair of sounds below, state what the sounds have in common and how they differ. (Start with the characteristics outlined in chapter 1; then add further details from more recent chapters, including this one. Your answer may need to include a description of what the articulators are doing or where the airstream is going, for example, "The tongue tip is moved forward slightly." or "The airstream is channeled through a groove.")

[s] and [t] *sibilant vs. stop   voiceless & place*
            grooved vs. flat

[d] and [ʒ] *sibilant vs. stop, alveolar vs. palato-alveolar,*
            grooved vs. flat

[ð] and [z] *interdental vs. alveolar, fricative vs. sibilant,*
            grooved vs. flat.

[s] and [ʃ] *alveolar vs. palato-alveolar | voiceless*
                                          sibilants

Transcription conversion exercise

Retranscribe each of the following, using only IPA symbols.

[žeˈšibɪkʰöp]

[šædɛˈgüžɑ]

10

Uses of Pitch Variation

Goals

⌘ You will be able to explain why proper use of pitch is as important to good pronunciation of a language as is proper production of the individual segments of the words.

⌘ You will be able to define *intonation* and *tone,* give examples of each, and explain several specific ways in which intonation and tone differ.

⌘ You will be able to represent *pitch contours* on utterances such that you can reproduce orally what you have heard and written down, using the *relative pitches* at which you heard them.

⌘ You will be able to explain the difference between *tone glides* and *vowel glides*.

⌘ You will be able to define *frame* as the term is used in studies of tone, and you will be able to explain how to construct a constant frame with which to compare the tones of words in a tonal language.

There is more involved in good pronunciation of a language than just saying the individual sounds correctly. In chapter 8 we talked in general terms about the prosodic features of a language. One such prosodic feature that is a very important aspect of good pronunciation is proper use of the PITCH of your voice. Maybe you need to speak in a high voice or a low voice or something in between, or perhaps you need to vary back and forth between pitch levels. In any case, in order to sound really right in the language, you need to reproduce the relative pitches used by native speakers just as carefully as you do the pronunciation of the individual segments. If you do not do this, you will sound funny and foreign, and you may easily communicate a message different from what you intend!

Pitch is used in languages in two different ways: intonation and tone.

Intonation

INTONATION is the pitch pattern over an entire utterance (for example, a sentence or phrase) and is usually used to indicate emotions, convey thoughts or attitudes, or to distinguish between such things as questions and statements but *not* to distinguish one word from another. It may be symbolized by a continuous line drawn just above, just below, or even right through the string of segments that you have written. The relative height of the line represents the relative pitch of the voice, higher lines indicating higher pitches and lower lines indicating lower pitches.

For example, in the sentence shown at the right, the first two words are depicted with low pitch, the third with a high pitch falling lower, the fourth and fifth words low again, and the last word higher but not as high as the third and then falling a bit. Try saying this sentence aloud, using the intonation pattern indicated. It sounds pretty emphatic, doesn't it?

Peter does not want to go!

Peter does not want to go

Say it again, using the pattern at the left instead. This time, the voice starts a bit high, drops for the next four words, then goes higher and falls during the last word. This way, it sounds more like a simple statement.

Now try one last intonation pattern, as shown at the right. Here, the voice starts quite low, rises quite high on the second syllable of the first word and stays up for the next four words, then climbs even a bit higher on the last word. From this intonation pattern, we get the definite impression that the speaker thought Peter really did want to go and is surprised to hear that he does not, and maybe does not believe it.

Peter does not want to go?

Intonation gives different shades of meaning to the same sequence of phonetic segments. Notice that, in the three preceding examples about Peter, punctuation was used to reflect the different intonation contours. Often on texts written down by other people, that will be the only clue you get concerning intonation contours for reading the material aloud, although the proper attitude or emotion may be clear from the context as well. When you write down samples of a language that is new to you, we strongly recommend that you always indicate the pitch contour of the sample, as well as the segments, so that your readers (and you yourself) will be able to reproduce that feature of the language as accurately as the individual segments.

Kenneth Pike (1948:16) gives the following examples of information conveyed by different intonation contours in the Rumanian phrase meaning "What is your name?"

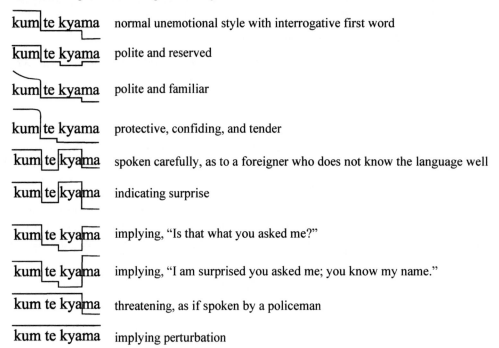

kum te kyama   normal unemotional style with interrogative first word

kum te kyama   polite and reserved

kum te kyama   polite and familiar

kum te kyama   protective, confiding, and tender

kum te kyama   spoken carefully, as to a foreigner who does not know the language well

kum te kyama   indicating surprise

kum te kyama   implying, "Is that what you asked me?"

kum te kyama   implying, "I am surprised you asked me; you know my name."

kum te kyama   threatening, as if spoken by a policeman

kum te kyama   implying perturbation

Note that in all the examples given in this chapter so far the intonation pattern never changes the basic meaning of the individual words. Instead its meaning is simply superimposed onto those meanings, conveying the attitude of the speaker in different circumstances. That is the key to the difference between tone and intonation.

Intonation is often one of the last things to be learned in language study, but it is one of the first things that will point someone out as a foreigner if it is used incorrectly. It is very common for a language learner to superimpose the normal intonation patterns of his or her own language onto utterances in the new language, often with unintended results.

As an example (adapted from Stockwell and Bowen 1965:30), if a Spanish speaker asks you where you are from and your response (which means 'I am from Minneapolis') has a normal English narrative intonation contour,

Soy de Minnea|polis

instead of the normal Spanish narrative intonation contour,

Soy|de Minneapolis

you could accidentally be indicating annoyance with having been asked.

On the other hand, if an English speaker asks a Spanish speaker what is for dinner and gets the reply with the normal Spanish narrative intonation contour

tuna|casserole and a salad

instead of the normal English one,

tuna casserole and a sa|lad

the implication is that you should not have asked or the speaker is not looking forward to that (perhaps often repeated) menu. Below are two more examples of English sentences involving this "annoyance or disgust" intonation contour.

Come|on.

What are you doing|now?

Tone

Thus far in our discussion of uses of pitch in language, we have limited ourselves to intonation patterns, which do not affect the basic meaning of words. However, in some languages the pitch of a word or syllable in a word contributes as much to the meaning of the word as do the individual segments; in fact, the pitches are intrinsic to the meanings of the words just as the segments are. Languages in which this is the case are called TONAL LANGUAGES or TONE LANGUAGES, and the pitches in such languages are called TONES.

Thai is a good example of a tonal language. The single syllable $[k^h aː]$[39] in Thai can have five different meanings, depending on the pitch of the voice that is used to say it (Ed Robinson, personal communication).

$k^h aː$	'to engage in trade'
$k^h aː$	'galangal, a cooking herb'
$k^h aː$	'a grass'
$k^h aː$	'to kill'
$k^h aː$	'leg'

Since the pitch of the voice actually determines the meanings of the words, the segments being identical in all five words, this is a clear case of tone, not intonation.

This is a very different situation from English, in which you can say, for example, the word "duck" with a high pitch, low pitch, high falling pitch, low rising pitch, or any other pitch or pitch combination you please, and still be communicating the basic meaning, 'quacking water fowl'.

---

[39]The symbol following a segment indicates that the segment is extra long. You will learn more about length in chapter 14.

Another big difference between intonation and tone is that intonation contours are distributed over entire phrases, for example,

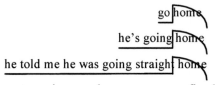

whereas tones in many languages are confined to syllables or words and do not spread to whole phrases.

Focus on pitch relative to context, not on absolute musical pitch

Note that with both intonation and tone, we are not concerned with the absolute pitch of the voice but rather with the pitch relative to the surrounding pitches. People do not all speak in the same voice register. Rather, women usually have a higher voice register than men do, and children's voices are usually higher yet. Of course, there is wide variation of register used within those groups as well and sometimes even by one person moving from one situation to another.

What we focus on as we study tone and intonation in languages is not the absolute musical pitch(es) used in a particular word or phrase but rather whether the pitch(es) used are higher or lower than, or the same as, those surrounding them. This focus on relative pitch is even more important in studying tone than it is in studying intonation. You will become very frustrated and sound very peculiar as you track or mimic tones if you try to speak in the same register as the person you are copying, especially if that person is of the opposite gender from you.

When you listen for tone, it is important to have some sort of FRAME, an adjacent word or two whose pitches are known and remain constant, so that tones on other words can be judged in relation to them. For example, in these Mandarin Chinese utterances (Floyd, field notes, transcription simplified), the

[ʃuɔ mi] say "secret" (same, falling)

[ʃuɔ mi] say "to charm" (somewhat lower, rising)

[ʃuɔ mi] say "meow" (same, level)

[ʃuɔ mi] say "rice" (much lower, rising)

frame [ʃuɔ] on a high tone, remains constant, and the [mi] syllables' tones can be compared with that high tone.

Types of tone languages

Not all tone languages are alike. Some tone languages utilize only LEVEL TONES (that is, the pitch is perceived to stay the same throughout an entire syllable). Others also utilize TONE GLIDES (that is, the pitch is perceived to rise or fall or both, within a single syllable).

Note: Be sure to note two different usages of the word *glide*. In this chapter, *glide* means *tone glide* and refers to a rise or fall in the pitch of the voice, while the vowel quality stays the same. In the vowel chapters, *glide* means *vowel glide* and refers to a change of vowel quality caused by a shift in the tongue and/or lip position, while the pitch probably stays the same.

When a language utilizes tone glides that have been analyzed as not being sequences of level tones, then that language is called a CONTOUR TONE LANGUAGE.

Languages also differ as to the number of tones used. Igbo (Nigeria) has two levels, high and low; Trique (Mexico) has five levels (Barbara Hollenbach, field notes; Thai has two levels and three glides (Floyd, field notes).

Decisions regarding the number and types of tones in a given language will depend on phonological analysis of the whole sound system of the language, that is, how the tones interact with each other and with the segments in the words, etc. Your concern as a phonetician is to write down what you hear, so that you have accurate data to work with in making those phonological decisions. Actually, that is true of your transcription of individual segments as well. Your analysis of the whole sound system may show that some phonetic detail is very predictable from context. However, you need to be able to write that detail down first, so that you have an accurate body of data to help you begin an intelligent, meaningful analysis.

Notation of tone

You may very possibly not know whether a new language you are starting to learn and transcribe is tonal or not,[40] but you should definitely start to write down the pitch patterns right from the start. After all, it is just as important to your overall pronunciation of an intonational language to reproduce intonation or tone correctly as it is to get the tones in a tonal language right. Initially, you may find it easiest to use the continuous pitch contour lines suggested in the previous section on intonation contours, filling that line in above or below the string of segments that you have transcribed first.

There are many ways to symbolize the tones. If you are using this book as part of a classroom course, your instructor will presumably specify which system you are to use for the course. If not, the choice is yours, at least until you find out what system is preferred in the area in which you are working. Table 10.1 summarizes some of the main systems that are in use worldwide.

Table 10.1. Some possible tone symbolizations

	Numbers System A	Numbers System B	Diacritics	Contours	Tone letters
Level tones					
extra high	a^5	a^1	$\acute{\acute{a}}$	$\bar{a}$	a˥
high	a^4	a^2	á	$\bar{a}$	a˦
mid	a^3	a^3	$\bar{a}$	$\bar{a}$	a˧
low	a^2	a^4	à	a	a˨
extra low	a^1	a^5	$\grave{\grave{a}}$	A	a˩
Glides					
extra high-low	a^{52}	a^{14}	$\hat{a}$	$\acute{a}$	a˥˩
high-low-mid	a^{423}	a^{243}	$\tilde{a}$	λ	a˦˧
mid-high	a^{34}	a^{32}	$\acute{a}$	$\bar{a}$	a˧˦
low-high	a^{24}	a^{42}	ǎ	$\acute{a}$	a˩˥

Most linguists who use numbered tone levels (see Numbers System A in table 10.1) start with 1 for the lowest pitch level and use higher numbers for higher pitch levels, which is mnemonically easy. Others, especially some in Mexico, use an opposite system for numbering tones (see Numbers System B in table 10.1); their highest tone level is usually numbered "1," and progressively lower tones are numbered "2, 3," etc. This system is also mnemonically easy if you think of the first drawer in a bureau or file cabinet as being the highest, the second as the next highest, the fourth or fifth or whatever drawer as the lowest, etc. In either case, the numbers are written as a superscript following the syllables to which they pertain. Note that the numbers used to denote glide sequences are to be read as a series of levels, for example, 423 in System A is a high-low-mid glide.

If diacritics are used, they should be written directly above the syllables to which they pertain, as shown in the following example, from San Miguel el Grande Mixtec of Mexico (Ruth Mary Alexander, personal communication; treat the raised "w" as a regular English "w" for now).

---

[40]Whenever you begin studying a new language, you need to research into what other people have learned about that language, or other languages that are closely related to it; otherwise you will be in considerable danger of "reinventing the wheel." Other linguists' written opinions regarding whether or not a language is tonal are very likely to be available in linguistic books or journals and are worth studying. However, you should not regard their findings as gospel truth and force your data to fit their analysis if your findings are at variance with theirs.

'kūù 'kɨ̄tɨ̄ 'kʷáá   'The blind animals will die.'

In general, tone diacritics "slant toward" the tone level that they denote, for example, the high tone diacritic (´) slants upward (toward high), the low tone diacritic (`) slants downward (toward low), and the mid tone diacritic (¯) "slants" straight toward the middle. One or more of these diacritics may be combined for contour tones, for example, (ˇ) combines the low and high tone diacritics, denoting a glide from a low pitch to a high pitch, and (^) is a high-low combination.

Tone letters can be used in several different ways. Usually a tone letter either consistently precedes or consistently follows the syllable to which it pertains, as in the same Mixtec example, rewritten below.

'ku˧ u˩ 'kɨ˧ tɨ˧ 'kʷa˥ a˥   'The blind animals will die.'

Alternatively, if you wish to keep the segmental and pitch transcriptions from interfering with each other, the tone letters or contour lines may be placed directly above the segmental transcription and aligned vertically with the characters representing the respective syllable nuclei, similar to the way tone diacritics are placed, as in the same Mixtec example, rewritten yet again below.

   ˧ ˩ ˧ ˧   ˥ ˥
'ku u 'kɨ tɨ 'kʷa a   'The blind animals will die.'

With this usage it can be very difficult to achieve ideal alignment. However, if the alignment is correct, we find tone letters easier to read if they are above the syllables rather than inserted directly into the line of segment symbols as is more standard.

Tone marking systems are adaptable to the number of levels being distinguished in the transcription. For example, if you have been marking four or more phonetic pitch levels of tones in the language with which you are working, and then you discover after a while that there are only three contrastive levels of tone in the language, you may adapt your notation system accordingly.

Often the practical orthography for a tone language leaves one ("default") tone unmarked, which simplifies the writing system. For example, the mid tone may be left unmarked, and a reader will interpret every syllable as having mid tone unless it has been specifically marked with some other tone. However, such shortcuts should be implemented only after much careful analysis of the language has been done.

Hints for deciding whether or not a language is tonal

Deciding whether or not a language is tonal involves application of analytical principles and techniques. Finding sets of segmentally identical words with different meanings reflected only in pitch differences, as in the Thai example in this chapter, is excellent evidence for claiming that the language is tonal.

E. Pike (1974:169ff) provides some additional guidelines to facilitate making such a decision.

- Most intonational languages have some correlation between stress (extra prominence to a syllable in a word or phrase; see chapter 11 for further explanation) and high pitch. This is not necessarily the case with tone languages. Hearing stress on a low pitch is a good indication that the language is tonal.
- In a language where high pitch tends to co-occur with stress, a stressed syllable is also frequently lengthened, as for example in English. Such languages are usually not tonal. However, in a tone language, syllables with high pitch are often shorter in duration than syllables with nonhigh pitches, as is the case in Cantonese, Thai, Fasu, Chatino, and Popoloca.

These are tendencies, not guaranteed absolutes, but their frequency of occurrence is noteworthy and should be kept in mind.

Hints for hearing pitch accurately

It is sometimes difficult for people to begin hearing contrastive voice pitches if they have never thought to focus their attention on pitch before.[41] Unfortunately, tonal languages rarely confine the tones they use to nice melodic intervals in the musical scale.

A very good starting place for training yourself to hear pitch is simply to compare one syllable's tone with another syllable's tone. Are they the same or different? If they are different, is the second syllable's tone higher or lower than the first? Is it a lot higher / lower, or is the difference quite small? Remember, you can almost always use a constant tone FRAME whose tone you know, so you can make comparisons like this.

When you are working with contour tone languages, the first question to ask is whether the pitch on the syllable changes or stays constant. If it changes, is it gliding up or down, or perhaps both? Is the glide in that direction a big one or a small one? Is the pitch at the start of the glide higher or lower than or the same as the pitch in your known frame for comparison? How does the ending pitch of the glide compare with that of your frame?

When you are not sure of the tone(s) on a word, make a list of several words that you guess probably have the same tone as your puzzling word. Then ask a speaker of the language to say all the words, one right after the other. If you guessed right, your word will seem to fit right into the list. If you guessed wrong, the tone of your word will probably stand out clearly as being different from the others. In that case you can set up another list of words with some other tone pattern, and keep trying until you get a match.[42]

Key concepts

pitch
    relative
intonation: mood, attitude
    intonation contour
    distributed over entire phrases
tone: contrastive meaning
    level tone
    contour tone
    glide
    pertaining to single word or syllable
frame

Exercises

1.   Read the following sentences aloud, using the indicated intonation contours. Write down for the first three what emotion or attitude its intonation communicates to you. For the fourth, draw onto the sentence the markings for an intonation contour that would indicate incredulity. Your answers on these may differ depending on what your native language is.

    John is not going to the circus   *aggravated* _____

---

[41]Actually, it is often difficult for people to notice any kind of pitch, not just the contrastive ones of a tone language. These hints can be useful for dealing with intonational contours as well as tone levels and contours.

[42]This list-making technique can be very effective in identifying difficult segments as well. As with tone, make a list of words that you know contain a segment that is very similar to the problem segment, and insert the word whose segment you are uncertain about. If that segment is the same as the others, it will blend into the list. If not, it will stand out as different and you can try moving it to a different list featuring another segment.

John is not going to the circus   *stern*

John is not going to the circus   *surprized*

John is not going to the circus. (incredulity)

2. Read the text at the right into a tape recorder, using the indicated intonation contours. Listen to the tape and compare your intonation with that on the paper. It would probably be helpful to you to practice reading it several times first without the tape recorder, so you can get used to the intonation contours that are prescribed.

3. Ask someone to read a brief paragraph of your choice aloud. Be sure that (s)he and you each have a copy. Your copy needs to have space between the lines like the circus story. As (s)he reads, draw intonation contour lines on your copy to depict the pitches (s)he used.

4. Read aloud the following words, being careful to use the correct tones.

Kikuyu of Kenya (Pat Bennett, personal communication)

ŋìmà   'complete'
ŋéà   'jog along'
ŋènì   'strange'

I really enjoy going to circuses. It is so exciting to watch the clowns and acrobats, and my favorite part is seeing the wild animals do tricks. Can you watch lions jump through flaming hoops without screaming for fear that their manes will catch fire?! Don't you hold your breath waiting to see if the elephants will fall and squash their trainer?! Oh, how I wish a circus would come to town soon!

Sui of China (adapted from E. Pike 1978:80; Fang-Kuei Li: 4 is extra high, 1 is low)

p^ha^2 'blue'
ba^3 'to add'
$ʔba^{34}$ 'wide'
$ɸa^2$ 'right (side)'
$ɸa^3$ 'cloth'
$ɸa^{43}$ or $ɸa^{42}$ 'father's younger sister'
$ɸa^{32}$ 'sheep'
pak^{43} or pak^{42} 'white'
mum^4 'fish'

11

Stress

Goals

⌘ You will be able to define *stressed* and *unstressed syllables, primary* and *secondary stress,* and *phrase stress.*

⌘ You will be able to list physiological and auditory correlates of stress, as well as several phonetically perceivable characteristics of stressed and unstressed syllables.

⌘ You will be able to indicate which syllable(s) of a word is/are stressed, and which stressed syllable in a phrase is stressed the most.

When we speak of a syllable as being STRESSED, we mean that that syllable is in some way more prominent than the others in the same word. According to Ladefoged (1993:249–250), a speaker stresses a syllable "by extra contraction of the muscles of the rib cage, and by extra activity of the laryngeal muscles," and perhaps also by "increases in the muscular activity involved in the articulatory movements." As is the case for most of the physiological aspects of speech, the speaker is almost certainly unconscious of these minor changes.

However, the hearer will not perceive stress in terms of the physiological changes in the speaker's chest or throat. Rather, the hearer may perceive stress on a syllable by means of several audible phenomena which vary from language to language. These phenomena may occur singly or in combination with others. A stressed syllable usually exhibits at least one or two of the following qualities:

- it is spoken more loudly[43]
- it has a higher pitch of voice
- it has a longer vowel
- it may contain any of the vowels used in the language

In contrast, an UNSTRESSED syllable is usually perceived phonetically as one which

- is spoken more softly
- has a lower pitch
- has a shorter vowel
- may contain one of a more restricted selection of vowels, often fairly neutral central vowels

---

[43]However, relative loudness of two syllables is difficult to measure accurately. Some people have attempted to measure the loudness component of stress by seemingly simple procedures such as noting the peak reading volume indicator on a tape recorder. Such a procedure to compare the loudness of various syllables may give a valid indication of relative stress only if the vowels of the syllables are of the same or nearly the same quality, but the results will be very misleading if the vowels differ significantly in quality. Other, more sophisticated acoustic instruments may be used with more reliable results; however, discussion of such instruments is outside the scope of this book.

One technique for determining which syllables are perceived by a mother-tongue speaker of a language as being stressed is to have the speaker tap with a finger while saying the word, phrase, or sentence in which you wish to determine stress placement. There is a strong tendency in at least some languages for the tapping to occur on the stressed syllable.

Stress is indicated with a small raised vertical line (') preceding the stressed syllable.[44] For example, the first syllable of the word "dishes" is stressed, so the word can be written phonetically as ['dɪʃɨz]. The stress mark can go anywhere within the stressed syllable as long as it precedes the vowel, but it is most common to place it at the very beginning of the syllable. Stress should be marked in any phonetic transcription of more than one syllable. Most phonetics instructors will probably ask you to put only one stress mark in each word, although you can also transcribe secondary stresses, to be discussed later in this chapter.

Languages may indicate stress in various ways. For example, in Swedish a higher pitch of voice on a syllable is the primary clue that that syllable is stressed. Some noun-verb pairs in English differ only in the pitches of the syllables, for example, "insult/insult," "export/export," "overflow/overflow" (Ladefoged 2001:22). In Serbo-Croatian, a lengthened vowel is the primary indicator. Several Russian vowels are reduced to a very neutral central quality when in unstressed syllables, and the placement of stress in Russian can even affect the qualities of vowels in surrounding syllables.

English uses a combination of pitch, vowel length (indicated below by a symbol similar to a colon, to be explained further in chapter 14), and vowel quality to indicate stress. Notice that, in the following pairs of words that we think of as differing only in stress, the pitch rises, and vowels lengthen on stressed syllables, while many vowels in unstressed syllables tend to be reduced to [ə]. These words contain a few symbols that you have not learned yet and which will be explained in later chapters, but it should be easy to guess what they represent since all the words and sounds are from American English. You can ignore them for now, as they are not the focus of the discussion here.

'combine	[ˈkʰaːmbaɪ̯n]	'a piece of farm machinery'
comˈbine	[kʰəmˈbaːɪ̯n]	'to mix together'
'reject	[ˈɹiːdʒɛktʰ]	'one who is rejected'
reˈject	[ɹɪˈdʒɛːktʰ]	'to refuse, shun'
'commune	[ˈkʰaːmi̯un]	'a collective farm'
comˈmune	[kʰəˈmi̯uːn]	'to communicate intimately'

Once you have figured out what the correlates of stress are in a language you are investigating, you can use the stress mark (') as a shorthand symbol representing them. However, until you have done considerable analysis in the language, it will be important to mark as much phonetic detail as possible (as in the preceding pairs) as well as the stress mark itself, even though that results in some redundancy.

Other types of stress

Words containing several syllables may have more than one level of stress. There will be one syllable that is the most stressed, but one or more of the other syllables will receive slightly more stress than the rest. In such a case, the most stressed syllable is said to have PRIMARY STRESS, while the somewhat stressed syllable(s) will be said to have SECONDARY STRESS. In the IPA, primary stress is marked with the small *raised* vertical line we just described and illustrated ('), while secondary stress is marked with a similar line just *below* the baseline of the segmental transcription (ˌ). In the Americanist system of transcription, primary stress can be marked with a *double* raised vertical line (") and secondary stress with a *single* one ('). When stress is noted in published linguistic data, there will most likely be an explanation of which system is used and what the symbols represent.

Some linguists even distinguish three or four levels of stress. Marking such fine detail might be overwhelming to you in your initial stages of language learning and transcribing, but it may be beneficial at some stage to focus on several levels of stress after you are more comfortable with recognizing and writing the segments.

---

[44]Pullum and Ladusaw (1996:237) call this symbol a vertical stroke (superior).

PHRASE STRESS[45] is another type of stress to be aware of. This looks beyond the scope of individual words to the whole phrase. Usually there is one stressed syllable in a phrase that has more prominence even than the other stressed syllables in the same phrase. Consider the following sentence.

The only kind of stress I can relate to right now is emotional!

Perhaps, as you pronounce this sentence to yourself, the syllable "I" stands out as being the most prominent, or perhaps "now" or the "mo" in "emotional." One of those three syllables, probably "I," has the sentence stress. (For English, you can probably make the decision based on which one you say with the highest pitch of your voice.) "I," being a one-syllable word, would not even need to be marked with the conventional word stress symbol. To mark it for phrase stress, you may use a small raised ° (an Americanist symbol).

The only kind of stress °I can re'late to right now is e'motional!

Stress and rhythm

The timing of stressed syllables in a phrase gives that phrase a distinctive rhythm. Consequently, variations in the use of stress cause different languages to have different rhythms. English and other Germanic languages are sometimes called STRESS-TIMED languages, meaning that they give the impression that stressed syllables occur at roughly even time intervals regardless of the number of intervening unstressed syllables. For example, in the phrase "'English and 'other Ger'manic 'languages" the stressed syllables tend to be evenly spaced in terms of time. This is accomplished by varying the duration of the unstressed syllables in between.

In contrast, other languages, such as French and Spanish, are sometimes called SYLLABLE-TIMED, meaning that all syllables tend to have approximately the same duration. Thus in the sentence, *A mí no me gusta eso* 'I don't like that', each syllable is given pretty much the same duration of time and the same amount of stress. Consequently, English speakers often think of Spanish as being a very rapid language, because there are no long syllables on which they can "catch up and rest," that is, the syllables come at a uniformly rapid rate.

Correctly mimicking the prosodic feature of rhythm of a language, that is, the relative pattern of stresses and duration allotted to syllables, is as important to having a good "accent" as is correct pronunciation of the individual phonetic segments of the language. It is also vital to utilize the correct technique or combination of techniques to signal stress in the language, rather than imposing those of your own language. For example, if a language utilizes only vowel length to indicate stress but you, as an American English speaker, also raise the pitch of your voice on each stressed syllable, you will sound "foreign" even if you pronounce every segment correctly and get the rhythm right. Your pronunciation of a language will sound best to mother-tongue speakers if you strive to mimic *every* aspect of the way that mother-tongue speakers speak the language.

Key concepts and symbols

stressed syllable
unstressed syllable
primary stress
secondary stress
phrase stress
stress-timed languages / syllable-timed languages

---

[45]Phrase stress, as the term is used here, corresponds to what Ladefoged calls "tonic accent" (Ladefoged 1993:116–117) and to what Crystal (2003:467) calls "tonicity."

Oral exercises

1. Do a tracking exercise such as that described on p. 56. Ask someone to tape a short paragraph for you in your mother tongue. Listen to the recording over and over then begin tracking it to the best of your ability focusings specifically on stress patterns.

2. Do the same exercise with a language *not* your own; find a mother-tongue speaker of that language to make the tape. Ignore the sounds that you have not yet covered in your phonetics course, focusing on stress patterns.

Written exercises

1. In the following sentence, identify which syllables are marked for stress within a word and which one syllable receives the main phrase stress. Which word is marked for two levels of stress and which syllables in that word have stress at the two levels?

    A 'highly 'capable 'acrobat fell ˌunex'pectedly to his ᵒdeath from the 'tightrope at the 'circus this after'noon.

2. Mark each of these words for primary and secondary stress.

    'appliˌcation   'supplemeˌntary   inˌcompreˈhensible

3. Write out an English sentence of your choice containing about ten words and twenty syllables. Mark the syllable with primary stress in each word of more than one syllable and the major phrase stress. Also mark secondary stress on long words, if your sentence contains any.

    A stupid, idioctic man named Andy Bernard sold his Extera to a smart and capable man named Dwight.

4. List several auditory characteristics of syllables that are perceived as being stressed. Do the same for unstressed syllables.

    Stressed syllables are louder, higher in pitch and contain common vowels
    Unstressed syllabus are quieter, softer, low pitched & contain more unusual vowels.

5. List two specific things that your vocal mechanism can do physically to cause a syllable to be perceived as being stressed.

    Push air out faster & more air through a smaller airway, tighten vocal cords

12

Nasalized Vowels

Goals

⌘ You will be able to define the major difference between *nasal* sounds and *nasalized* sounds in terms of air flow and resonant cavities—*nasalized* sounds have air flow and resonance in both the oral and nasal cavities.

⌘ You will be able to explain what is meant by *contrastive* differences between sounds, what *minimal pairs* are, and how they help to demonstrate whether or not differences are indeed contrastive.

⌘ You will be able to recognize, produce, and symbolize all vowels made with the *modification* of *nasalization,* and give the technical name for each nasalized vowel.

The MODIFICATION of NASALIZATION can be added to any vowel by lowering the soft palate (the velum). As you may recall from chapters 1 and 6, this creates a velic opening that allows the sound to resonate in the nasal cavity. Both nasal and nasalized sounds are made with velic opening (velum lowered). However, there is an important difference between these two categories of sound.

- A nasal segment is produced with a complete closure in the mouth which completely impedes the airstream through the mouth.
- A nasalized vowel is produced with passageways for the airstream through both the mouth and nose, allowing the sound to resonate in both the nasal and oral tracts.

We see nasalization as a modification of a vowel rather than considering nasalized vowels to be totally unique sounds from their non-nasalized counterparts. This is because not all languages employ nasalization *contrastively*, that is, they do not all have pairs of words with contrasting meanings that differ phonetically only in whether or not a particular vowel is nasalized. However, virtually all languages do use tongue and lip position on vowels contrastively. In that sense, then, tongue and lip position are more intrinsic to vowel quality than is the presence or absence of nasalization.

The vocal tract resonates at different frequencies, depending on its size and shape (which a speaker can control and manipulate by moving and shaping the lips and tongue), resulting in a wide variety of vowel qualities. In contrast, the size and shape of the nasal tract are essentially fixed. Thus, a speaker can control whether or not the resonances of the nasal tract are involved at all in determining the quality of a vowel (by lowering or raising the velum) and the degree of nasalization involved in a vowel (by varying the size of the velic opening), but not the resonating frequencies of the nasal tract itself.

The qualities of nasalized vowels are often more difficult to identify than the qualities of non-nasalized vowels. This is partly due to the fact that resonances in the nasal tract interact with resonances in the oral tract, altering them or even canceling them out. Nasal resonances may also change the perceived quality of a vowel, often making it sound as if the tongue is articulating the vowel in a somewhat lower (more open) position than what it really uses.

Notation of nasalized vowels

In the IPA notation system, nasalization on vowels is indicated by placing a tilde (˜) directly above the normal vowel symbol, for example, ã, ẽ, etc. In the Americanist system, a Polish hook (˛) is placed directly below the normal vowel symbol, for example, ą, ę. You may occasionally see nasalization symbolized by a comma (ˌ), cedilla (˒), or reversed comma (ˏ) under the vowel symbol, for example, ą, ǫ ę. In this book, we use the tilde and Polish hook.

Contrast involving nasalization

The presence or absence of nasalization on a vowel can be the only difference between two words with different meanings. Pairs of words that differ in only one segment but have different meanings are called MINIMAL PAIRS. The difference between the pronunciations of the two words in a minimal pair is said to be CONTRASTIVE. Below are three minimal pairs from the Ewe language spoken in Ghana (Westermann and Ward 1933:43).[46] Notice that in each pair, the words have different meanings and the only phonetic difference between the two words is whether or not the vowel is nasalized; this suggests that nasalization on vowels is contrastive in Ewe.

dɔ	'belly'
dɔ̃	'be weak'
du	'in heaps'
dũ	'staring'
ma	'not'
mã	'divide'

In a few languages, there may be more than two degrees of nasalization (nasalized versus non-nasalized), at least phonetically. For example, in Palantla Chinantec of Mexico (Merrifield 1963:14; tone notation: 3 is high, 1 is low), vowels may be non-nasalized, lightly nasalized, or heavily nasalized.

ʔe^{12}	'teach'
ʔẽ^{12}	'count'
ʔę̃^{12}	'chase'

Technical names

Technical names for nasalized vowels are the same as for the vowels taught thus far, except for the insertion of the word "nasalized" just before the word "vowel."[47] Thus, [õ] is a "(voiced) close-mid back rounded *nasalized* vowel." "Non-nasalized" is the default characteristic for vowels so it is not included in the technical names for purely oral vowels.

---

[46]This Ewe data has been simplified by omitting notation of length, which will not be taught until chapter 14.

[47]Other vowel modifications will be introduced in later chapters.

Production hints

To gain control and awareness of velic opening or closure, say the word "hidden," without putting a vowel in the second syllable at all. The only physical difference between the sounds [d] and [n] is presence or absence of velic opening. Say just the second syllable of "hidden" repeatedly, [dndndndndn], again without any intervening vowels. You should be able to feel your velum moving down and up, opening and closing that doorway to your nasal cavity that was described in chapter 1, the velic opening. The same feeling should be present if you say [bmbmbmbmbm] or [gŋgŋgŋgŋgŋ].

Now that you have gained awareness of what your velum is doing, say [mĩmĩmĩmĩmĩ], being sure that you never feel your velum rise to close off the velic opening. Try it with other nasalized vowels. Next try it with an alveolar nasal [n] instead of the bilabials. Now try it with a velar nasal [ŋ]; if you feel a bit of movement in the back of your mouth on this one, that is probably the back of your tongue rising to meet your velum, not the velum rising to close off the velic opening.

It is usually not difficult for people to produce nasalized vowels adjacent to nasal consonants, and non-nasalized vowels adjacent to oral consonants. The challenge comes in producing consonant / vowel combinations that differ in nasality. For example, try saying [mɑmɑmɑ] without any nasalization on the vowels, or [pɑ̃pɑ̃pɑ̃] with full nasalization on the vowels. If you find that difficult, say the words very slowly, being sure to lengthen both the consonants and the vowels. Hold a finger or two lightly on each side of your nose, where you can feel hard bone just below the bridge of your nose. You will probably feel some vibration there during nasal and nasalized sounds but not during purely oral sounds. This is a useful test for velic opening as you learn to control nasalization of vowels. Fortunately, in many languages, vowels that occur next to nasals, and especially those that occur between two nasals, are likely to include at least some nasalization.

You can also use a mirror to help you master this skill. Open your mouth so you can see your soft palate rise and lower to close and open the velic opening. Now say a series of vowels, alternating between nasalized and non-nasalized ones: [ɑãɑã], [iĩiĩ], etc. You should be able to see quite a bit of movement of the velum up and down. But beware: sometimes students think they are seeing movement of the velum when in fact it is the tongue back moving up and down toward the velum, producing the velar nasal consonant [ŋ] instead of a vowel.

Key concepts

modification
nasal / nasalized / non-nasalized / nasalization
contrastive feature / minimal pair

Oral exercises

1. Say each vowel in figure 7.1 (in chapter 7) with and without nasalization. Since nasalization somewhat blurs the distinctiveness of the vowel qualities, start first with a series of vowels that differ considerably in quality, for example, [i e a o u]. Then later go to a series of vowels that are closer together on the chart, for example [i ɪ e ɛ æ].

2. Practice the following phrases from San Miguel el Grande Mixtec of Mexico (Ruth Mary Alexander, personal communication). Note that the raised figures indicate tone: ˥ is high, ˦ mid, ˩ low. However, concentrate more on controlling your velum than on the tone. Feel free to omit the tones completely if they are too confusing. Treat the raised "w" as a regular English "w" for now.

      ˧˩ ˨˧ ˦˦   ˥˥
'ku u 'kɨ tɨ 'kʷa a   'The blind animals will die.'

      ˧˩ ˨˧ ˦˦   ˥˥
'kũ ũ 'kɨ tɨ 'kʷa a   'four blind animals'

      ˧˩ ˨˧ ˦˦   ˥˥
'ku u 'kɨ tɨ 'kʷã ã   'The yellow animals will die.'

      ˧˩ ˨˧ ˦˦   ˥˥
'kũ ũ 'kɨ tɨ 'kʷã ã   'four yellow animals'

3.   Practice saying aloud the following words.
     French (Bickford, personal notes)

     mõ fis   'my son'
     mon a'mi   'my friend'[48]
     ma   'my (feminine)'
     mo'mã   'moment'
     mõ nõ   'my name'
     mon o   'my water'

Written exercise

Write out the technical names for the following vowels.

[ã] *open front unrounded nasalized vowel*

[ũ] *close back unrounded nasalized vowel*

[ɛ̃] *open-mid front unrounded nasalized vowel*

[ỹ] *close front rounded nasalized vowel*

[æ̃] *near-open front unrounded nasalized vowel*

Transcription conversion exercise

Rewrite each of the following, using only IPA symbols.

[ɑ'kʰ ɪ m̩ i̯]

[ɓ̈ü̈tʰ ë 'ɡ̊o̥š]

---

[48]It is quite probable that many speakers of French will include at least some nasalization on the vowels that occur between two nasals.

13

Laterals

Goals

⌘ You will be able to define a *lateral* as a sound in which there is an air passageway over one or both sides of the tongue and not over the center.

⌘ You will be able to define an *approximant* as a sound produced by two articulators coming close to each other, but not so close as to produce the audible turbulence characteristic of a fricative nor the complete impedance which defines a stop.

⌘ You will be able to recognize, produce, symbolize, and give a technical name for each sound in the lateral table.

A LATERAL is an oral speech sound in which there is an air passageway over one or both sides of the tongue and not over the center. The most common lateral is [l], as in English "long," "lie," and "low."

All laterals are either fricatives or approximants. An APPROXIMANT is a sound produced by two articulators coming close to each other. The airstream for approximants is directed by the articulators but not impeded; thus, approximants are CONTINUANTS and not stops. The airstream is not impeded sufficiently to produce audible turbulence between the articulators; thus, approximants are sonorants, not fricatives. The term approximant is derived from the articulation involved: the active articulator (or some part of it—in the case of laterals, the tongue *sides*) "approximates" or approaches the passive articulator. All laterals are consonants, since they fail to meet the vowel's criterion of "central." Fricative laterals also lack the vowel criterion of "sonorant."

The shape of the tongue for a lateral is in one sense the inverse of that for a sibilant. Recall that for [s] the sides of the tongue curve upward to contact the alveolar ridge along its sides, and a constriction between the tongue tip and the alveolar ridge produces the fricative noise. In contrast, for alveolar lateral fricatives the tongue tip contacts the alveolar ridge, and a constriction between one or both sides of the tongue and the alveolar ridge produces the fricative noise. The diagrams in figure 13.1 show front-view cross-sections of the shape of the tongue for flat fricatives, sibilants, and lateral fricatives.

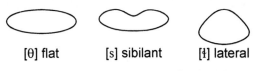

[θ] flat   [s] sibilant   [ɬ] lateral

Figure 13.1. Tongue shapes for fricatives.

As with sibilants, we do not represent laterals on face diagrams because we have no convention for indicating the position of the tongue sides, which are crucial to distinguish flat fricatives, sibilants, and laterals, for example, [θ], [s], and [ɬ].

Table 13.1. Laterals

	Alveolar	**Velar**	
voiceless	ḷ̥	ʟ̥	lateral approximant
voiced	l	ʟ	
voiceless	ɬ		lateral fricative
voiced	ɮ		
active articulator	tongue tip	tongue back	

Technical names and notes about the symbols

As before, to derive technical names for these sounds, read the labels on the table clockwise. For example, [ɮ] is a "voiced alveolar lateral fricative" and [l̥] is a "voiceless alveolar lateral approximant".[49]

When you write lateral symbols by hand, it is best to use a cursive-style "ℓ," to help avoid confusion with other handwritten symbols that look similar, such as "t." This is especially true for the Americanist symbol "ɬ," which looks very much like a "t" if it is not written cursive-style. Be sure that your cursive "ℓ" is tall enough not to be confused with a cursive "e."

Production hints

[l] is the sound that most English speakers use in the pronunciation of words such as "long," "live," and "low," in which a lateral occurs at the onset of a syllable. The syllable-initial lateral approximant [l] in English is sometimes called a "clear l" to distinguish it from the syllable-final lateral approximant in words such as "bill" or "null". This so-called "dark l" will be introduced in chapter 31.

[l̥] is produced with the same articulation as [l], but without voicing. Say the sequence [lɑlːɑlːɑ], pausing on the laterals, then repeat the entire sequence without voicing [l̥ɑl̥ːɑl̥ːɑ].[50] In practicing to produce this sound, be careful not to introduce noisy turbulence.

[ɬ] is produced with an articulation similar to that of [l], but with sufficient constriction and air flow to cause audible noise due to air turbulence. Start with the voiceless lateral just described, then squeeze the sides of your tongue toward the roof of your mouth to narrow the constriction and thus produce noise. The tip of your tongue must remain on the alveolar ridge.

[ɮ] is produced in the same way as the voiceless alveolar lateral fricative [ɬ], but with the voicing. It sounds similar to [ʒ], but with the addition of a lateral quality. Beware of rounding your lips for this voiced lateral, just as you need to beware of rounding your lips for the sibilant [ʒ].

Very few English speakers make velar laterals [ʟ] in their normal speech. To practice making these sounds, say words that start with "gl," such as "glue" and "glow," being careful to keep your tongue tip glued to the floor of your mouth. (Your tongue tip will probably really want to sneak up to your alveolar ridge.) Say the words again, giving extra length to the laterals. Then try saying just the velar lateral in isolation. Now put it between [ɑ] vowels: [ʟɑʟɑ], etc. To get the voiceless velar lateral sound, try that same sequence by whispering "cl" words such as "clue" and "class," then whisper the [ʟɑʟɑ] sequence. Then, finally, try the voiceless velar lateral in isolation and then between two voiced vowels.

---

[49]Sometimes you will see the order of the two parts of the manner of articulation reversed—"fricative lateral" instead of "lateral fricative." Either order is acceptable.

[50]Note that the same small circle that is used under the [l] to indicate a voiceless alveolar lateral approximant [l̥] can also be placed under a vowel symbol [ạ] to indicate that the vowel is voiceless. We will work with voiceless vowels in more detail in chapter 15.

Table 13.2. Common alternative symbols

IPA symbol	Alternative symbol
l̥	ɬ
ʟ	L
ʟ̥	Ł
ɫ	ł
ɮ	ɭ

Key concepts

lateral
approximant
continuant

Oral exercises

1. Practice the following frame drill aloud three times.

    ʟula
    ʟul̥a
    ʟuɮa
    ʟuɬa
    ʟuʟa
    ʟuʟ̥a

2. Practice saying aloud the following words.
    English

    ləkʰ   'luck'
    pl̥əkʰ   'pluck'
    lɪpʰ   'lip'
    kl̥ɪpʰ   'clip'

    Mid-Wahgi of Papua New Guinea (Ladefoged and Maddieson 1996:190)

    alala   'speak incorrectly'
    aʟaʟe   'dizzy'

    Zulu of South Africa (Westermann and Ward 1933:71)

    isiɬaɬa   'bush'
    ɮula   'pass'
    iɮelo   'pasture ground'

    Suto and Pedi of South Africa (Westermann and Ward 1933:71)

    ɬɛɬa   'to trot'
    ɬɔla   'to create'
    ɬola   'to overpower'
    ɬapa   'to wash'

Nii of Papua New Guinea (Larry and Ann Cates, personal communication)

nokʟ̥	'water'
eg nakʟ̥	'next door language'
moʟəm / sæʟəm / pæʟəm	'it's there (different positions)'
paʟa	'fence'
wakʟ̥	'knitted bag'

Written exercise

Write all six lateral symbols. Give the technical name for each one.

[l̥] _voiceless alveolar lateral approximant_
[l] _voiced alveolar lateral approximant_
[ɬ] _voiceless alveolar lateral fricative_
[ɮ] _voiced alveolar lateral fricative_
[ʟ̥] _voiceless velar lateral approximant_
[ʟ] _voiced velar lateral approximant_

Transcription conversion exercise

Rewrite each of the following, using only IPA symbols.

šɬaf _____

žüʝæp _____

bʊtʰ _____

ɖuʟɔŋ _____

ʟaɬəŋ _____

14

Length

Goals

⌘ You will be able to define the concepts of *duration* (the amount of time used for articulation of an individual speech sound or a sequence of speech sounds) and *length* (the modifying characteristic segments have in a language which uses degrees of duration contrastively).

⌘ You will be able to recognize, control, and transcribe varying degrees of length on vowels and consonants.

In phonetics, DURATION refers to the amount of time used for articulation of an individual speech sound or a sequence of speech sounds, such as a syllable. The duration of a consonant or a vowel may be the normal minimal amount of time required to articulate the sound at a normal rate of speech, or it may be significantly longer. When different degrees of duration are used contrastively in a language, we refer to SEGMENTAL LENGTH. In this chapter we are concerned primarily with length of individual segments, not with that of larger phonological units such as syllables. Sometimes it is difficult to determine the length of a segment, especially in the case of two consecutive vowels or two consecutive consonants (most notably a stop followed by a fricative), because the two sounds seem to blend together to form one sound. In such cases, we must carefully compare their duration with that of neighboring segments.

Segments are significantly long or short only relative to each other, just as the pitch of one syllable is significantly high or low only in relation to the pitch of neighboring syllables.

If you began learning to read English using a "phonics" teaching method, you may have been taught that a "short vowel" is one that occurs in the middle of a word spelled with a consonant-vowel-consonant sequence such as "mat," "pet," "rid," "hop," and "tub," and that a "long vowel" is one that occurs in the middle of a word spelled with a consonant-vowel-consonant-silent "e" sequence, such as "mate," "Pete," "ride," "hope," and "tube." By now you will probably recognize that the difference between these "long and short vowels" is primarily a difference in vowel quality resulting from differences in oral cavity shape. For example, the vowel in "mat" is [æ] and the vowel in "mate" is a glided vowel [ei̯]. So, it is important for you to abandon those definitions from phonics (at least while you are in "phonetics mode") and realize that in phonetics the terms "long" and "short" refer to duration of segments, not to vowel qualities.

Symbolizing length

The symbols most frequently used to represent length are either a pair of triangles (ː) called a LENGTH MARK, or a colon (:), following the symbol for the lengthened segment. The IPA symbol is the pair of triangles, but a plain colon is easier to write and so much more commonly available on word processors and computers;

triangle-style length mark is rarely used except in professionally printed materials. Linguists from both the IPA and Americanist traditions usually use a colon. IPA also has the symbol [ˇ] for extra short.

Contrastive versus noncontrastive length in languages

In English, we distinguish three significantly different degrees of phonetic duration of a vowel, depending on whether the syllable ends with a voiceless consonant, a voiced consonant, or no consonant at all. However, two English words with different meanings never have the duration of the vowel as the only phonetic difference between them. Consider the words "bee," "bead," and "beet." The [iː] vowel in "bee" is the longest, the [iˑ] in "bead" is next longest, and the [i] in "beet" is shortest. There is a phonological rule in English that vowels in open syllables (syllables that end in vowels) will be the longest, those preceding voiced consonants will be next longest, and those preceding voiceless consonants will be shortest. Because these three degrees of phonetic length on vowels in English are entirely predictable by that rule, length is not a contrastive feature of English vowels.

However, in some languages length *is* a contrastive feature. In the minimal pairs given here, from Hausa of Nigeria (Westermann and Ward 1933:116), the words have different meanings even though they differ phonetically only in the length of the first vowel.

da	'(relative particle)'
daː	'formerly'
dafa	'to cook'
daːfa	'to hold'
duka	'all'
duːka	'to beat'

Here is another minimal pair, two phrases from Ganda of Uganda and Tanzania (Westermann and Ward 1933:117; tone omitted), again involving a phonetic difference only in the length of one vowel.

okuzika	'to go out of cultivation'
okuziːka	'to bury'

Mixe of Mexico (Ladefoged and Maddieson 1996:320 quoting from Hoogshagen 1959) has three degrees of phonetic vowel length. Below are three sets of words demonstrating these three lengths.

pet	'climb (n.)'
peˑt	'broom'
peːt	'Peter'
poʃ	'guava'
poˑʃ	'spider'
poːʃ	'knot'
piʃ	'flea'
piˑʃ	'marigold'
tʃiːt	'cat'

When three degrees of length occur contrastively and thus need to be symbolized, the shortest one is represented by just the segment symbol itself, the middle-length one is denoted by a raised triangle (ˑ) called a HALF-LENGTH MARK or a RAISED PERIOD (·) following the segment symbol, and the longest one is symbolized by double triangles (ː) or a colon (:) following the segment symbol. However, languages with three contrastive degrees of length are rare.

All the examples given so far have shown length on vowels. Consonants can also occur with contrastive degrees of length, as exemplified in these Estonian words (Laver 1994:14)

vaka	'pious'
vak·a	'bushel'
kana	'hen'
kan·a	'heel'
kamin	'fireplace'
kam·in	'comb'

and these Pattani Malay words (Ladefoged and Maddieson 1996:94 quoting from Abramson 1986).

bulɛ	'moon'
bːulɛ	'many months'
katoʔ	'to strike'
kːatoʔ	'frog'
labɔ	'to make a profit'
lːabɔ	'spider'
makɛ	'to eat'
mːakɛ	'to be eaten'
siku	'elbow'
sːiku	'hand tool'

Regardless of whether or not length is used contrastively in a language, as soon as you notice that it occurs at all, it is important to include it in your phonetic transcription.[51]

Production hints

Higher pitch and increased length tend to co-occur as the phonetic manifestation of phonological stress in English. Therefore, if you are a mother-tongue speaker of English, you need to practice controlling these elements independently of one another. Practice the following words from Comanche of Oklahoma (E. Pike 1978:55; Elliott Canonge), noting that the syllable containing a lengthened vowel is not the one that has stress and higher pitch.

| ˈmásìːtò | 'fingernail' |
| ˈhánìːβì | 'corn' |

Key concepts and symbols

duration
length / segmental length
length mark (ː) / colon (ː)
half length mark (·) / raised period (·)

---

[51]Then, based on analysis of your phonetic transcription, you will be able to decide whether or not length is a contrastive feature in the language and thus whether or not you need to continue transcribing it indefinitely. In general, features that are not contrastive can eventually be omitted from nonphonetic transcription, whereas features that are contrastive need to be represented explicitly.

Oral exercises

1.   Practice saying aloud the following words.

Zuni of New Mexico (Carolyn and Bill Murray, personal communication)

'mula	'parrot'
'muːla	'mule'
'hopːi	'where is it?'
'ʔopi	'it's sour'
'ʃotonːɛ	'abalone shell'
'ʃotːonːɛ	'a rib'
'latanːɛ	'feather'
'tatːanːɛ	'a tree'
'ʔoːlo	'gold'
'holo	'no!'

Finnish (Kari Ranta, personal communication)

kuːla	'bullet'
kuːlːa	'to hear'
kuola	'drool'
kuolːa	'to die'

15

Voiceless Vowels

Goals

⌘ You will be able to explain the similarities and the differences between voiced and *voiceless vowels*.

⌘ You will be able to control and give the technical name for each voiceless vowel.

⌘ You will be able to explain the notion of *predictable* quality of a voiceless vowel adjacent to a voiced vowel.

⌘ You will be able to explain when the symbol [h] may be used to transcribe a voiceless vowel and when a symbol making explicit the quality of the voiceless vowel must be used.

For every voiced vowel there is a voiceless counterpart that is produced with the same vocal tract shape, but without vocal fold vibration. These VOICELESS VOWELS use the same base symbol as for a voiced vowel of the same quality, but with a small circle underneath (or above) the base symbol, for example, [ḁ], [ẙ], [u̥].

Since the default characteristic for vowels is "voiced" we specify "voiceless" in the technical name when necessary. In all other respects names for voiced and voiceless vowels are the same. For example, [e̥] is a "*voiceless* close-mid front unrounded vowel."

When a voiceless vowel occurs adjacent to a voiced vowel in the same syllable, the two vowels are articulated with essentially the same tongue and lip positions. In such cases, the quality of the voiceless vowel is PREDICTABLE—it will be the same as that of the voiced vowel adjacent to it. When the quality of a voiceless vowel is thus predictable from its environment, the symbol "h" may be used instead of an explicit voiceless vowel symbol.[52] English has many predictable voiceless vowels. Note the two ways that can be used to write these English words phonetically in the following examples.

[æ̥æm]	[hæm]	'ham'
[i̥ip]	[hip]	'heap'
[ɔ̥ɔg]	[hɔg]	'hog'

However, there are many languages in the world that use voiceless vowels in positions where their qualities cannot be predicted. Where the quality of a voiceless vowel cannot be assumed from the environment, the

---

[52]This is a phonological decision. It is quite likely that voiceless vowels adjacent to voiced vowels (either preceding or following them), and sharing all features with those voiced vowels except voicing, are actually functioning as consonants ("h") rather than as syllable peaks. In a phonetic transcription, "h" represents a tentative judgment in favor of this decision.

vowel should be written with an explicit vowel symbol, not [h]. Consider these two words from Comanche of Oklahoma (data from Rick Floyd).

[tɯpi̥]   'lips'
[tɯpe̥]   'stone'

The only phonetic difference between these two words with different meanings is in the quality of the final voiceless vowel. There is nothing in the environment of the final vowel to give a clue as to its vowel quality. Naturally, if we were to write these words using an "h" for the voiceless vowel, the transcriptions of the two words would be the same ([tɯph]) for the two different pronunciations with different meanings, and we would not know which pronunciation nor which meaning was intended. Thus it is important, when the quality of voiceless vowels is not predictable from the phonetic environment, to indicate the explicit nature of its quality with the appropriate symbol.

You will probably find that the consonant immediately preceding a word-final voiceless vowel will also be voiceless.

Production hints

In a classroom situation, voiceless vowels may be overemphasized to make their presence and quality obvious to the students. However, languages such as Comanche and Cheyenne have voiceless vowels at the ends of words that are pronounced so softly that a newcomer to the language may not hear them at all. The only clue to their presence may be a slight lip movement. You will probably want to overemphasize the voiceless vowels somewhat at first, just to remind yourself that they are there, but avoid putting excessive audible turbulence on them.

When pronouncing voiceless vowels in the middle of an expression (word, phrase, or sentence), you may have to exercise care not to omit any of the voiceless vowels. For example, consider this Cheyenne word (E. Pike 1978):

[βɪ̥po̥tsɪ̥]   'leaf'

and these Comanche words (E. Pike 1978):

['kaḁpe]   'bed'
[ma'muɸi̥siɨka]   'when he blew his nose'

Take care to include every vowel in such words, not just the voiced ones.

Common alternate symbols

In the Americanist transcription system, voiceless vowels are written as upper case letters which correspond to the lower case letters of the voiced vowel counterparts, for example, [E], [I], [Ö].

Key concepts

voiceless vowel
predictable quality [h]
nonpredictable quality (explicit symbol)

Oral exercises

Practice saying aloud the following words.

Shoshone of Utah (Floyd 1981:38)

[ˈtɪmpe̥]	'mouth'
[ˈtɪmpi̥]	'stone'
[ˈnəmpe̥]	'foot'
[ˈnəmpḁ]	'shoe'
[ˈsapu̥ɪ]	'belly'
[ˈtaɸe̥]	'sun'
[ˈtuku̥]	'flesh'

Enga of Papua New Guinea (E. Pike 1978:41; Sheila Draper and Nan Shaw)

[ˈaŋki̥]	'pineapple'
[ˈkamʊŋko̥]	'chief'
[pɛnˈdoko̥]	'Adam's apple'
[ˈipu̥]	'come'
[ˈkɛŋke̥]	'hand'

Written exercises

Match an Americanist symbol from the left-hand column with the appropriate IPA symbol from the right-hand column. Then write out the technical name for each IPA vowel listed.

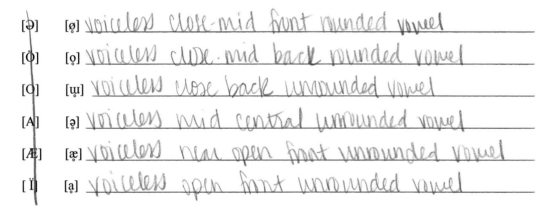

Americanist	IPA	
[Ə]	[ø̥]	voiceless close-mid front rounded vowel
[Ó]	[o̥]	voiceless close-mid back rounded vowel
[Ǫ]	[ɯ̥]	voiceless close back unrounded vowel
[A]	[ə̥]	voiceless mid central unrounded vowel
[Æ]	[æ̥]	voiceless near-open front unrounded vowel
[Ï]	[ḁ]	voiceless open front unrounded vowel

16

Affricates

Goals

⌘ You will be able to define an *affricate* as a stop released into a fricative, both sounds typically articulated at the same or nearly the same place of articulation and having the same voicing characteristic.

⌘ You will be able to explain the difference between the terms *homorganic* and *heterorganic* and to give examples of stop-fricative sequences of each type.

⌘ You will be able to give a technical name for any homorganic affricate, deriving its place of articulation from that of the fricative release involved.

⌘ You will control all the affricates presented in the chapter.

Recall that a stop is a sound in which a moving airstream is completely impeded by the meeting of an active articulator and a passive articulator. The air pressure that builds up behind that complete closure for a voiceless stop may be RELEASED in any of three ways: directly into a vowel (for example, [pa], [ta], [ka]) and called simply a stop; into aspiration (for example, [pʰa], [tʰa], [kʰa]) and called an aspirated stop; or into a fricative (for example, [pfa], [tθa], [kxa]) and called an AFFRICATE.

In the case of a stop with fricative release, the movement of the active articulator away from the passive articulator is sufficiently slow as to produce audible turbulence. The duration of the resulting fricative is usually not as long if the affricate functions as a single phonological unit as it is if the stop and fricative function as two independent phonological units. By definition, the stop and the fricative in an affricate share the same voicing characteristic, that is, they are either both voiced or both voiceless.

As you might expect, concerning release of the articulation of a stop, the most frequent type of affricate is HOMORGANIC; that is, the place of articulation of the fricative release is the same or very nearly the same as that of the stop, for example, [bβ], [dʒ], and [kx]. However, you will occasionally encounter discussion of HETERORGANIC affricates, in which the place of articulation of the fricative release is quite distant from that of the stop, for example, [ps], [kʃ], and [tf] . While some languages make frequent use of heterorganic affricates, for our purposes we define an affricate as a stop released into a fricative, at the same or nearly the same place of articulation, and having the same voicing characteristic as the stop.

89

Symbols and technical names

Table 16.1. Homorganic affricates

	Bilabial	Labiodental	(Inter)dental	Alveolar	Palato-alveolar	Velar	
vl.				tsʰ	tʃʰ		aspirated
vl.	pɸ	pf	tθ	ts	tʃ	kx	affricate
vd.	bβ	bv	dð	dz	dʒ	gɣ	
vl.				tɬʰ			aspirated
vl.				tɬ		kʟ̥	lateral affricate
vd.				dl		gʟ	

Table 16.1 lists some of the homorganic affricates that may be produced. The technical names for affricates are derived, as usual, by reading the labels clockwise on the table. Since a stop can be released into more than one fricative at nearly the same place of articulation, the sounds have been organized according to the place of articulation of the fricative. For example, [pf] is listed as labiodental, even though the stop is bilabial. Thus, the technical names specify the point of articulation of the fricative release.

Notice that, as with stops, affricates can be released with aspiration, as in the first and fourth lines of the table.[53] However, only the alveolar and palato-alveolar ones are commonly found with aspirated release. Another unique characteristic of alveolar and palato-alveolar affricates is that they involve no flat fricatives but rather either sibilants or lateral fricatives.[54] The term "lateral" is included in the technical names for the three alveolar affricates involving lateral fricatives, in order to distinguish them from [ts] and [dz], which may be described as "sibilant affricates" or "grooved affricates."

If for some reason you wish to discuss heterorganic sequences of stops and fricatives, you can either give the technical names for the stop and fricative separately or coin a new term for the unit. For example, [ks] could be referred to as a "voiceless velar stop followed by a voiceless alveolar sibilant" or perhaps as a "voiceless velo-alveolar heterorganic affricate."

You may encounter affricate notations such as [t͡θ] (employing a ligature) or [tθ] (superscripting) to reflect the linguist's phonological hypothesis concerning the unit nature of these affricates. We avoid such notations since phonological analysis is beyond the scope of a phonetics book.

We will not draw face diagrams of affricates, since affricates involve a sequence of articulations, and a face diagram represents only one moment in a single articulation.

Lateral affricates

The sequence [dl] occurs in many languages. According to the definition of affricate given above, [dl] is not technically an affricate since [l] is an approximant rather than a fricative. The expected affricate would be [dʒ]. However, [dʒ] has been found to occur very rarely in languages, whereas [dl] occurs fairly frequently and in similar contexts to other affricates.

---

[53]We have not included in the table all the logically possible aspirated affricates, as some rarely if ever occur in languages. The Beembe language of Congo is reported to have voiceless labiodental affricates with and without aspiration, contrastively (Ladefoged and Maddieson 1996:91, quoting French linguist, André Jacquot).

[54]A few languages also use dental lateral affricates, but they are rare enough that we chose not to include them in this chapter. See Ladefoged and Maddieson 1996:185 for a discussion of laterals found in the Kaititj language of Australia. They say that several other languages of Australia use laterals at many different places of articulation as well.

Production hints

Be sure that your affricates have the stop releasing directly into the fricative without any intervening vowels or aspiration. For example, you want [tθa], not anything like [tǝ'θa] or [tʰθa]. Here are a few English phrases containing alveolar and palato-alveolar affricates:

[tsʰ]	'the ca*t's h*ere'	[tʃʰ]	'*ch*ange'
[ts]	'the ca*t's* ear'	[tʃ]	'ex*ch*ange'
[dz]	'the la*d's* ear'	[dʒ]	'See *J*ames'

Alveolar lateral affricates may be relatively easy for you to produce. Try substituting [d] for the initial voiced velar stop in English words like "glad" (for example, [dlæd]) and [t] for the initial voiceless velar stop in words like "clock" (for example, [t̥lakʰ]; then add friction to the lateral which yields [t̥ɬakʰ]). Do not allow your tongue back to get involved in the affricate, resulting in a stop that is velar rather than alveolar.

It is sometimes difficult to *hear* the difference between [dl] and [gl] or between [tɬ] and [kɬ]. Fortunately, these two pairs of sounds have not been found to contrast in any language. Remember that in this book we deal primarily with homorganic affricates. Do not allow yourself to be fooled into writing heterorganic affricates simply because the homorganic ones sound a lot like English heterorganic consonant clusters.

Key concepts

release
affricate
homorganic / heterorganic
lateral affricate

Oral exercises

1. Practice the following frame drills three times each.

    'dlopɸi
    'dlobvi
    'dlodʒi
    'dlotʃʰi

    'gɣabvu
    'gɣakxu
    'gɣatθu
    'gɣatɬʰu

    'tʃigɣæ
    'tʃidlæ
    'tʃitʃʰæ
    'tʃitsʰæ

2. Practice saying aloud the following words from various languages in Africa.

    Shona of Zimbabwe (Bickford, field notes)

    pfumo   'spear'

Fante of Ghana (Rick Floyd, field notes)

ɔtsɪ	'he heard'
midzidzi	'I eat'
adzɪ	'a thing'

Gã of Ghana (Westermann and Ward 1933:87, 89)

tʃɛ	'father'
tʃo	'to burn'
dʒa	'to divide'
dʒi	'to be'
dʒu	'to wash'
tʃi	'to move'

Chuana of South Africa (E. Pike 1978:36)

leʼtsatsi	'sun'
ʼtɬɔla	'to smear oneself'
ʼtɬʰɔma	'to plant'
ʼtɬɔxa	'to depart'
ʼtɬʰɔxa	'to spring up, begin to grow'

3. Practice the following words from Highland Mazatec of Mexico (E. Pike 1978:31; Eunice Pike; tone omitted).

tʃa	'lacking'
tʃʰa	'brother-in-law'
tse	'big'
tsʰe	'clean'
tʃʰe	'thief'

Written exercise

Consider each of the following clusters of consonants. Is it an affricate, according to the definition given in this book? If so, give its technical name. If it is not an affricate, explain why not.

[pɸ] _Yes, voiceless bilabial affricate_

[tx] _No - ~~voiced velar affricate~~ not made at same place._

[gɣ] _Yes; voiced velar affricate_

[kʰx] _No - aspiration out of place moves to ~~voiced~~ an affricate._

[dʒ] _Yes; voiced palato-alveolar affricate_

[bg] _No - two stops_

[bf] _No - voiced vs voiceless_

[tsʰ] _Yes; voiceless alveolar aspirated affricate_

[vb] _No - air pressure doesn't complete closure_
[tɬ] _Yes, voiceless alveolar lateral affricate_
[dəð] _No - vowel_
[kx] _Yes, voiceless velar affricate_
[zv] _No - no stop_
[kɬ] ~~No~~ _Yes, hetero_

Transcription conversion exercise

Rewrite each of the following, using only IPA symbols.

dʒitšʰæ'tɬʰu _____

'dlopᵽibbu _____

ɠgo'dɖəv _____

17

Glottal Consonants

Goals

⌘ You will be able to describe [h] as a segment that may function either as a consonant or as a vowel.

⌘ You will be able to control two glottal consonants, [h] and [ʔ], in various positions relative to other consonants and vowels.

The voiceless glottal fricative

You will recall from chapter 15 on voiceless vowels that [h] may be used as a symbol for a voiceless vowel of predictable quality. For example, "head" may be written phonetically as [hɛd] rather than [ɛ̥ɛd] because the quality of the voiceless vowel is predictable from the adjacent voiced [ɛ]. In that chapter, we explained that all nonpredictable voiceless vowels need to be written with a symbol explicitly specifying vowel quality.

[h] may also be used as a symbol for a "voiceless glottal fricative." [h] is not a fricative in the same sense as [s] or [f]. The difference is that [s] and [f] are produced by local turbulence at the articulators, whereas for [h] the turbulence is distributed throughout the vocal tract. Thus, when [h] is called a fricative, the term is being used in a broader sense than our earlier definition.

The glottal stop

The glottal stop, [ʔ], was introduced in chapter 4 on stops. Recall that for [ʔ] the pulmonic airstream is completely impeded at the vocal folds (which are the articulators). Consequently, nothing above the vocal folds in the vocal tract, for example, velic closure, tongue, and lip positions, is involved in the definition of [ʔ]. The only pertinent parts of the face diagram of [ʔ] are the straight line through the larynx, signifying closure of the vocal folds, and the arrow below it, signifying an egressive pulmonic airstream.

Figure 17.1. [ʔ]

The technical name for [ʔ] is simply "glottal stop." It consists of a complete and sustained closure of the glottis produced by pressing the vocal folds together with sufficient force to prevent the air pressure from below from forcing them apart. Since voicing involves a repeated rapid opening and closing of the glottis as the vocal folds vibrate, it is physically impossible to produce a voiced glottal stop. Consequently, there is no need to include the word "voiceless" in the technical name for [ʔ].

Like other stops, [ʔ] can be released with aspiration, resulting in [ʔʰ]. Try saying [aʔ], then [aʔʰ].[55]

Production hints

Neither of the glottal consonants, [ʔ] and [h], is difficult for an English speaker to articulate. The only difficulty is to become aware of times when you *are* making a [ʔ] and avoid putting one in where it does not belong. Most English words that are spelled with a vowel as the first letter actually begin phonetically with [ʔ]. However, many languages do not work that way. To eliminate a habitual glottal stop before an initial vowel, try one or more of these techniques:

- Say [ha]; then gradually shorten the [h] until you have [a] in isolation.
- Think [h] but say [a].
- Yawn and say [a].

Hints for detecting the presence of glottal stops

It is sometimes difficult for English speakers to hear and reproduce glottal stops next to other consonants. Hints for detecting the presence of [ʔ] include listening for any of the following three things:

- abrupt onset
- abrupt cutoff
- interruption of either voicing or the "continuity" of a segment

For example, in a sequence such as [aʔkʰ], the presence of the glottal stop is made apparent by the abrupt cutoff of the voicing of the vowel. Likewise, in a sequence such as [ʔfa], the abrupt onset of the fricative reveals the presence of the glottal stop, even though the fricative is voiceless.

Key concepts

voiceless glottal fricative [h]
glottal stop [ʔ]

Oral exercises

1. Practice the following sequences twice as written, then a third time substituting vowels of your choice.

[a]	[hma]	[hla]	[hna]	[ʔma]	[anʔ]
[ʔa]	[m̥ma]	[ɬla]	[n̥na]	[ʔba]	[alʔ]
[aʔ]	[amh]	[alh]	[anh]	[ʔla]	[azʔ]
[ʔaʔ]	[amm̥]	[alɬ]	[ann̥]	[ʔfa]	[avʔ]

2. Practice the following sequences.

[okʰ]	[oʔkʰ]	[ohkʰ]
[epʰ]	[eʔpʰ]	[ehpʰ]
[utʰ]	[uʔtʰ]	[uhtʰ]

---

[55]Unlike other stops, the glottal stop has not (to our knowledge) been found to occur with aspiration intervening between it and a following vowel, for example, [ʔʰo]. However, it does occur with aspirated release preceding other consonants, for example, [ˈbahoʔʰtʰ] 'they see them' in Chichimeca Pame of Mexico (Lorna Gibson, personal communication) and word finally, such as [loʔʰ].

3.   Practice saying aloud the following words.
     Tabasco Chontal of Mexico (James Walker, personal communication)

[tʰi]	'maybe'
[tʰiʔ]	'mouth'
[tʰɯ]	'to'
[tʰɯʔ]	'very'
[tʰaʔa]	'yours'

     Choapan Zapotec of Mexico (Larry Lyman, personal communication)

[biu]	'dove'
[biuʔ]	'moon, month'
[biʔu]	'flea'
[zi]	'only'
[ziʔ]	'injury'
[ziʔi]	'heavy'

     Tzeltal of Mexico (Floyd 1981:47)

[shol]	'his head'
[naht]	'tall'
[htat]	'my father'
[hlap]	'I put on'
[hpat]	'my back'
[hbiːl]	'my name'

18

Central Approximants

Goals

⌘ You will be able to define the terms *central approximant, semivowel, nonsyllabic vowel, rhotacized,* and *retroflex.*

⌘ You will control the central approximants given in the tables.

As you may recall from chapter 13, "Laterals," the term APPROXIMANT implies that the airstream is directed by the articulators but not impeded sufficiently to produce either stoppage of the airstream or audible turbulence at the place of impedance. Thus, an approximant is defined as a frictionless oral speech sound involving shaping but not obstruction of the airstream. In chapter 13 we introduced lateral approximants, sounds in which the passageway for the airstream is over one or both sides of the tongue. In the present chapter, we introduce various CENTRAL APPROXIMANTS, that is, approximants in which the passageway for the airstream is over the *central* part of the tongue rather than over the sides.

The central approximants introduced in this chapter are also called SEMIVOWELS or NONSYLLABIC VOWELS.[56] Although they fit the definition for vowels, that is, they are central oral sonorants, they do not hold the syllable nuclear position held by prototypical vowels but instead function as non-nuclear elements in a syllable. Semivowels are very similar in quality to their syllabic counterparts, because the lip and tongue positions are very similar. However, semivowels often are shorter in duration and made with greater constriction between the articulators than vowels.

Table 18.1. Central approximants

	Labiodental	Alveolar	Palatal	Labial-palatal	Labial-velar	Velar	
vl.	ʋ̥	ɹ̥	j̊	ɥ̊	w̥	ɰ̊	approximant, nonsyllabic vowel, or semivowel
vd.	ʋ	ɹ	j	ɥ	w	ɰ	
art.	lower lip and upper teeth	tongue tip to alveloar ridge	palate and tongue front	lips, palate and tongue front	lips, tongue back and velum	tongue back and velum	

The labial-velar and labial-palatal approximants each involve two essential constrictions, one produced by rounding the lips and the other by a part of the tongue. The technical name for a sound symbolized in table 18.1

---

[56]Lateral approximants are not semivowels, as they are lateral rather than central.

is derived, as usual, from reading clockwise around the labels. For example, [j] is a "voiced palatal nonsyllabic vowel" or a "voiced palatal approximant" or a "voiced palatal semivowel." Note that the term "central" need not be included in the technical names of central approximants, as "central" is the default characteristic unless "lateral" is specified.

Some examples of alveolar approximants as they occur in American English words are shown below.

[tʰʊɹ]	'tour'
[aɹ]	'are'
[iɹ]	'ear'

The following are some examples of palatal and labial-velar semivowels in English.

[ju]	'you'	[wu]	'woo'
[jat]	'yacht'	[wat]	'watt'
[ji]	'ye'	[wi]	'we'

Notice that in "ye" and "woo" there is more constriction on the semivowel than on the syllabic vowel, which helps to distinguish between them.

You may recall from the chapters on vowels that we emphasized unglided vowels. When a vowel is glided, it is preceded or followed by a semivowel, most commonly one from table 18.1. However, nonsyllabic counterparts of other vowels can also occur as vowel glides. Thus, table 18.1 is definitely not an exhaustive inventory of semivowels. Any semivowel, including those given in table 18.1, may be symbolized with a superscript version of the symbol for its syllabic counterpart or with the symbol of the syllabic counterpart itself with a subscript arch [̯] beneath it. For example, [w] is equivalent to [ᵘ] or [u̯], and a nonsyllabic [o] can be symbolized [ᵒ] or [o̯].

Production hints

Many English speakers do not distinguish in their speech between voiced and voiceless labial-velar approximants, making only voiced ones. For example, they pronounce the words "where" and "wear" identically. Such people will need to listen and concentrate carefully to distinguish between [w] and [w̥]. To articulate the voiceless labial-velar sound [w̥], think of saying [h] and [w] simultaneously, or perhaps [hw]. This same technique also facilitates saying [j̊]: think of saying [h] and [j] simultaneously, or perhaps [hj].

Retroflex approximants

RHOTACIZED speech sounds are ones that have an "r" quality. The mid central rhotacized vowel is the syllable nucleus in American English words such as "her," "fur," and "sir." Rhotacized vowels and semivowels can be produced in two rather different ways—with the tongue tip curled up or with the center of the tongue humped up. Lip rounding may be important in producing rhotacized sounds; the lips are usually rounded for articulation of English "r."

Retroflex sounds of various kinds usually have some rhoticity. The term RETROFLEX refers to sounds made with the tip of the tongue curled back toward a place on the hard palate just behind the alveolar ridge, whether or not it actually makes contact there. In the case of the RETROFLEX APPROXIMANTS, the tongue tip does not actually touch the hard palate but only turns backward toward that place. Retroflexion is discussed in more detail in chapter 24.

One technical name for [ɹ] is "voiced alveolar approximant." As is the case for other central approximants, the term "semivowel" or "nonsyllabic vowel" can be substituted for "approximant."

Production hints

Rhotacization, the acoustic effect of [ɹ] and [ɻ], can be articulated in either of two distinct ways:

- position the tip of the tongue in a retroflex manner, or
- keep the tongue tip low and bunch up the body of the tongue.

If you try saying the word "red" both ways, you may not be able to hear the difference. This difference is almost certainly not contrastive in any language, but it would be good to be able to produce the sounds both ways so you can utilize the same articulation that is used by indigenous speakers of the language you study.

The sound symbolized by the letter "r" in English usually involves rounding of the lips. However, such is not the case for retroflex approximants in all languages, so you will need to be able to produce unrounded ones as well. Simply becoming aware of English lip-rounding habits usually solves this problem. You can also try saying English words containing "r" and no other labial sounds (for example, "try," "cry," "gray," "stray," etc.) in front of a mirror. Be careful not to allow any lip-rounding throughout the entire word.

Vowel / semivowel correspondence

Most central approximants have syllabic counterparts (see table 18.2) to which they exhibit similarities.

Table 18.2. Vowel / semivowel correspondence

Place of articulation or quality of semivowel	Voiced vowel	Voiced semivowel	Voiceless semivowel
alveolar (rhotacized)	ɚ	ɹ	ɹ̥
palatal	i	j	j̊
labial-palatal	y	ɥ	ɥ̊
labial-velar	u	w	w̥
labiodental		ʋ	ʋ̥
velar	ɯ	ɰ	ɰ̊

Note: Rhotacized vowels such as [ɚ] will be discussed more fully in chapter 24.

Common alternative symbols

The common alternative symbols are given in table 18.3

You may also encounter the symbol [ɹ̢], which is sometimes used as an equivalent to [ɹ]. However, [ɹ] most precisely refers to an alveolar approximant while the IPA calls [ɻ] a retroflex approximant, which is probably articulated further back in the mouth. These two symbols are also used inconsistently by various linguists who attempt to distinguish between syllabic and nonsyllabic approximants.

Also, beware confusion over the [y] which is used by the IPA for a close front rounded vowel.

In this chapter, we are not yet making distinctions based on places of articulation for retroflex approximants, nor on syllabicity. These two sounds are not likely to be contrastive in any language.

Table 18.3. Alternative symbols for central approximants

IPA symbol	Alternative symbol
j	y
j̊	Y
ɚ	ǝ
w̥	W
ɹ	r
ɹ̥	r

Key concepts

approximant / central approximant
semivowel / nonsyllabic vowel
rhotacized
retroflex / retroflex approximant

Oral exercises

1. Practice saying aloud these English words, reading across the rows.

[ju]	'you'	[wu]	'woo'	[ɹu]	'rue'
[jat]	'yacht'	[wat]	'watt'	[ɹat]	'rot'
[ji]	'ye'	[wi]	'we'	[ɹi]	're-'
[tʰʊɹ]	'tour'	[tʰaɹ]	'tar'	[tʰiɹ]	'tear'
[tɹ̥ɛjn]	'train'	[pɹ̥aw]	'prow'	[kĵɪw]	'cue'
[wɛɹ]	'wear'	[w̥ɛɹ]	'where'		
[wɪtʃ]	'witch'	[w̥ɪtʃ]	'which'		
[ju]	'you'	[ĵu]	'hue / Hugh'		

2. Practice saying aloud the following words.
    French (Marquita Klaver, personal communication)

[ɥit]	'eight'
[lɥi]	'(to) him/her'
[kɥ̥i]	'cooked'

Mandarin Chinese (Andy Eatough, personal communication)

[ɥɛn ˦]	'wrong, injustice'
[ɥɛn ˦]	'primary, original, former'
[ɥɛ ˩]	'moon, month, music'

Transcription conversion exercise

Rewrite the following, using only IPA symbols.

[Wɛr] _____

[Yu] _____

[kÜ̥i] _____

[pr̪ɛy] _____

19

Review Exercises and Tables (I)

Goals

⌘ These exercises review the material through chapter 18.

⌘ The tables at the end of this chapter are cumulative, including most of the consonant and vowel symbols introduced thus far in the book.

Exercises

1. Explain the difference between *active* and *passive articulators*.

An active articulator is a part of the mouth that moves as the sound is being articulated.
A passive articulator is a fixed part of the mouth where an active articulator touches or closely gets close to touching

2. How are articulators different from places of articulation?

An articulator is a part of the mouth that comes in contact to make a sound, a place of articulation is the relationship between the articulators in order for them to produce airstreams.

3. List the three airstream mechanisms and the initiator of each.

Pulmonic - muscles of the rib cage, diaphram
Glottalic - larnyx & closed glottis, walls of the pharnyx
Velaric - back of the tongue, tongue body.

103

4. Define *egressive* and *ingressive airstream*. In which direction does the pulmonic airstream almost always move?

    egressive is an outward airstream
    ingressive is an inward airstream
    pulmonic air almost always moves egressive.

5. Give symbols for four sounds with each of the following manners of articulation.

    stop   [b], [p], [t], [d]

    fricative   [h], [f], [v], [x]

    vowel or approximant   [ɹ], [ɑ], [e], [ɪ]

6. Circle the symbols of sounds made with velic closure.

    [n] [p] [β] [o] [s] [m̥] [ŋ] [f] [kʰ] [gɣ] [ỹ] [i̥] [h]

7. Circle the symbols of sounds made with vocal folds vibrating.

    [z] [f] [b] [ø] [kx] [ɬ] [L] [ɪ] [i̥] [m] [l] [w] [j]

8. Write out the technical name for each of these sounds. Circle the word in each consonant name that indicates place of articulation.

    [z] voiced alveolar sibilant

    [æ] near-open front unrounded vowel

    [l] voiced alveolar lateral approximant

    [pʰ] voiceless bilabial aspirated stop

    [gɣ] voiced velar affricate

    [ỹ] close front rounded nasalized vowel

    [d] voiced alveolar stop

    [ʃ] voiceless palato-alveolar sibilant

    [n̥] voiceless alveolar nasal

    [ʔ] voiceless glottal stop

    [o̥] voiceless close-mid back rounded vowel

    [dʒ] voiced palato-alveolar affricate

    [h] voiceless glottal fricative

9. Give the articulatory phonetics definition for the term *vowel*.

    A speech sound that that is a central oral sonorant.

10. Write the symbols for the sounds depicted in these face diagrams.

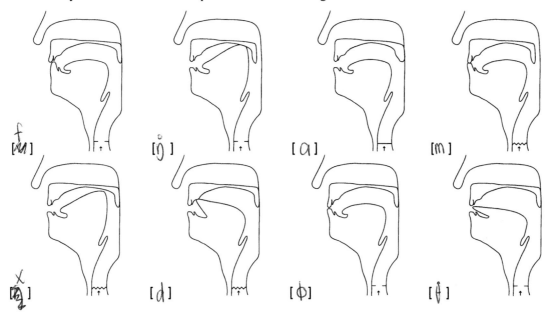

[ʍ]   [ɳ̊]   [ɑ]   [m]

[ɣ̽]   [ɖ]   [ɸ]   [ɟ]

11. Complete face diagrams for the following sounds.

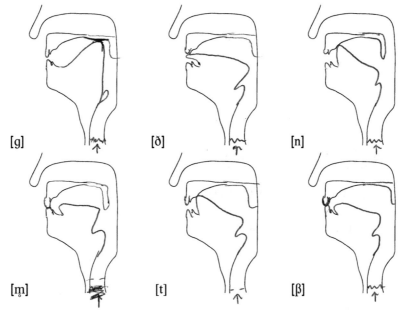

[g]   [ð]   [n]

[m̥]   [t]   [β]

12. Following are listed the three resonating cavities in the speech mechanism that are employed in the sounds described so far in the book. Consider each class of sounds described on the right and place on the blanks the letter of each cavity in which the sound resonates for those sounds (for example, fricatives—A; nasals—B; vowels—A, B, and/or C, depending on specifics).

A. oral cavity   ___A___ stops (not including nasals)

B. nasal cavity   ___A___ rounded non-nasalized vowels

C. labial cavity   ___B___ unrounded nasalized vowels

___A, C___ sibilants

13. Give the symbols that correspond to the following technical names.

[ɯ̥] a voiceless close back unrounded vowel

[b̪͡ð] a voiced bilabial affricate

[ɹ̥] a voiced alveolar approximant

[ǀ] a voiceless alveolar lateral affricate

[ɣ] a voiced velar fricative

[ʔ] a glottal stop

[ɛ] a mid open front unrounded vowel

14. In [boṵtʰuːkʰ], what does the little vertical line before the "t" indicate? *stress*

What do the brackets [ ] mean? *an Ipa transcription*

What does the subscript arch under the first "u" mean? _____

What do the little triangles after the second "u" mean? *lengthen*

What does the superscripted "h" mean? *aspirated*

How many syllables does the word have? *2*

How many vowels? *3*

How many consonants? *3*

15. Do the symbols below represent phonetic vowels? If you say "no," explain why those are not phonetic vowels.

[o] *yes*

[ʟ] *no, touches articulators & interupts airstream*

[m̩] *no, touches articulators*

[z] *no, touches articulators*

[ɤ] *yes*

[æ] *yes*

[h] *no, touches articulators*

[ʔ] *no, touches articulators*

[u] *yes*

[ɡ] *no, touches articulators*

[ɹ] *no, touches articulators*

[w̥] *no, touches articulators*

16. Thinking of the six main parameters used in this book to identify speech sounds, plus other articulatory details such as lip rounding, position of tongue sides, etc., what difference(s) is/are there in the following pairs of sounds.

[l] and [d] _lateral approximant, stop_

[o] and [ø] _back, front_

[o] and [ɤ] _rounded, unrounded_

[p] and [ɸ] _stop, fricative_

[m] and [m̥] _voiced, voiceless_

[z] and [ʒ] _alveolar, palato-alveolar_

[k] and [ɣ] _voiceless, voiced_

17. What do *all* the sounds from the preceding exercises have in common?

They are IPA symbols,

18. For each set of sounds below, what characteristic(s) do all the sounds in the set share (in addition to the one mentioned in question 17)?

[b β o f l θ ɯ kʰ] _____

_____

[æ̃ w ĵ ɹ o i̥ ỹ e] _____

_____

[v x ɣ ʒ ʂ θ s β] _____

_____

[m n̥ õ ŋ ỹ m̥ æ̃] _____

_____

[p d kʰ g b tʰ ʔ] _____

_____

[f t kx i̥ pʰ h] _____

_____

[l d s tʰ dz t ʂ] _____

_____

Table 19.1. Cumulative table of consonants, chapters 1–18

	Bilabial	Labiodental	(Inter)dental	Alveolar	Palato-alveolar	Velar	Glottal	
vl.	pʰ			tʰ		kʰ		aspirated
vl.	p			t		k	ʔ	stop
vd.	b			d		g		
vl.	ɸ	f	θ			x	h	fricative
vd.	β	v	ð			ɣ		
vl.				s	ʃ			sibilant
vd.				z	ʒ			
vl.				ɬ				lateral fricative
vd.				ɮ				
vl.				l̥		ʟ̥		lateral approximant
vd.				l		ʟ		
vl.				tsʰ	tʃʰ			aspirated
vl.	pɸ	pf	tθ	ts	tʃ	kx		affricate
vd.	bβ	bv	dð	dz	dʒ	gɣ		
vl.				tɬʰ				aspirated
vl.				tɬ		kʟ̥		lateral affricate
vd.				dl		gʟ		
vl.	m̥			n̥	ñ̥ / n̥	ŋ̥		nasal
vd.	m	ɱ		n	ñ / n̠	ŋ		

Table 19.2. Central approximants (nonsyllabic vowels)

	Labiodental	Alveolar	Palatal	Labial-palatal	Labial-velar	Velar	
vl.	ʋ̥	ɹ̥	j̊	ɥ̊	ʍ̥	ɰ̥	approximant
vd.	ʋ	ɹ	j	ɥ	w	ɰ	

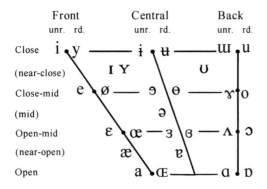

Figure 19.1. IPA vowels.

nasalized	ẽ
length	eˑ or eː
voiceless	e̥

Figure 19.2. Vowel modifications.

20

Palatal and Uvular Consonants

Goals

⌘ You will control the consonants presented in this chapter and will be able to explain how the *palatal* and *uvular* places of articulation differ from the velar.

⌘ You will be able to read and draw face diagrams depicting these consonants, focusing especially on how they differ from face diagrams depicting velar sounds.

In previous chapters, you have encountered consonants involving the velar place of articulation, that is, with the tongue back as the active articulator and the front of the velum as the passive articulator. In this chapter we introduce consonants articulated either slightly forward of or slightly behind the front of the velum. Sounds articulated by the tongue front coming close to or contacting the hard palate, forward of the velum, are said to have a PALATAL place of articulation; those articulated by the tongue back coming close to or contacting the back part of the velum, including the uvula, are said to have a UVULAR (or BACK VELAR) place of articulation.

The consonants introduced in this chapter are all the stops, fricatives, affricates, nasals, and lateral approximants at the palatal and uvular places of articulation. Table 20.1 gives the IPA symbols that represent these sounds.

Table 20.1. Palatal, velar, and uvular sounds

	Palatal	**Velar**	**Uvular**		
voiceless	cʰ	kʰ	qʰ	aspirated	
voiceless	c	k	q	stop	
voiced	ɟ	g	ɢ		
voiceless	ç	x	χ	fricative	
voiced	ʝ	ɣ	ʁ		
voiceless	cç	kx	qχ	affricate	
voiced	ɟʝ	gɣ	ɢʁ		
voiced	ɲ	ŋ	ɴ	nasal	
voiced	j	ɰ		approximants	
voiced	ʎ	ʟ		lateral approximant	
articulators	tongue front and hard palate	tongue back and front of velum	tongue back and uvula		

Note: The official IPA symbol for the voiced palatal nasal is the same symbol that many linguists, especially in Africa, use for a palato-alveolar nasal. Because the IPA uses this symbol for a palatal nasal we, in this book, avoid the use of this symbol for the palato-alveolar, reserving it instead for a palatal nasal.

The face diagram in figure 20.1 simultaneously depicts three different fricatives: [ç], which is palatal; [x], which is velar; and [χ], which is uvular.

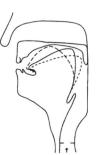

Figure 20.1.
[ç],[x], and [χ]

Production and recognition hints

Starting with [x], move your tongue forward and backward in your mouth such that you glide through a series of voiceless fricatives: [x ç x χ x ç x χ x ç x χ]. Even if you are careful to keep your lips from changing position, you will hear the pitch move up and down as your tongue moves forward and backward. The different positions of your tongue vary the size of the oral cavity. Different sizes of cavities have different resonances that help the hearer to distinguish between the different places of articulation, as shown in table 20.2.

Table 20.2. Effect of place of articulation on size
of sound chamber and fricative quality

Place of articulation	**Cavity size**	**Quality of sound**
palatal	small	high pitch
velar	medium	medium pitch
uvular	large	low, hollow-sounding pitch

English speakers usually use a palatal aspirated stop in pronouncing the word "key" [cʰi]. In anticipation of the high front vowel, the tongue moves forward; the tongue front presses against the palate, producing closure at a position further forward than that of the velar stop beginning the word "cop" [kʰap]. Likewise, some English speakers use a uvular stop in pronouncing the word "caw" (imitating a crow), especially if they use a vowel that is very far back and pulls the tongue back in anticipation of its enunciation. If you speak German, say the two words *ich* 'I' and *auch* 'also'. The first is phonetically [iç] (palatal fricative) and the second is [aʊ̯x] (velar fricative).

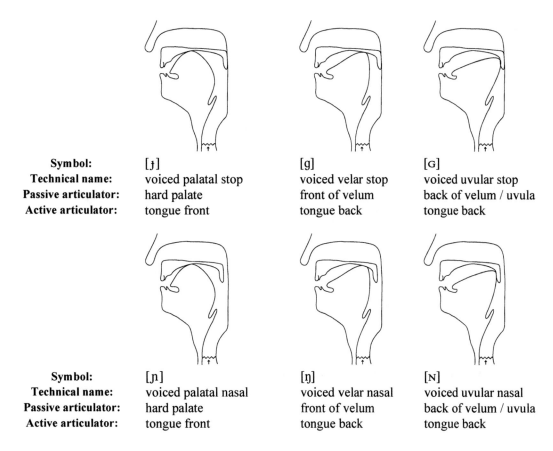

Symbol:	[ɟ]	[g]	[ɢ]
Technical name:	voiced palatal stop	voiced velar stop	voiced uvular stop
Passive articulator:	hard palate	front of velum	back of velum / uvula
Active articulator:	tongue front	tongue back	tongue back

Symbol:	[ɲ]	[ŋ]	[ɴ]
Technical name:	voiced palatal nasal	voiced velar nasal	voiced uvular nasal
Passive articulator:	hard palate	front of velum	back of velum / uvula
Active articulator:	tongue front	tongue back	tongue back

Figure 20.2. Face diagrams showing palatal, velar, and uvular places of articulation.

Table 20.3. Common alternative symbols

Palatal speech sounds		Uvular speech sounds	
IPA symbol	**Alternative symbol**	**IPA symbol**	**Alternative symbol**
ç	x̬	χ	x̣
ʝ	g̬	ʁ	g̣
cʰ	k̬ʰ	qʰ	ḳʰ
c	k̬	q	ḳ
ɟ	g̬	ɢ	g̣
cç	k̬x̬	qχ	ḳx̣
ɟʝ	g̬g̬	ɢʁ	g̣g̣
ɲ	ŋ̬	ɴ	ŋ̣
ʎ	L̬		

It may be helpful to notice that, in the alternative (Americanist) notation system, a subscript arch [ˬ] is used under a velar consonant symbol to indicate a palatal place of articulation. Likewise, an underdot [̣] is placed under a velar consonant symbol to indicate a uvular place of articulation. It may also help to think of all the sounds presented in this chapter as the "velar family," since they all involve articulation of the tongue either right in the velar position or shifted forward or backward from there.

Key concepts

palatal
uvular / back velar

Oral exercises

1. Practice saying aloud the following words
    Dutch, Rotterdam dialect (Floyd 1981:61)

dʁi	'three'
fyχ	'fire'
maχ	'but'
fχintʰ	'friend'
ʁœym	'space'
ʁøˈzɪn	'giantess'
xχax	'gladly'
ˈandəʁə	'other'

Quiche of Guatemala (David G. Fox, personal communication)

kukʰ	'squirrel'
kuqʰ	'their skirt'
quqʰ	'our skirt'
kaˈtʃotʃʰ	'their house'
qaˈtʃotʃʰ	'our house'
cinuˈmikʰ	'I'm hungry'
wiˈkan	'my uncle'
tsɪx	'word / truth'
ikʰ	'chili pepper'

Written exercises

1. Write the phonetic symbol for the sound depicted in figure 20.3.   [ɟ]

2. Give technical names for the following sounds.

    [ɴ] _voiced uvular nasal_
    [cʰ] _voiceless palatal aspirated stop_
    [ɢʁ] _voiced uvular affricate_
    [x] _voiceless velar fricative_

Figure 20.3.

3. Draw a face diagram simultaneously depicting [ɲ], [ŋ], and [ɴ] or draw three separate face diagrams if you prefer.

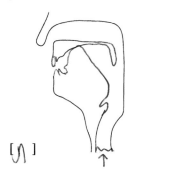

[ɲ]

[ŋ]

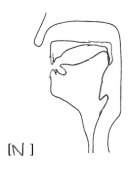

[ɴ]

Transcription conversion exercise

Rewrite each of the following using only IPA symbols.

kʰḁtsʰoɡi

kʰukʰ ŋɔ

wik̬ʰan

ɡöümbɪŋ

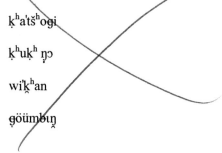

21

Syllabic Consonants and Prenasalization

Goals

⌘   You will control *syllabic consonants*.

⌘   You will be able to define *prenasalization* of an oral stop or affricate as a very brief velic opening preceding an oral stop (or the stop portion of an oral affricate), during which the primary articulators of the nasal and the stop remain constant.

⌘   You will be able to explain and symbolize the difference between *syllabic nasals* and *prenasalized stops*.

In many languages, certain consonants can be SYLLABIC, that is, they function as the nucleus of a syllable, like vowels. Placing a small vertical line (called a SYLLABICITY MARK) beneath a consonant symbol [m̩], indicates that that consonant is syllabic.

Syllabic consonants typically have a duration similar to that of vowels, and they may carry tone. By far the most common syllabic consonants are voiced sonorants (especially nasals, and lateral and retroflex approximants). Here are several examples of syllabic sonorants that occur in American English words.

ˈhɪdn̩	'hidden'	ʔm̩ˈm̩m̩	'(affirmative)'
ˈpʰədl̩	'puddle'	bɹ̩d	'bird'
ˈlæʔn̩	'Latin'	ˈbænɹ̩	'banner'
ˈkʰaʔn̩	'cotton'	ʔæbˈsɹ̩d	'absurd'
ˈm̥m̩ʔm̩	'(negative)'	ˈsɪstɹ̩	'sister'

Note: The [ɹ] is a symbol for a nonsyllabic vowel (see chapter 18). Thus, putting the syllabicity mark underneath [ɹ] changes it from a "nonsyllabic vowel" into a "syllabic vowel." [ɹ̩] can alternatively be written as [ɚ], the IPA right hook indicating rhoticity. The schwa symbol represents a sound that is already syllabic, so the syllabicity mark would be redundant.

Here are some more examples of syllabic nasals.

Igbo of Nigeria (Floyd 1981:72)

ḿbà	'no'
ńnònò	'bird'
ádīm̄à	'I'm fine'
áhām̄bò	'my name'

Gumuz of Ethiopia (Peter Unseth, field notes)

m̩ ŋ̍ ga sa	'to tell'

Djuka of Suriname (Floyd 1986:72)

n̩'kola	'snail'
n̩'zau	'elephant'
m̩'pij	'cuckoo'
m̩'bomba	'anaconda'
ŋ̍goni'ni	'harpy eagle'
n̩dʒuk'da	'Djuka'

Usila Chinantec of Mexico (Skinner 1962:253; tone 1 is high and tone 5 is low; stress is omitted)

$m̩^{43}$	'medicine'
$ʔm̩^{34}$	'new'
$o^{1}m̩m̩^{43}$	'rain'
$m̥m̩^{34}$	'river'
$m̩^{4}m̩^{3}m̩m̩ʔ^{5}$	'plum'
$m̩^{4}m̩m̩ʔ^{43}$	'tomato'
$a^{2}ʔm̩ʔ^{3} ʔm̩ʔ^{2} ʔm̩^{34} m̩ʔ^{2}m̩^{3}$	'you will order the thick new clothing'

Fricatives can also be syllabic, as shown in these examples from Lendu of the Democratic Republic of the Congo and Uganda (Tucker 1940:384).

kāzź̩	'fire'
dzz̩̄	'ground, flour'
rítsż̩	'thing'

There may be some voiceless syllabic consonants as well, but no examples are available at this time. Oral stops cannot be syllabic.

Prenasalized stops and affricates

Some languages, especially in Africa, have a series of PRENASALIZED stops and affricates which contrast with other stops and affricates by including a brief nasal onset during the first part of the articulation. The nasal onset is at the same place of articulation as that of the following stop or affricate. Prenasalization is symbolized by a superscripted nasal symbol preceding the normal stop or affricate symbol, for example [^{m}b], [^{n}dʒ], or [^{ŋ}k].[57]

Since the nasal onset is so brief, it does not carry contrastive tone. It is virtually always voiced, whereas the stop may be either voiced or voiceless.

---

[57]A prenasalized stop in the middle of a word (e.g., [a^{m}ba]) would indicate a likely syllable boundary after the first [a]. Written as [amba] there is no definite indication of syllable boundary. As differentiating between these two is a phonological question, you need not attempt to distinguish between these two situations for phonetics class. The phonetic distinction between them is slight.

Below are some examples of prenasalized stops.

Ocotepec Mixtec of Mexico (Ruth Mary Alexander, personal communication)

ᵐbâ:	'comrade'
ⁿdīkā	'banana'
ᵑgó̃ʔõ̀	'let's go'
ʔĩ̄ᵑgà	'another'
ⁿdʒáʔākā	'not yet'
ⁿdúʔù	'I'
ⁿdōkō	'zapote (a kind of fruit)'
ⁿdĩ̄ʔà	'fruit'

Tiv of Nigeria (Jockers 1991:20)

áⁿdzó	'debts'
áⁿdzá	'reasons'

Key concepts

syllabic consonant
syllabicity mark
prenasalized stop

Oral exercise

Practice saying aloud all the words listed earlier in the chapter that demonstrate syllabic consonants and prenasalized stops.

Written exercise

Write out phonetically three to five other English words containing syllabic consonants (or use your own native language, if it is not English and contains syllabic consonants). Show them to someone else in the class and see if (s)he can read what you have written.

cattle → kæt!

listen → lɪsn̩

risen → rɪzn̩

drizzle → drɪz!

cuddle → kʌd!

22

Transition and Release of Consonants

Goals

⌘ You will be able to explain the difference between *released consonants* and *unreleased consonants*, and between *open transition* and *close transition* between consonants.

Released and unreleased consonants

A consonant in utterance final position may be either RELEASED or UNRELEASED. The releasing or unreleasing of a consonant refers to what happens immediately following the articulation of the closure. In an unreleased consonant the active articulator maintains contact with the passive articulator or perhaps releases inaudibly.[58] On the other hand, a released consonant will be followed by aspiration and symbolized with a superscripted "h," [ap^h], if the consonant is voiceless, or by a very short schwa and symbolized with a superscripted schwa, [ab^ə], if the consonant is voiced.

To indicate that a final consonant is unreleased, you may use a superscripted diacritic called a corner [˺], following the consonant symbol, [ap˺].[59]

A transcription which fails to symbolize the release or nonrelease of a consonant, for example, [ap] without any diacritic, is ambiguous. For example:

Released	Unreleased	Ambiguous
ap^h	ap˺	ap
ab^ə	ab˺	ab
iv^ə	iv˺	iv
iz^ə	iz˺	iz

Word finally, if release is not explicitly indicated in a transcription, we will assume unrelease.

---

[58]While there is actually a slight articulatory difference between these two styles of unreleased consonants, a difference which is even somewhat perceptible, it is unlikely that any language will use them both contrastively. Therefore, it is very common to merge the two, representing them both the same way. However, you will want to notice which style of unreleased consonants is used in the language you study and match your pronunciation as much as possible to that of native speakers in that detail.

[59]Another rare Americanist option to denote an unreleased final consonant is to superscript the consonant symbol itself, [a^p].

Try saying each of the foregoing syllables, focusing on whether or not you are releasing the consonants. Notice that the voicing on unreleased consonants, especially fricatives, tends to fade into voicelessness.

Open and close transition

Whereas release refers to an utterance-final articulation, transition refers to a parallel phenomenon between contiguous consonants, either within a word or across word boundaries. We refer to transition as either OPEN or CLOSE. OPEN TRANSITION involves audible release of one consonant's articulators before the articulation of the next consonant. After voiceless consonants, open transition is aspiration. After voiced consonants, open transition is heard as a nonsyllabic schwa. Read the following English examples, paying special attention to the open transitions.

sɪkʰmæn	'sick man'
hædᵊgɔn	'had gone'
hatʰpʰaɪ̯	'hot pie'
laktʰtʰɐɪ̯tʰ	'locked tight'

In CLOSE TRANSITION between two consonants, the articulation of the second consonant is initiated before the articulation of the first consonant is released. Close transition is indicated simply by letting the consonant symbol stand alone. In other words, in a consonant cluster, if open transition is not specifically indicated then close transition is assumed. Try those same English phrases again, this time with close transition.

sɪkmæn	'sick man'
hædgɔn	'had gone'
hatpʰaɪ̯	'hot pie'
laktʰːɐɪ̯t	'locked tight'

Key concepts

released consonants (audible release)
unreleased consonants (no release or inaudible release)
open transition
close transition

Oral exercises

Practice reading aloud the following words, focusing on release and transition of the consonants.

Seri of Mexico (Mary Moser and Steve Marlett, personal communication)

ptkamn	'lobster'
ʔɛ ˈkɛkt ˈktam	'father-in-law'

Central Pame of Mexico (Lorna Gibson and Norma Smith, personal communication)

kənˈhæʔʰ	'baby'
kənˈhæʔʰtʰ	'babies'
kənˈhæʔʰkʰ	'I'm a baby'
ˈbahoʔʰ	'they see it'
ˈbahoʔʰkʰ	'they see me'
ˈbahoʔʰtʰ	'they see them'

English

ˈbɹei̯k:ʰei̯bl̩	'brake cable'
ˈbɹei̯kʰkʰei̯bl̩	
ˈgʊdmæn	'good man'
ˈgʊdᵊmæn	
ˈfætbɔi̯	'fat boy'
ˈfætʰbɔi̯	
dɛˈdːɔg	'dead dog'
dᵊˈdɔg	
ˈʍɪplæʃ	'whiplash'
ˈʍɪpʰlæʃ	
ˈbei̯klakʰ	'bike lock'
ˈbei̯kʰlakʰ	

Chinook of Canada (cited in Floyd 1981:76)

iɬˈtʃkʷa	'water'
ˈitʰkʷʰti	'house'
ˈitʰkʰpʃ	'feet'
iˈgei̯çtʃutkʰ	'flint'
oˈʔolɛptʃkiç	'fire'
ˈekʰtʰkʰ	'head'
ˈektʃxam	'he sang'
aˈtʃokʰtsʰkʰtamitˀ	'he roasts'
ˈtʰgakʰtʰkakʃ	'their heads'
ʃˈtxaxamuks	'our dogs'
olˈxakxalpʰtʃʰkiç	'our fire'
ˈetʃamxtʃ	'my heart'
ˈnukstx	'smallness'
aˈklokʃtʰpʰtʃʰkʰ	'she carries it up from the beach'

23

Speech Styles

Goals

⌘ You will be able to list the various *speech styles* given in the chapter and likely combinations of more than one speech style.

⌘ You will be able to impose various speech styles on a brief passage of text that you read aloud in your own native language.

⌘ You will be able to recognize and imitate various speech styles when they are used in foreign language texts that you hear.

Most of this phonetics book is devoted to introducing you to the many individual speech sounds utilized in the languages of the world. If you learn to produce, symbolize, and categorize them all correctly (or even just the subset of those sounds that actually occur in the language you want to learn), you will have taken many giant steps toward speaking the new language in a way that will enable meaningful communication between you and native speakers of that language.

However, there is more to acquiring a native-like accent than just getting the individual segments right. You also need to be aware of the overall characteristics or speech styles used in the language that you are trying to learn and in your own native language. You will need to take on the SPEECH STYLES of the new language and shed any speech styles of your own language that are not used in the new one. Failure to do this may result in your communicating wrong attitudes or wrong meanings. This chapter introduces several speech styles to increase your awareness of the types of things to look for in language besides individual segments.

Some speech styles are used consistently whenever a given language is spoken. Others are used only by certain subgroups of people or only in certain social situations. Therefore, information presented in this chapter should be useful in triggering ideas for ethnographic and sociolinguistic study as well as for improving your accent in the spoken language and facilitating your becoming less of an outsider to the culture.

A partial inventory of speech styles

The speech styles introduced in this chapter are organized into general categories, according to what is involved in producing that style: position or range of movement of the tongue, lips, or jaw; use of the nasal cavity; rhythm; speed; pitch register; pitch modulation; volume; and state of the vocal folds. There may be other types of speech styles as well; this is not an exhaustive inventory of possibilities.

Position of the tongue: The whole body of the tongue may be shifted slightly, either forward or back in the mouth, with the result that all the segments are articulated slightly ahead of or behind the "normal" positions for them. For example, with a FRONTED TONGUE POSITION, the vowels will likely be fronted slightly, alveolar sounds may be fronted toward a dental place of articulation, palato-alveolar sounds may involve articulation with the tongue blade closer to the alveolar region,[60] there may be more palatal sounds than velars, few or no uvulars, etc. In Mixtec of Mexico (Ruth Mary Alexander, personal communication), there is a fronted tongue position, resulting in [n], [t], [k], [a], and [u] all being fronted. Spanish and Seminole of Florida (Dave and Virginia West, personal communication) are also spoken with a fronted tongue speech style. With a BACKED TONGUE POSITION, the vowels will likely be backed slightly, there may be few or no dental sounds, more velars and uvulars than palatals, etc. These two speech styles are mutually exclusive. Clearly, the tongue cannot be simultaneously fronted and backed.

A third overall speech style that involves the tongue is RETROFLEXION, in which the tongue tip tends to be curled up and back much of the time, resulting in many retroflexed vowels and retroflexed alveolar and palato-alveolar consonants.[61] Many languages in India utilize retroflexion contrastively, but that is different from a retroflexed speech style. Retroflexion is rarely used as a speech style, but one example is an English speaking humorist imitating an old man.

If you note that the language you are learning has one of these overall speech styles involving tongue position, you can eventually discontinue tedious notation of such minute phonetic detail. For example, after noting that the tongue seems to be somewhat fronted for everything, you can stop writing ['tine̩][62] and simply write ['tine], as long as you state somewhere in your notes that you are no longer using narrow (that is, very detailed) phonetic transcription and that the overall language uses a fronted tongue position, including details of how that is consistently manifested in individual segments. Any phonetic or phonological papers that you write about the language also need to include a clear description of the speech style utilized. As for correctly pronouncing the words, it is easiest to simply "change gears" by shifting the tongue forward or back rather than thinking about changing the tongue position for individual segments.

Position of the lips: The lips may be rounded, squared, or spread. You have already encountered the notion of rounded and unrounded lips on vowels. When a language uses a ROUNDED LIPS speech style, even the normally unrounded vowels tend to involve some lip rounding, as do many consonants.[63] A SQUARED LIPS speech style is much like rounded lips; however, the lips tend to extend outward more and to assume a squared shape. Squared lips are used in Shona of Zimbabwe and some other languages of Africa. In contrast, the SPREAD LIPS speech style involves little or no lip rounding; even the vowels that are normally rounded will not be greatly rounded. Seminole of Florida (Dave and Virginia West, personal communication) is spoken with spread lips.

As with speech styles involving altered tongue position, once you determine that the language consistently uses a special lip shape and that there is no contrast between sounds with and without that lip shape, you can stop writing tedious phonetic detail, such as [t_wop_wɔ][64] for a language involving rounded lips, simply writing [topɔ], as long as your notes contain a clear explanation of the speech style involved and how it manifests itself on individual segments. Occasionally lip position can reflect certain emotions, moods, or social situations. For example, some English speakers use lip rounding to show pity, for example, "Oh, the poor little thing," said with very rounded lips throughout.

---

[60]See chapter 24 for more details concerning individual dental and fronted palato-alveolar consonants.

[61]See chapter 24 for more details concerning individual retroflexed vowels and consonants.

[62]See chapter 24 for more details concerning fronted (dental) consonants. In this chapter, we are not concerned with how to write down the individual segments that manifest certain speech style characteristics. For now, suffice it to say that the symbol [̪] under a basic vowel or consonant symbol or [̺] under an alveolar consonant indicates that that consonant is articulated with the tongue farther front than usual.

[63]See chapter 31 for more details concerning rounded consonants, for example, *labialization* and *palato-labialization*.

[64]See chapter 31 for a fuller explanation of proper notation of lip rounding and other modifications on consonants. In this chapter, we are not concerned with how to write down the individual segments that manifest these speech style characteristics. For now suffice it to say that a subscript "w" following a base consonant symbol indicates that that consonant is articulated with rounded lips.

Position of the jaw: For some languages, the jaw is kept in a fairly set position involving little vertical motion (SET JAW). For others, the jaw can move more freely, involving significant amounts of vertical motion (FREE JAW). These jaw positions affect the tongue height of vowels more than anything else. Languages with a set jaw speech style (such as Seminole; Dave and Virginia West, personal communication)[65] tend to have vowels in a narrower, higher area, while languages with a free jaw will vary their vowels over a wider range of vertical tongue position possibilities. How freely the jaw moves can sometimes be determined by the mood of the speaker or the formality of the situation or some other nonlinguistic factors. People sometimes exaggerate the amount of jaw motion when speaking to foreigners, perhaps thinking that that will enhance the clarity and comprehensibility of their speech.

Use of the nasal cavity: In some languages, the velum tends to be somewhat lowered much of the time, resulting in at least slight nasalization of many vowels and perhaps greater frequency of nasal consonants than might be considered average for languages. Such languages are said to have a NASALIZED speech style, for example, the English spoken in and near the state of Wisconsin. (Again, awareness of the overall nasality of the speech style can eliminate the need for tedious notation of nasalization on all vowels. Phonetic notation is intended to denote distinctions, not phonetic detail for its own sake.) Other languages may have the velum raised preventing resonation in the nasal cavity most of the time, resulting in virtually no nasalization of any vowels, and perhaps more oral stops and fewer nasals than might be considered average. Such languages are said to have a NON-NASALIZED speech style. However, these are only tendencies, and one would not expect to find a language that contains all nasalized vowels and no oral stops, nor a language using no nasal consonants at all.

Rhythm: Languages may tend to be STRESS-TIMED or SYLLABLE-TIMED. See chapter 11 on stress for a reminder of what these terms indicate. Spanish and French are syllable-timed, while English and other Germanic languages tend to be more stress-timed. Many linguists do not consider these rhythmic characteristics to be special speech styles, since they would be fully covered by the phonological analysis in any case.

Speed: The general speech style for some languages or situations may be characterized by being quite RAPID or quite SLOW. Zuni of the southwestern United States (Curtis Cook, personal communication) is spoken quite slowly, while Italian is often quite rapid.

Pitch register: In some languages or certain situations, the voice may mainly be used in relatively HIGH pitch registers; in others, mainly fairly LOW pitch registers may predominate. In Mixtec of Mexico (Ruth Mary Alexander, personal communication), high pitch is often used to indicate politeness. In Totonac of Mexico (Aileen Reid, personal communication), the pitch of the voice goes up and up if the speaker is about to ask for a favor.

Pitch modulation: How wide a range of pitch is utilized can be another speech style characteristic. In some languages, a very WIDE RANGE of pitch is used, varying extensively from quite high to quite low within one utterance. In others, only a very NARROW RANGE of pitch is used. It is possible but quite rare for speech to be completely MONOTONE, that is, no pitch variation at all. Again, speech styles involving modulation of pitch can reflect individual moods or situations or social classes rather than being a consistent characteristic of the language as a whole. In Mixe of Mexico (John Crawford, personal communication), people who are angry or excited will speak in a monotone with the pitch diving downward at the end.

Volume: Likewise, how LOUDLY or SOFTLY a person speaks can be determined by social class, mood, or situation, or it can be characteristic of a language as a whole. The Mazatecs of Mexico (Dan and Peggy Agee, personal communication) speak very quietly, women never raising their voices. The Seminoles of Florida (Dave and Virginia West, personal communication) speak quietly, sometimes so quietly that they are inaudible the first time and need to repeat what they have said. The Zunis of the southwestern United States (Curtis Cook, personal communication) are also a soft-spoken people, so much so that they have very few heavy stresses and little voicing. In contrast, the Kiowa language of Oklahoma uses quite a loud speech style.

State of the vocal folds: Some speech styles involve a high degree of either "breathiness" or "creakiness". These, predictably, are called BREATHY and CREAKY speech styles. These unusual speech qualities are

---

[65]However, although Seminole is usually spoken with very little jaw action, speakers deviate from this speech style when they are excited or when they are trying to speak exactly and precisely to a stranger that they think will not understand.

articulated by particular states of the vocal folds which differ from the voiced and voiceless states introduced in chapter 1.[66] As for some other styles mentioned previously, breathy or creaky speech styles can be characteristic of a language as a whole, or they can be used for special effect in certain situations. These two speech styles are mutually exclusive as they involve two incompatible states of the vocal folds. However, they can be used in the same language in different situations. For example, in the Mixe language of Mexico (John Crawford, personal communication), breathiness is used to show excitement and for emphasis, whereas a creaky voice is used when the speaker wants to borrow money. Zuni has an overall tendency toward a creaky speech style (Curtis Cook, personal communication).

How to acquire a good accent

We end this chapter with a few recommendations adapted from *An Intensive Course in English for Latin-American Students*, Volume 1: "Pronunciation," by Kenneth L. Pike, 1942:1–3.

A person who wishes to learn to speak any language with an accent like that of its native speakers must constantly focus his attention on three things:

He must listen attentively. In every conversation he must listen to individual sounds and to the sentence melodies of the language. He can compare these sounds and melodies with [those of] his own [language]. He can then use features native to the language he is learning rather than sounds foreign to that language.

He must learn to be a mimic. If we mimic our friends in our own language, we may insult them. They won't like it. But in a foreign language the opposite is true. The more we can mimic the people whose language we wish to learn, and the closer we can come to their pronunciation, the better. If we sound exactly like them, they are pleased—never offended. They don't like to have us sound different...So do not be afraid to mimic the...people you listen to. Repeat utterances after them, [do simultaneous tracking with tapes,] and try to sound exactly the same. People will not mind but will be [honored].

Learn how sounds are made. We need to know how the sounds of our own language are made. We can then make a transfer from our own sounds to those of the language we are learning. Further, we must know the patterns in which the voice seems to 'sing' as it talks, so we can learn the intonation of the native speakers.

Above all, we must listen, listen carefully, and mimic well. *"If we wish to have a good accent, we must not be afraid to mimic people."*

"Readjustment of habits. The intricate movements used to make the sounds of one's own language form themselves into ironclad patterns, nearly unbreakable habits. It is very difficult to change them. In order to turn from one language to another and have a good accent in each, one must be able to make rapid changes both in the basic, sweeping articulatory placements, and in the detailed differences. To prepare for this change, one needs some type of articulatory calisthenics to weaken old muscular habits. Oral gymnastics help prepare the way for the readjustment of old methods of forming sounds, so as to produce new habits."

---

[66]See chapter 27 for further details on the states of the vocal folds.

Key concepts

speech styles
tongue position
>   fronted
>   backed
>   retroflexed

lip position
>   rounded
>   squared
>   spread

jaw position
>   set
>   free

use of nasal cavity
>   nasalized
>   non-nasalized

rhythm
>   stress-timed
>   syllable-timed

speed
>   rapid
>   slow

pitch register
>   high
>   low

pitch modulation
>   wide range
>   narrow range
>   monotone

volume
>   soft
>   loud

state of vocal folds
>   breathy
>   creaky

Oral exercise

Find brief paragraphs or poems in your native language to read aloud several times, incorporating different speech styles and combinations of styles. This might be more fun to do with a fellow student.

Written exercise

List at least three combinations of speech styles that are impossible or mutually exclusive, for example, "monotone and wide range of pitch." Then list at least five likely combinations of speech styles, for example, "soft volume and narrow range of pitch."

① creaky and high pitch
② loud volume and high pitch range
③ low and rapid

① loud and slow
② monotone and creaky
③ wide range of pitch and high pitch
④ soft and low/breathy
⑤ narrow range and monotone

24

Fronting and Retroflexion

Goals

⌘   You will be able to define the terms *fronting* and *retroflexion*.

⌘   You will control the *dental, retroflex alveolar, palato-alveolar, fronted palato-alveolar, retroflex palato-alveolar,* and *interdental* sounds presented in the chapter.

⌘   You will become aware of the existence of the *interdental, retracted alveolar, retroflex palato-alveolar, retracted palato-alveolar,* and *alveolo-palatal* sounds presented.

⌘   You will be able to read and draw face diagrams for the sounds presented in the chapter and be able to state the technical name and articulators for each sound.

⌘   You will control *retroflexed vowels* and be able to symbolize them and give their technical names.

In this chapter we introduce two variants of alveolar and palato-alveolar consonants, articulated: (1) by shifting the active articulators slightly forward—called FRONTING; and (2) by curling the tongue tip backwards to make contact with an area slightly behind the prototypical alveolar or palato-alveolar positions—called RETROFLEXION. In retroflexion, the underside of the tongue tip is what makes contact with the roof of the mouth.

There is some question as to whether fronting and retroflexion should be considered truly separate places of articulation or simply as modifications of alveolar and palato-alveolar consonants. The passive articulators are the same for both alveolar and fronted palato-alveolar sounds; for both, some portion of the tongue contacts the alveolar ridge. Likewise, the passive articulators for retroflex alveolars and palato-alveolars are the same; for both, some portion of the tongue contacts the area behind the alveolar ridge.

In this book we treat fronting and retroflexion as processes that result in separate places of articulation rather than as modifications of alveolar and palato-alveolar consonants. However, we recognize that not all linguists share this view.[67]

---

[67]In spite of the fact that it is possible to produce sibilants at virtually any point along the roof of the mouth between the teeth and the palate, most languages do not contrast more than two or three places of articulation. We recommend that you concentrate on learning the ones included in table 24.1 as "canonical" reference points against which variants in your particular language of study can be gauged.

Dental and retroflex alveolars

Because of its flexibility, the tongue tip is the active articulator for several different places of articulation, two of which, alveolar and interdental, you have already encountered. In this chapter you encounter DENTAL consonants, for which the tongue tip touches the back of the upper front teeth or the roof of the mouth just behind the upper teeth or both,[68] and RETROFLEX ALVEOLAR consonants, for which the tongue tip curls backward toward an area just behind the alveolar ridge. Dental sounds are common in Spanish and French, and retroflex alveolars in languages of India.

Figure 24.1 shows face diagrams contrasting the tongue positions used for the dental, alveolar, and retroflex alveolar places of articulation. For consistency, all the face diagrams depict voiceless stops.

Dental	Alveolar	Retroflex alveolar
passive articulator: upper teeth	alveolar ridge	behind alveolar ridge
active articulator:	tongue tip	tongue tip or its underside

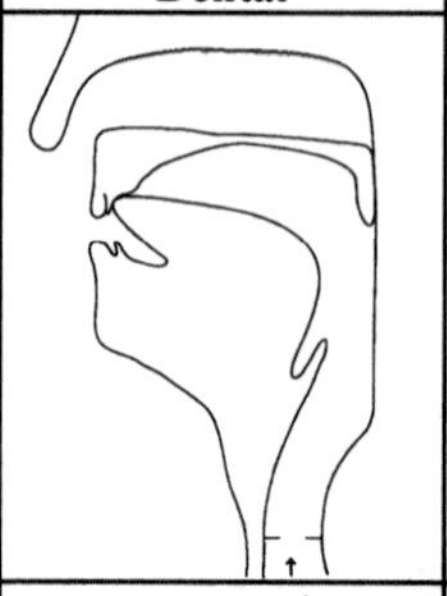

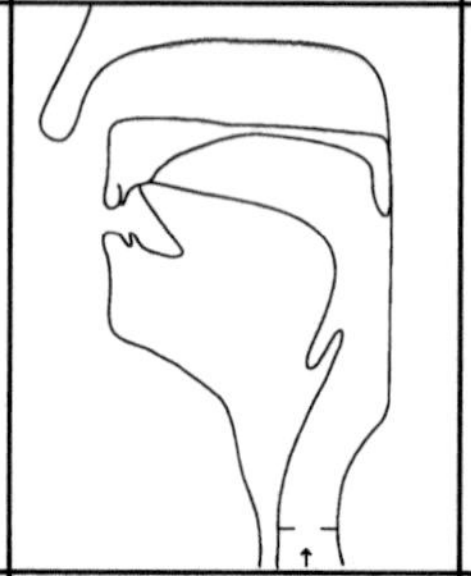

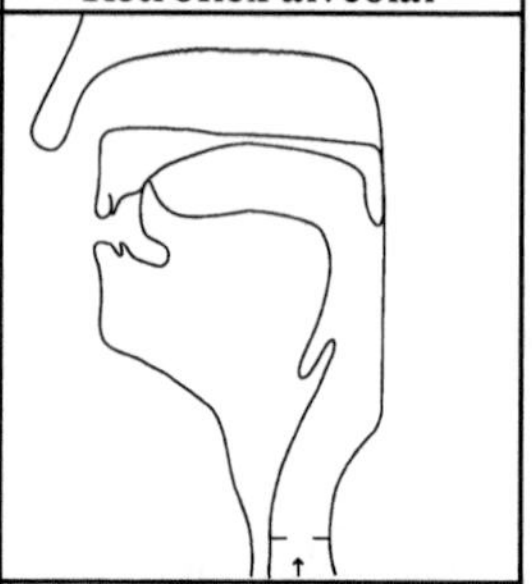

Figure 24.1. Contrast of dental, alveolar, and retroflex alveolar tongue positions.

Fronted palato-alveolars and retroflex palato-alveolars

The body of the tongue can also shift forward or the tongue tip can curl backwards on sounds which involve the tongue blade as active articulator, resulting in consonants at the FRONTED PALATO-ALVEOLAR and RETROFLEX PALATO-ALVEOLAR places of articulation, respectively.

Fronted palato-alveolar	Palato-alveolar	Retroflex palato-alveolar
passive articulator: alveolar ridge	behind alveolar ridge	behind alveolar ridge
active articulator:	tongue blade	underside or end of tongue tip

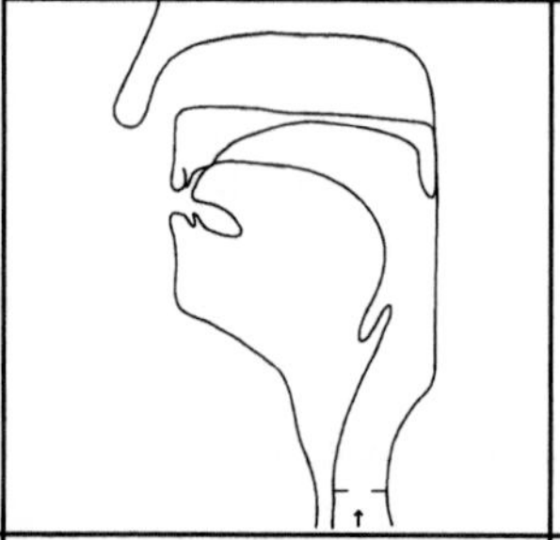

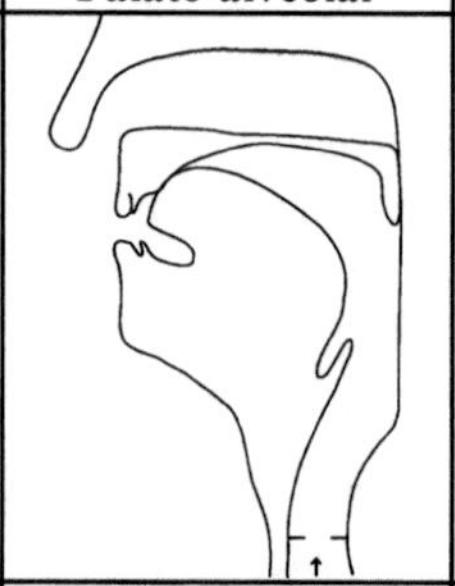

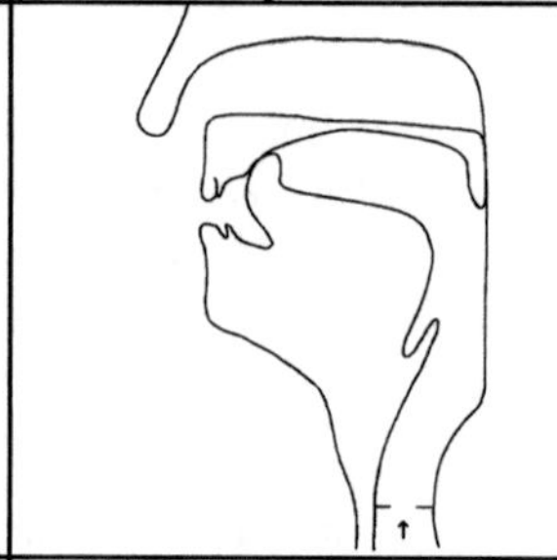

Figure 24.2. Contrasting palato-alveolar tongue positions.

The face diagrams in figure 24.2 contrast the tongue positions for PALATO-ALVEOLAR, FRONTED PALATO-ALVEOLAR, and RETROFLEX PALATO-ALVEOLAR consonants. However, please note that those face diagrams represent stops, and also note that the only fronted palato-alveolar sounds included in the table are sibilants and

---

[68]Another term that you may encounter, which is equivalent to dental, is FRONTED ALVEOLAR.

sibilant affricates, which cannot be depicted well in face diagrams since the tongue sides are salient in their production. Thus, these face diagrams of stops are included only to depict for you the relative tongue positions on the three types of palato-alveolar consonants.

Fronted palato-alveolars are sometimes referred to as laminal alveolars, since the tongue blade can be called the lamina. They could then be symbolized in table 24.1 in two different ways: to depict a fronted palato-alveolar, a plus, indicating advancing (fronting), is placed under a palato-alveolar symbol, [ʃ̟]. And to depict a laminal alveolar, on the other hand, an underbox is used with an alveolar symbol, [s̺]. (Editor's note: This underbox is usually more rectangular than the symbol used in this book.) For our purposes, we will use only the plus notation for sibilants.

Retroflex palato-alveolars, occur relatively rarely in the world's languages and for this reason the IPA does not have a symbol for them. (The IPA uses the "right tail" in conjunction with alveolar symbols.) However, linguists are beginning to recognize that a representation for such sounds is needed, and so we recommend the "right tail" added onto palato-alveolar symbols to indicate retroflexion from that place of articulation. For example, [ʃ̣], [ʒ̣], [t̠ʃ̣ʰ], [t̠ʃ̣], and [d̠ʒ̣].

Table of symbols

Table 24.1 gives symbols for sounds in the most common places of articulation discussed in this chapter. All of the alveolars and some palato-alveolars have already been presented in previous chapters.

Table 24.1. Summary of dental, alveolar, and palato-alveolar symbols

	Dental	Alveolar	Retroflex alveolar	Fronted palato-alveolar or laminal alveolar	Palato-alveolar	Retroflex palato-alveolar	
voiceless	t̪ʰ	tʰ	ʈʰ		t̠ʰ		aspirated
voiceless	t̪	t	ʈ		t̠		stop
voiced	d̪	d	ɖ		d̠		
voiceless	s̪	s	ʂ	ʃ̟	ʃ	ʃ̣	sibilant
voiced	z̪	z	ʐ	ʒ̟	ʒ	ʒ̣	
voiced	l̪	l	ɭ		l̠		lateral approximant
voiceless	ts̪ʰ	tsʰ	tʂʰ	tʃ̟ʰ	tʃʰ	tʃ̣ʰ	aspirated
voiceless	ts̪	ts	tʂ	tʃ̟	tʃ	tʃ̣	affricate
voiced	dz̪	dz	dʐ	dʒ̟	dʒ	dʒ̣	
voiceless					ɲ̥ / n̠̥		nasal
voiced	n̪	n	ɳ		ɲ / n̠		
voiced		ɹ	ɻ				approximant
passive articulator	upper teeth	alveolar ridge	just behind alvr. ridge	alveolar ridge	behind alveolar ridge		
active articulator	tongue tip		underside or end of tongue tip	tongue blade		underside or end of tongue tip	

Production hints

Fronted and retroflex sounds can often result automatically by simply adopting either a fronted or retroflexed overall speech style (see chapter 23). For example, try saying "She sells seashells by the seashore" three times: first, in normal English tongue position; second, with a fronted tongue position (as if your tongue tip is lisping on each sibilant) throughout; third, with a retroflexed tongue position (the tip of your tongue turned up and back) throughout. The second time through, you probably used no alveolar or palato-alveolar consonants, instead substituting dentals and fronted palato-alveolars. The third time through, you probably used retroflex alveolars and retroflex palato-alveolars. Next, try reading down each column in the table, putting each sound between two vowels, [aṣa], [aẓa], [aṯsʰa], [aṯṣa], etc.

Once you have mastered production of consonants with these places of articulation within the context of a speech style, the next step is to produce the sounds in contrast to one another. Read through the whole table again, but this time moving across, row by row, [aṣa], [asa], [aṣa], etc. Do the same with each row.

If the palato-alveolar stops, nasals, and lateral give particular problems, try hooking your tongue tip behind your lower front teeth, forcing the tongue blade to rise to make closure behind the alveolar ridge. However, take care not to produce more of a fronted palato-alveolar consonant than a true palato-alveolar.

Common alternative symbols

In place of the subscript bridge [̪] used by the IPA, Americanists use a subscript arch under an alveolar symbol [s̯] to indicate fronting to the dental place of articulation or under a palato-alveolar symbol [š̯] to indicate fronting for the fronted palato-alveolar place of articulation. Many linguists use an underdot to indicate retroflexion, for example, [ṣ], [ḍ], or [ʃ̣].

Palato-alveolar stops and laterals can be symbolized by placing an extra "tail" onto the side of a base alveolar symbol, thus: [ʈ], [ɖ], [ɭ]. Another option for symbolization of palato-alveolar stops, laterals, and nasals that you may find is to place a subscript box beneath a regular alveolar symbol, for example [t̠] or [n̠], to indicate that a sound is laminal, that is, a sound at the alveolar ridge is articulated by the tongue blade rather than the tongue tip.

Retracted consonants and alveolo-palatals

When the entire tongue is shifted backward slightly, we refer to this phenomenon as RETRACTION; this is common in Chinese and Polish. A short underline [_] is used to indicate retraction: for example, [s̠] is a retracted alveolar sibilant, and [ʃ̠] is a retracted palato-alveolar sibilant.

Another rare sound worth mentioning in this context is voiceless alveolo-palatal median laminal fricative [ɕ] which occurs in Polish and Mandarin Chinese. According to Pullum and Ladusaw (1996:33), [ɕ] is a "voiceless alveolo-palatal median laminal fricative, articulated further forward than [ç]...but not as far forward as [ʃ]...and articulated laminally...rather than apically [i.e., with the tongue blade rather than the tongue tip]." They also mention a voiced alveolo-palatal central fricative, [ʑ].

These sounds are rare enough that we have chosen not to complicate table 24.1 by including them. Just know that they exist, and you can return to this chapter of the book for a reminder if you encounter them in your language of study.

Another way to conceptualize all these places of articulation

It may be helpful to you to think in terms of all of these sounds as falling into two large categories that overlap slightly, the "alveolar family" and the "palato-alveolar family." Figure 24.3 demonstrates this overlap.

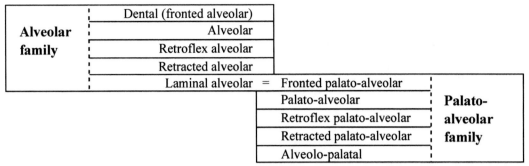

Figure 24.3. Overlap of sounds.

Additional interdental consonants

In chapter 3, you encountered interdental fricatives, [θ] and [ð]. Two stops, a nasal, and a lateral approximant at the interdental point of articulation have been reported for several languages of Australia and Malayalam of India (Dixon 80:135ff.; Ladefoged and Maddieson 1996:20). Such sounds can be symbolized by placing a subscript plus under an alveolar symbol, [t̪], [d̪], [n̪], [l̪], indicating that the articulation of the sound is "over-fronted." These sounds are produced by "over-fronting" the tongue tip, so that it protrudes between the front teeth as for interdental fricatives, rather than touching the roof of the mouth at the alveolar ridge or behind the upper front teeth.

Fronted and retroflexed vowels

A basic principle of phonetics / phonology is that articulations affect each other in terms of their quality. This is clearly seen in the case of the quality of vowels that surround retroflexed consonants. As the tongue tip begins to curl up and back in anticipation of the retroflexed consonant, preceding and following vowels may likewise be retroflexed. Retroflexing of vowels produces the sound quality called RHOTICITY that can be indicated by placing either a right hook (ˇ), a superscript inverted "r" symbol (ʴ), or an underdot (.) with a vowel symbol, for example, [ɚ], [əʴ], or [ə̣].[69]

Key concepts

fronting
retroflexion
dental
retroflex alveolar
fronted palato-alveolar
retroflex palato-alveolar
retraction
interdental
rhoticity
laminal / apical

---

[69]The right hook is used for retroflex vowels by the IPA, e.g., [ɚ] and [ɝ]. The underdot is commonly used by Americanists.

Oral exercises

1. Read aloud the following words, focusing your attention on the place of articulation of the dental, alveolar, retroflex alveolar, and palato-alveolar consonants.

    Hindustani of India (E. Pike 1978:118)

aṭa	'coming'
aṯa	'whole wheat flour'
ḍal	'pulse (porridge)'
ṯali	'palm of hand'
ṯʰali	'plate'
kaṭʰ	'wooden bed'
kaṭ	'bite'
uṯʰṭa	'rising'

    Gujerati of India (E. Pike 1978:119)

'dʒoḍɔ	'shoe'
'mata	'mother'
'maṭi	'dust'
tal	'chance of revenge'
ṭal	'bald'
'miṯʰu	'salt, sweet'
ṯʰaṯʰ	'show-off'

    Zoque of Mexico (E. Pike 1978:119)

'tata	'father'
'ṯata	'his father'
ṯʊkʰ	'his house'
tʊkʰ	'house'

    Southern Mixe of Mexico (E. Pike 1978:90)

piʃ̟	'cotton'
pɪʃ	'flea'
naʃ̟	'earth'
maˑʃ	'a fruit'
poʃ̢	'guava'
poˑʃ	'knot'
poːʃ̢	'spider'

French (Marquita Klaver, personal communication)

t̪ɔʁo	'bull'
ʁut	'road'
kat̪χ	'four'
lɛt̪χ	'letter'
bʁyt	'brute'
dəʁiẽ	'you are welcome'
pø'ṭɛt̪χ	'perhaps'

Malayalam of India (Ladefoged 1982:145; 1993:159)

mut̪ːu	'pearl'
mutːu	'density'
muʈːu	'knee'
kut̪ːi	'stabbed'
kutːi	'peg'
kuʈːi	'child'
kʌmːi	'shortage'
kʌnːi	'Virgo'
kʌṇːi	'link in chain'
kʌɲːi	'boiled rice and water'
kʌŋːi	'crushed'
eṇːʌ	'named'
enːe	'me'
eɳːʌ	'oil'
teːɲːʌ	'worn out'
teːŋːʌ	'coconut'

2. Read the sounds in table 24.1 twice, once reading down the columns and once reading across the rows. Put a vowel of your choice on each side in all cases. As you read across the rows, focus on how fronting and retroflexion affect the surrounding vowels.

Written exercises

1. Give the phonetic symbol for the sound depicted in each of these face diagrams.

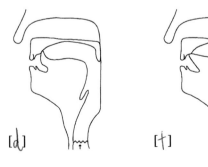

[ɖ]   [ţ]

2.   Draw face diagrams for [t̪], [ɳ̊], and [n̪].

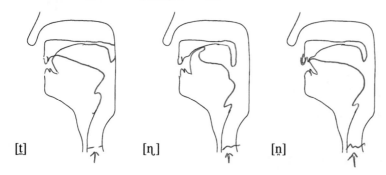

[t̪]   [ɳ̊]   [n̪]

Transcription conversion exercise

Rewrite each of the following using only IPA symbols.

ut̪ʰt̪a   pö̤t̪ɛt̪x

bɡ̊üt   dəɟiʕ

t̪ikʰ   dʒodɔ

t̪ʰat̪ʰ   ɖɑɭ

25

Ejectives

Goals

⌘ You will be able to explain what *ejectives* are (speech sounds produced with an egressive glottalic airstream) and how they differ from sounds made with the pulmonic airstream mechanism.

⌘ You will control the ejective sounds presented in this chapter.

⌘ You will be able to read and draw face diagrams of ejectives, noting especially the representation of the glottalic air mechanism.

You may recall from chapter 1 that three different airstream mechanisms can be used in producing speech sounds: pulmonic, glottalic, and velaric. So far we have introduced only sounds produced with the pulmonic airstream mechanism. The sounds called EJECTIVES and IMPLOSIVES are produced with the glottalic airstream mechanism (which is sometimes called "pharynx air").

In the formation of [ʔ], the vocal folds come together, and the air above the glottis is separated from the air below the glottis. If there is a constriction in the oral cavity, by raising the larynx with closed glottis, the air above the glottis is compressed. When the constriction is released the compressed air is "ejected" from the mouth. If the larynx with closed glottis is moved downward, the air above the glottis is sucked inward, resulting in an implosive sound. (We will present these more fully in chapter 28.) There is velic closure for all sounds involving the glottalic airstream mechanism.

Ejectives, sometimes called GLOTTALIZED sounds, are very common in many of the languages of the Americas. Implosives are common in languages of Africa, Vietnam, Central America, and the Caucasus. In this chapter we introduce only ejectives, reserving implosives for chapter 28.

Ejectives

Table 25.1 lists ejective sounds. Their technical names may, as usual, be derived by reading the labels clockwise around the table. For example, [k'] is a "velar ejective stop" or "velar stop with egressive glottalic air," and [ɬ'] is an "alveolar ejective lateral fricative" or "alveolar lateral fricative with egressive glottalic air." Note that the egressive glottalic airstream is represented by an apostrophe ['] following the basic symbol. Notice, also, that no voiced ejectives are included in the table since it is physically impossible to produce them.

Table 25.1. Ejective sounds

Bilabial	Labiodental	Interdental	Alveolar	Palato-alveolar	Retroflex (alveolar)	Palatal	Velar	Uvular	
p'			t'		ʈ'	c'	k'	q'	ejective stop
	f'	θ'	s'	ʃ'		ç'	x'	χ'	ejective fricative
	pf'	tθ'	ts'	tʃ'	tʂ'	cç'	kx'	qχ'	ejective affricate
			ɬ'						ejective lateral fricative
			tɬ'						ejective lateral affricate

Figures 25.1, 25.2, and 25.3 depict [k], [k'], and [ʔ], respectively. Diagrams of glottalic sounds differ from those of pulmonic sounds only in the region of the larynx. Note the representation of the air mechanism: the vocal folds are drawn completely closed (that is, with an unbroken straight line clear through the glottis), and the upward arrow is drawn *through* the vocal folds line (rather than below it as for pulmonic sounds), indicating that the vocal folds are the initiator of the glottalic airstream.[70]

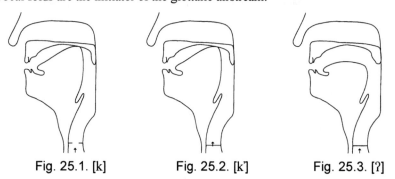

Fig. 25.1. [k]   Fig. 25.2. [k']   Fig. 25.3. [ʔ]

Production and recognition hints

The (inter)dental fricative [θ'] and affricate [tθ'] are probably the easiest ejectives to produce. Simply hold your breath and pretend to scrape something off the end of your tongue using your upper teeth as you articulate a [θ] or [tθ]. The other ejectives can be produced by analogy with the (inter)dental ones: Hold your breath while saying [k] or [p] or [t] to produce [k'], [p'], and [t'].

Try saying a long glottal stop between vowels, [aʔːa]. Progressively lengthen the glottal stop so that you can articulate a consonant in the mouth while maintaining the glottal closure. For example, if you superimpose [k] on [aʔːa], you get [aʔkʔa]. When you can produce that sequence, you can then eliminate the glottal stop preceding the ejective by ending the vowel with a velar closure, and you can eliminate the glottal stop following the ejective by reducing its length until it is just a necessary result of producing the ejective. Any number of ejectives can be produced during a long glottal stop with no depletion of the air in the lungs, as pulmonic air is not being used.

It is usually not too difficult to distinguish ejectives from sounds with egressive pulmonic air. Ejectives sound much sharper than their pulmonic-air counterparts.

---

[70]Recall that a face diagram of [ʔ] also has the straight unbroken line through the glottis, as its articulation also involves closure there; however, the airstream arrow goes *below* the glottis for [ʔ] since it is produced with a pulmonic airstream mechanism.

Alternative symbols

You will sometimes encounter ejectives written with a superscripted glottal stop symbol instead of the apostrophe, for example, [t$^{\textipa{P}}$] or [kx$^{\textipa{P}}$].

Key concepts

ejective
egressive glottalic airstream mechanism

Oral exercises

1. Practice the following sound drills.

ap^{h}a	ap'a
at^{h}a	at'a
ak^{h}a	ak'a
aθa	aθ'a
asa	as'a
afa	af'a

2. Practice saying aloud the following words
    ### Aguacatec of Guatemala (E. Pike 1978:99)

k^{h}a?	'grinding stone'
k'a?	'bitter'
q^{h}a:?	'our water'
q'a?	'bridge'
?ak'	'wet'
?aq'	'vine'
sak'	'grasshopper'
sak^{h}	'gunny sack'
saq^{h}	'white'

    ### Tabasco Chontal of Mexico (E. Pike 1978:100)

tʃ^{h}ɛŋ	'do it!'
tʃ'ɛŋ	'hole, well'
p'os	'sweepings'
p^{h}os	'it is pale'

Tlingit of Alaska (E. Pike 1978:102)

s'ix   'dirt'
t'ix'   'ice'
x'at'   'island'
tʰiɬ'   'dog-salmon'
kx'utɬ'   'boiling tide'
kʰutʃ'et'a   'ball'

Written exercises

1.   For the three sounds depicted in these face diagrams, give their symbols and their technical names.

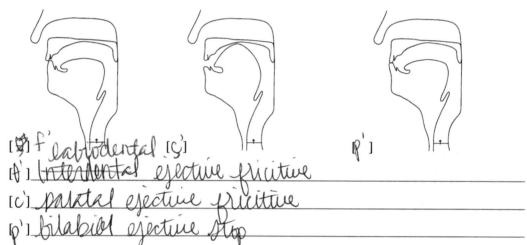

[θ̣] f' *labiodental* [ç̣]

[θ'] *Interdental ejective fricative*

[c'] *palatal ejective fricative*

[p'] *bilabial ejective stop*

2.   Draw face diagrams for [x'], [ʔ], and [t'].

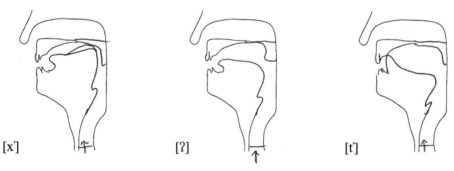

[x']   [ʔ]   [t']

Transcription conversion exercise

Rewrite each of the following, using only IPA symbols.

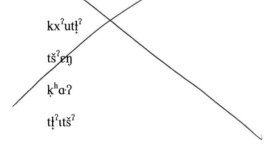

kxˀutɬˀ

tšˀɛŋ

ḳʰaˑʔ

tɬˀutšˀ

26

Flaps and Trills

Goals

⌘ You will be able to explain the articulatory difference between stops, *flaps,* and *trills.*

⌘ You will control the flaps and trills presented in the chapter, and be able to give a technical name for each.

The articulation of a stop involves three fairly controlled steps. The active articulator approaches the passive articulator, touches it, and is then released, all in a controlled, deliberate manner. In contrast, the articulation of FLAPS and TRILLS is much less controlled. Flaps involve a single rapid movement with momentary contact between two articulators as one is thrown against the other, as one might tap with a pencil eraser. Trills involve the rapid uncontrolled vibration of an articulatory organ as it is loosely held against another in a moving airstream, sometimes described as "flapping in the breeze."[71]

Table 26.1. Flap and trill symbols

	Bilabial	Labiodental	Dental	Alveolar	Retroflex	Uvular	
voiceless		f̌		ɾ̥	ɽ̥		flap
voiced	ƀ*	ⱴ		ɾ	ɽ		
voiced	m̌			ň	ň̢		nasal flap
voiced				ɺ	ɺ̢		lateral flap
voiceless	ʙ̥		r̥̪	r̥		ʀ̥	trill
voiced	ʙ		r̪	r		ʀ	

*The symbols in the table with a breve (˘) over them are pseudo-IPA symbols. The IPA uses the breve to indicate extra short length.

Pike (1978:92–93) reports lateral flaps in Wagi and Enga of Papua New Guinea and Moru of Sudan. Nasal flaps are used in American English. The existence of three labial flaps has been reported by Olson and Hajek (2003) in languages throughout Nigeria, Chad, Cameroon, Central African Republic, Democratic Republic of the Congo, Sudan, Zimbabwe, and Malawi, though not all may be phonologically contrastive. In table 26.1 we include the complete array of flaps and trills of which we are aware, even though the IPA has no official symbols for two of them. The voiced labiodental flap symbol was approved by the IPA council in 2005.

---

[71]Although simple vocal fold vibration fits this definition of a trill, it is not considered to be a trill.

Flaps

There are three types of articulatory movement possible for alveolar flaps.

> A. The active articulator taps the passive articulator and returns (this one is sometimes called a TAP instead of a flap).

> B. The active articulator flicks past the passive articulator, moving from front to back.

> C. The active articulator flicks past the passive articulator, moving from back to front.

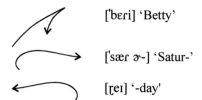

['bɛɾi] 'Betty'

['sæɾ ɚ-] 'Satur-'

[ɽeɪ] '-day'

Type A occurs between two vowels in many English words: 'booty' ['buɾi], 'ghetto' ['gɛɾoʊ], 'city' ['sɪɾi], etc. Type B occurs in many English words, immediately preceding a syllabic "r," such as 'butter' ['bəɾɚ], 'manner' or 'manor' ['mænɚ] (at least in fast speech), 'reader' ['ɹiɾɚ], etc. Type C occurs in many English words, immediately following an "r," such as 'party' ['pʰaɹɽi], 'dirty' ['dəɽi], 'Barney' ['baɹɳi], etc. As for the two flaps in 'Saturday,' the first is type B and the second is type C.

Lateral and nasal flaps may just be nasals and laterals of extremely short duration.

Trills

In attempting to learn to articulate trills, it is important to realize that they involve a rapid series of automatic closures brought about by the pressure of the moving airstream on the relaxed active articulator. Only the starting and stopping of the trill are under the speaker's neuromuscular control. In between, the dynamics of the airstream keep the trill going. In other words, you cannot expect to produce a trill by firing off a rapid series of controlled short stops or flaps. In fact, attempting to do so will create sufficient tension in the articulator that it cannot vibrate in the airstream, preventing the trill from happening.

Production hints

[ɾ] Say [tə'da] faster and faster to [tɾa]. Do the same for [gə'da] to [gɾa] and for [də'da] to [dɾa].

[ɾ̥] Some speakers of English make a distinction between 'ladder' ['læɾɚ] and 'latter' ['læɾ̥ɚ]. Try thinking or articulating [h] during the voiceless flap.

[ɺ] Say 'Millie' ['mɪli] or 'Sally' ['sæli] rapidly.

[ɾ̃] Say 'painting' ['pʰeɪɾ̃ɪŋ] rapidly.

[ʙ̥] Imitate the voiceless snort of a horse.

[ʙ] What you might say when it is cold. Your lips need to be looser than for [β]. This trill is used in Mixtec of Mexico (Ruth Mary Alexander, personal communication) to call turkeys.

[ʀ] Snoring uses the same articulators as this trill but with an ingressive airstream. Gargling produces an egressive uvular trill, voiced for some people, voiceless for others. Some people produce this sound quite easily when they are actually aiming at a voiceless uvular fricative, [χ].

[r] Your tongue *must* be relaxed to produce this trill correctly, because it needs to be set in vibration by the moving airstream. Keep your jaw fairly closed. Some people find it helpful to lie on their backs with their heads hanging off the edge of a bed; this allows gravity to help relax the tongue. Try saying "butted up" or "put it on," more and more rapidly, until they become [bɾəp] and [pɾan].

Alternative transcriptions

You may encounter a wedge (ˇ) instead of a breve (˘) to indicate a flap, for example [ř] or [ň]. You may also encounter some trills written with a tilde; for example, [r̃] is the Americanist equivalent of IPA [r], and [b̃] is the Americanist equivalent of IPA [ʙ].

Key concepts

flap / tap
trill

Oral exercise

Practice saying aloud the following words.

Kreish of Sudan (Westermann and Ward 1933:76–77)

gev̆e	'arrow'
gev̆umu	'to shoot with a bow'
eɾe	'hen'
ere	'beans'
iɾi	'kind of tree'
iri	'death'

Gã of Ghana (Westermann and Ward 1933:76)

mˌlihilɛ	'kindness'
mˌlamˌla	'quickly'

Spanish, various dialects

ˈsɛɾo	'zero'
ˈsɛro	'mountain range'
ɛnseˈɾaðo	'waxed'
ɛnseˈraðo	'enclosed'
fɛreteˈria	'hardware store'
ɛraˈðuɾa	'horseshoe'
rɛŋˈglon	'line'
ˈroro	'nursing child'
fɛrokaˈril	'railroad'
ˈpɛɾla	'pearl'
ˈkaɾo	'expensive'
ˈkaro	'car; vehicle'

Mura-Pirahã of Brazil (Floyd 1981:85: Dan and Keren Everett, personal communication)

aʙoi̯	'lake'
ɪʙogɪ	'milk'

Seri of Mexico (Floyd 1981:85; Mary Moser: uvular trills include some friction)

ˈkaʀaʀ̥	'loud sound'
ʀ̥aˈpoː	'sea lion'
ˈn̥aːpʀ̥a	'buzzard'

Malayalam of India (Floyd 1981:85; Laura Gillette, personal communication)

ˈɔrɔ	'room'
ˈɔr̥ɔ	'half'

English (Kenneth L. Pike, personal communication)

'Dead headed Ed had edited it.'

Written exercise

Write technical names for the following sounds.

[ʙ] Voiced bilabial trill

[ɾ] Voiced alveolar flap

[ʀ] Voiced uvular trill

[ɳ̆] Voiced retroflex nasal flap

[r̥] Voiceless alveolar trill

Transcription conversion exercise

Retranscribe the following using only IPA symbols.

[ɛřiňa]   [p̃iřa]

27

States of the Glottis

Goals

⌘ You will be able to explain four main *states of the glottis: voiceless, breathy, voiced, creaky.*

⌘ You will be able to recognize, symbolize, reproduce, and give technical names for sounds articulated with each of those four glottal states.

You have already encountered two states of the glottis: VOICED and VOICELESS. This chapter introduces three more states of the glottis: BREATHY, CREAKY, and WHISPERED.[72] Except for whispered, which is probably just a speech style, the states of the glottis have been found cross-linguistically to distinguish word meanings. In this chapter, we describe and give the symbolization for each of these states of the glottis, as well as production hints for breathy and creaky voice. See Ladefoged (1982:128) for photographic depictions of the various glottal states. The front of the larynx is at the top of each photo included there.

Voiceless

The vocal folds are apart and not vibrating for all voiceless sounds involving only the pulmonic airstream; when the vocal folds are apart, air passes through the glottis relatively unimpeded. The vocal folds are closed (still not vibrating) for glottal stop, ejectives, and voiceless implosives; you will soon see that glottal stop is technically not voiceless.

Voicelessness has been represented in two ways: either assumed as an intrinsic quality associated with a particular symbol (for example, [t], [k], [x], [s], etc.) or with a diacritic under-ring, for example, [n̥], [e̥], [w̥].

---

[72]Breathy and creaky have already been mentioned superficially in chapter 23 on speech styles. You were probably able to mimic the sounds of those speech styles without knowing exactly what your vocal folds were doing differently. These glottal states can be used contrastively on individual speech sounds, especially vowels, to determine the meanings of words. That is, there can be pairs of words with different meanings which differ phonetically only in whether or not a vowel is breathy, creaky, voiced, or voiceless. In other words, these states of the glottis are not only a stylistic detail of speech but can be as vital to contrastive meanings as is manner or place of articulation.

Breathy

Breathy sounds,[73] like voiced ones, involve some form of vocal fold vibration. However, the glottis is open during more of the cycle of vibration than for the voiced state, resulting in audible turbulence. Even though the vocal folds are vibrating in the front on breathy sounds, they may be slightly apart and stationary in back. Breathiness can also occur when the vocal folds do not come together completely during vibration, instead vibrating or flapping randomly.

Breathiness has been found as a feature of both consonants and vowels. Breathy vowels are reported to be contrastive in Dinka (Pike 1978), Maasai, Nuer, and probably other Nilotic languages of Africa. Many languages of India have a series of breathy consonants (stops and affricates) that contrast with voiced ones.[74] These breathy consonants are sometimes called "voiced aspirated" because they involve a very quickly articulated breathy vowel release. However, applying the term "voiced" to breathy consonants is technically a contradiction, since voiced and breathy are mutually exclusive glottal states.

Breathiness of vowels and consonants is symbolized in the IPA by a subscript umlaut (̤), for example, [e̤] or [b̤]. The symbol [ɦ] may be used for a breathy vowel if its quality is predictable, being the same as that of an adjacent voiced vowel, for example, [ɦa].

At first, the breathy state of the glottis can be achieved simply by imitating the speech of a "sexy" movie actress. Then try saying a word with two nearly identical syllables that differ only in that the first vowel is voiced and the second is breathy, for example, [ˈdidi̤]. Try this with several two-syllable "words," until you can control the breathiness, putting it only on individual segments rather than using it as an overall speech style.

Voiced

For voiced sounds, the vocal folds vibrate back and forth along their entire length. Many consonant and vowel symbols assume a voiced glottal state. For example, these symbols represent voiced speech sounds: [a], [g], [β], [z], [w], [l]. There is no particular diacritic (equivalent to the under-ring which "devoices" the base symbol under which it is written) to "add voicing" to an inherently voiceless symbol.[75]

Creaky

Like voiced, the creaky state of the glottis involves vocal fold vibration. However, instead of vibrating along their entire length, the vocal folds vibrate only in front, being together and stationary in back. The vibrations are irregular, often a strong pulse alternating with a weaker pulse. This state of the glottis is sometimes referred to as "laryngealization." You encountered this glottal state in chapter 23, in the creaky speech style. However, the creaky state of the glottis can also be used contrastively on individual segments (primarily vowels and other sonorants), not only as part of an overall speech style.

To symbolize the creaky state of the glottis, the IPA uses a subscript tilde (̰), for example, [a̰], [m̰].

Creaky speech sounds are easiest to produce at low pitch. However, they also occur at high pitches in many languages, for example, Mazatec and Zapotec of Mexico. If you have difficulty producing creaky sounds, try imitating the voice of a tired person or someone who has just gotten up in the morning and has not used his or her voice much yet. It is sometimes helpful to imitate the sound of a door creaking open or a stick being run along a picket fence. Then try saying a word with two nearly identical syllables that differ only in that the first vowel is creaky and the second is voiced, for example, [ˈba̰ba]. Try this with several two-syllable "words," until you can control the creakiness, putting it only on individual segments rather than using it as an overall speech style.

---

[73]The term "murmured" is sometimes substituted for "breathy" in the technical names of breathy consonants and vowels, for example, by Ladefoged (1993).

[74]See chapter 29 for a more detailed discussion and a symbol table of these breathy stops and affricates.

[75]However, the IPA does permit use of a subscript wedge [̬] to indicate voicing in certain circumstances. For example, [s̬] can be used to denote [z] in a language having no phonemic contrast between [s] and [z], but where the phonemic /s/ is phonetically somewhat voiced in some special environment, perhaps intervocalically. Such a symbol is outside the realm of ordinary phonetic transcription.

Whispered

The whispered glottal state is similar to glottal stop in that there is no vibration of the vocal folds because they are held tightly together. However, there is a very narrow glottal opening at the back of the vocal folds, between the arytenoid cartilages, through which air is forced, creating turbulence. The whispered glottal state probably applies mainly to vowels, perhaps to other sonorants as well.

The whispered glottal state differs from the voiceless speech sounds in the configuration of the vocal folds. For voiceless speech sounds they are apart and relaxed, with no vibration, and virtually no impedance of the airflow. For whispered speech sounds, they are tightly together for about the front two-thirds to three-fourths, then apart for the back portion, and the opening between them there is sufficiently small to result in some friction. It is highly unlikely that any language would contrast the two.

There is no IPA symbol to indicate whispered sounds. They apparently choose not to provide a symbol for this state of the glottis since it is not used contrastively in any known language, being used rather as an overall speech style in certain circumstances.

Glottal stop—<u>not</u> a state of the glottis

The glottal stop [ʔ] is not a state of the glottis, even though it involves the glottis. Rather, it is a unique consonant articulated separately from the states of the glottis. The vocal folds come tightly together as active articulators, completely impeding the pulmonic airstream from below. In chapter 4, we said it was redundant to include "voiceless" in the technical name for this stop. You can now realize that it would actually be incorrect to do so, since the glottal stop is very different from the voiceless state of the glottis. However, glottal stop is perceived auditorily as being voiceless since there is no vibration of the vocal folds.

Technical names

The first "slot" in the technical name for any speech sound is reserved for the label specifying the glottal state involved. In the case of voiced vowels, that slot can remain empty, as we assume voiced to be the default state of the glottis for vowels. For all other speech sounds (except [ʔ]), insert the state of the glottis term into that slot. For example, [e̤] is a breathy close-mid front unrounded vowel.

Table 27.1. Common alternative transcriptions

State of glottis	IPA symbols	Common alternative symbols
voiceless	n̥ e̥ w̥	N E W
breathy	e̤ b̤ ɦ	e̤ bʱ ɦ
creaky	ḛ	ẻ

Key concepts

state of the glottis
voiceless
breathy / murmured
voiced
creaky / laryngealized
whispered
glottal stop

Oral exercise

Practice reading aloud the following words.

Isthmus Zapotec of Mexico (Velma Pickett, personal communication; 3 is high, 1 is low)

'na̰²¹	'I, me'
'naː²¹	'he says'
za²kou̯ʔ²³	'you will receive'
gu²laʔ²kiʔ¹	'put'
'gi̤²u³	'lime'
'ŋgi̤²u¹	'man'
't͡ʃṵ²³	'let's go'
't͡ʃa̰ʔ²³	'I go'

Shilluk of Sudan (Tucker and Bryan 1966:403)

tsàːgē̠	'his milk'
tsàːgéː	'our milk'
tsāːkɔ̠	'to begin'
kó tsàkṳ̀	'don't begin! (pl.)'
nēːnɔ̠	'to see'
nè̠ːná	'my sight'

Lango of Sudan (Tucker and Bryan 1966:404–405)

kɔ́m	'chair'
kɔ́mê̤	'chairs'
kɔ́mːí	'your chair'
pé̤ː àpɔ̤̀á	'it is not a feeble-minded man'

Written exercises

1. Give technical names for the following speech sounds, specifying the state of the glottis appropriately for each one.

    [ɯ] breathy, back unrounded vowel ~ close

    [ø] close-mid front rounded vowel

    [ɪ] creaky near-close front-central vowel ~ unrounded

    [ʍ] voiceless labial-velar approximant

    [ʔ] glottal stop

2.   Write a phonetic symbol for each technical name.

[ɪ̤] a breathy close front unrounded vowel

[l̰] a creaky alveolar lateral approximant

[y] a close front rounded vowel

[j̊] a voiceless palatal nonsyllabic vowel

3.   How would you arrange the four main states of the glottis (breathy, creaky, voiced, voiceless) along a continuum of decreasing airflow at the glottis, due to increasing glottal constriction?

voiced, creaky, breathy, voiceless ~~voiced~~ *voiceless, breathy, creaky*

4.   Arrange the elements within the following two sets of symbols according to their position along this continuum of decreasing airflow at the glottis.

[ɑ̤, w̰, e̥, ɪ]   [I, a̰, w̥, e̤]   [e̤, w̰, ɪ, a̰) *voiceless, breathy, voiced, creaky*

[n̥, j, t̬, ɹ̰]   [j, t, n̥, ɹ̰]   [t̬, w̰, j, n̥]

Transcription conversion exercise

Retranscribe the following words, using only IPA symbols.

kȯtsɑ̇kǔ

yá líŋā gṳök

28

Implosives

Goals

⌘ You will be able to explain implosives as speech sounds produced with an ingressive glottalic airstream, and how they differ from ejectives and from sounds made with a pulmonic airstream.

⌘ You will control the implosive sounds presented in the chapter.

⌘ You will be able to read and draw face diagrams of implosives, noting especially the location and direction of the arrow through the vocal folds.

Implosives are the first sounds introduced in this book to involve an ingressive airstream. Like ejectives, they involve a glottalic airstream. However, they are the "reverse" of ejectives because of the direction of that airstream. The glottis is closed (or nearly closed, in the case of voiced implosives), and the larynx is pulled downward while some other articulation is being formed in the mouth. Whereas with ejectives the air above the glottis is compressed and forced out of the mouth, with implosives the air in this chamber is rarefied, causing a partial vacuum.

Table 28.1 lists the implosives that have been found in languages. Unlike ejectives, implosives can be either voiced or voiceless. The voiced series of implosives is more common than the voiceless series. There appear to be no implosive fricatives used in any language, although a voiced implosive affricate [ʤ] is reported to occur in Roglai of Vietnam (Norris McKinney, personal communication) and Komo of the Democratic Republic of Congo.

Table 28.1. Implosive sounds

	Bilabial	Alveolar	Palato-alveolar	Retroflex (alveolar)	Palatal	Velar	Uvular	
vl.	ɓ̥	ɗ̥		ʈ		ɠ̊	ɠ̥	implosive stop
vd.	ɓ	ɗ		ᶑ	ʄ	ɠ	ʛ	
vd.			ʤ					implosive affricate

The ingressive glottalic airstream mechanism is symbolized by adding a hook to the top of the basic symbol of the corresponding pulmonic sound.

The action of the larynx in producing voiced implosives is sometimes described as being similar to that of a leaky piston in a vacuum pump. The downward movement of the larynx produces a partial vacuum, but the vocal folds are not held as tightly together as they are for ejectives or voiceless implosives, and so some pulmonic air leaks through the glottis, causing the vocal folds to vibrate. Thus, voiced implosives use a combination of two air mechanisms, an egressive pulmonic airstream and an ingressive glottalic airstream.

The face diagrams in figures 28.1 and 28.2 depict the implosives [ɠ̊] and [ʄ]. For voiceless implosives, the ingressive glottalic airstream mechanism is represented by a downward arrow through a straight line across the glottis. Depicting voiced implosives is more complex, since they involve two airstream mechanisms. This combination of airstream mechanisms is depicted by drawing a straight line halfway across the larynx with a downward arrow drawn through it representing the ingressive glottalic airstream mechanism and a wavy line the rest of the way across the larynx area with the usual upward arrow below the vocal folds representing the egressive pulmonic airstream.

Figure 28.1. [ɠ̊]   Figure 28.2. [ʄ]

The technical name for [ɠ̊] is "voiceless velar implosive" or "voiceless velar stop with ingressive glottalic air." Note that all the implosive sounds are either stops or an affricate that includes a stop, so it is unnecessary to specify the manner of articulation in technical names for implosives.

Hints for production and recognition of implosives

For most people, voiced implosives are easier to produce than voiceless ones. Many people can produce voiced velar implosives by imitating a frog: [ɠə ɠə ɠə ɠə]. Try this. If you can produce a voiced velar implosive this way, you can probably do the other three by analogy.

If you are not one of the fortunates who can "frog" their way into voiced implosives, try this technique instead: Say [a] with *ingressive* pulmonic air. Close your lips, but continue sucking air inward to produce [a]. Make sure that there is a velic closure to prevent air from entering your lungs after your mouth is closed. At this point, you should be able to feel your larynx dropping. Open your lips suddenly and [ɓ] should result. Do the other implosives by analogy.

There are two other tricks to try to help you learn to produce voiceless implosives. The first assumes that you can already produce ejectives. The second assumes that you can already make voiced implosives. Choose the one that fits you best.

If you can already produce ejectives, try a "rocking" exercise by alternately raising and lowering the larynx, thus alternating between articulation of an ejective and an implosive: [k' ɠ̊ k' ɠ̊ k' ɠ̊ k' ɠ̊]. Your larynx might be more easily pulled downward if it has just been pulled upward to produce an ejective.

If you can already produce voiced implosives, then whisper a sequence such as [ɓaɓa]. The result will be [ɓ̥aɓ̥a]. The next step is to work on producing a voiced vowel following the voiceless implosive. Try to do it by analogy, perhaps saying [ɓaɓa], then immediately [ɓ̥aɓ̥a].

To produce the difference between ejectives and implosives correctly, you will need to gain muscular control of the upward and downward movement of your larynx. Ladefoged (1993:131) suggests: "You can recognize what it feels like to raise the glottis by singing a very low note and then moving to the position for singing the highest note you possibly can."[76] Put your fingers on your throat to feel the movements of the larynx.

---

[76]Such extreme larynx movement upward and downward does not actually occur in trained singers as they vary between high and low pitches. However, this suggestion can be useful even for singers if they just think of *speaking* as low and high as possible rather than of singing. For nonsingers, the mental suggestion of singing seems to help more than speaking at the pitch extremes.

Try holding your breath during a [ʔ]. Meanwhile, push and pull the airstream by muscle action, being sure to keep the glottis closed. Try articulating an [f] while pushing and pulling the airstream.

As for hearing the difference between voiceless implosives and ejectives, the lower position of the larynx for implosives makes the cavity above the glottis longer (and the forward position of the tongue root makes that cavity larger) for implosives than for ejectives. Consequently, implosives have a more hollow quality (a lower-pitched sharp "pop") than do ejectives.

Alternative symbols

You will sometimes encounter implosives written with a backwards superscripted glottal stop, for example, [kˤ] or [dʒˤ].

Key concepts

implosive
ingressive glottalic airstream

Oral exercises

1. Practice the following sound drills.

apʰa	atʰa	akʰa	aqʰa
ap'a	at'a	ak'a	aq'a
aɓ̥a	aɗ̥a	aɠ̊a	aʛ̥a
aɓa	aɗa	aɠa	aʛa
aba	ada	aga	aɢa

2. Practice the following words with voiced implosives.
    Nancere of Chad (E. Pike 1978:106)

ɗɛgɛ	'covered them'
dɛgɛ	'with them'
di	'with him'
ɗi	'negative'
bei	'pour out'
ɓɛl	'lead'
ɓaŋ	'he'

3. Practice these voiceless implosive sounds.
    Tojolabal of Mexico (E. Pike 1978:106)

'ɓ̥oɓ̥	'to be able'
sk'aɓ̥il	'her sleeve'
ɓ̥a'k'ɛtʰ	'meat'
tʃa'ɓ̥ɛkʰ	'beeswax'

Written exercises

1. Write a symbol for each sound depicted in these three face diagrams, and give their technical names.

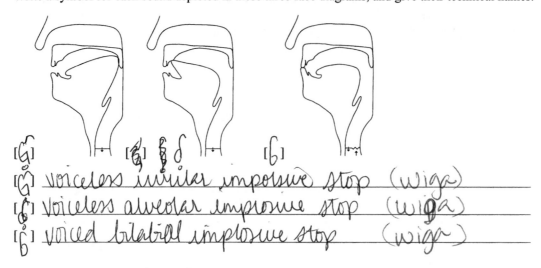

[ɢ̊]
[ɢ̊] *voiceless uvular implosive stop (wiga)*
[ɗ̥] *voiceless alveolar implosive stop (wiga)*
[ɓ] *voiced bilabial implosive stop (wiga)*

2. Draw face diagrams for [ɓ̥] and [ʄ].

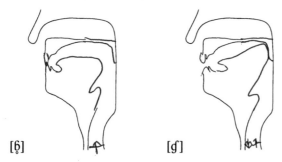

[ɓ̥]   [ʄ]

Transcription conversion exercise

Rewrite each of the following, using only IPA symbols.

gˤaˈbˤɛl
ˈdˤɛged
aˈkˤɪlɪʔ
bˤou̯gˤəm
kˤɛˈpˤotˤi

29

Breathy Stops and Affricates

Goals

⌘ You will control the *breathy stops* and *affricates* presented in the chapter.

⌘ You will be able to give technical names for all the symbols in the table.

You may recall from chapter 27 that breathiness involves vibration of the front part of the vocal folds but a greater airflow than is the case for voiced sounds since the vocal folds are apart and stationary in back. This increased airflow results in a "softer" quality of sound.

Many languages of India have a series of breathy stops and affricates that contrast with the voiced stops and affricates at the same places of articulation. These breathy stops and affricates have sometimes been referred to as "voiced aspirated" because their very quickly-articulated breathy vowel release somewhat parallels the voiceless vowel release following a voiceless aspirated stop or affricate. However, recall from chapter 27 that the states of the glottis for voiced and breathy sounds are actually quite different. Therefore, in this book we will refer to breathy stops, not to "voiced aspirated" stops.

Table 29.1.Breathy stops and affricates

	Bilabial	Dental	Alveolar	Retroflex alveolar	Palato-alveolar	Velar	
voiceless	pʰ	t̪ʰ	tʰ	ʈʰ		kʰ	aspirated
voiceless	p	t̪	t	ʈ		k	stop
voiced	b	d̪	d	ɖ		g	
breathy	b̤	d̪̈	d̤	ɖ̤		g̤	
voiceless					tʃʰ		aspirated
voiceless					tʃ		affricate
voiced					dʒ		
breathy					d̤ʒ		

You may occasionally encounter the terms "murmured stop" and "murmured affricate." These are acceptable equivalents to "breathy stop" and "breathy affricate."

Table 29.1 contains breathy stops and affricates alongside voiceless aspirated, voiceless, and voiced stops and affricates. You may encounter other breathy consonants, but these are the ones most commonly used contrastively in languages. Technical names, as usual, can be found by reading the labels on the table clockwise. For example, [b̤] is a breathy bilabial stop, and [d̤ʒ] is a breathy palato-alveolar affricate. We do not draw face diagrams of breathy stops.

Alternative transcription

Americanists use a superscript hooked h [ʰ] following a symbol for a stop or affricate, to indicate a breathy segment, for example [bʱ] or [džʱ], rather than the subscript umlaut [̤] used by the IPA.

Key concepts

breathy stop / murmured stop
breathy affricate / murmured affricate

Oral exercise

Practice reading aloud these words from Hindi of India (Laura Gillette, personal communication), moving across the rows.

baːl	'hair'	b̤aːl	'forehead'
ɖaːl	'branch'	ɖ̤aːl	'shield'
ɖaːn	'charity'	ɖ̤aːn	'paddy'
gaːnaː	'song'	g̤aːn	'hammer'
dʒəl	'water'	d̤ʒələk	'glimmer'

Written exercise

Write technical names for the following sounds.

[g̤] *breathy, velar stop*

[b] *voiced bilabial stop*

[tʰ] *voiceless dental aspirated stop*

[d̤ʒ] *breathy palato-alveolar stop*

Transcription conversion exercise

Rewrite each of the following using only IPA symbols.

[džʱɔtʰɑ] _____

[bʱɔgʱi] _____

30

Pharyngeal and Epiglottal Consonants

Goals

⌘ You will control the *pharyngeal* and *epiglottal* consonants presented in this chapter.

⌘ You will be able to read and draw face diagrams of pharyngeal and epiglottal consonants and give technical names for them.

Pharyngeal and epiglottal sounds are articulated between the uvular and glottal places of articulation.[77] Several pharyngeal and epiglottal consonants have been reported for a number of languages in the Middle East and the Caucasus, as well as a few Salish languages of North America. Since the pharyngeal and epiglottal places of articulation are so very low in the vocal mechanism (between the uvula and glottis), it is especially difficult to distinguish between the fricatives. Consequently, there is considerable disagreement among linguists as to which ones actually occur in the various languages that include such sounds at all.[78] Even though the official IPA charts relegate the epiglottals to "other symbols," we provide the following array based on the discussion in Laufer and Condax (1979 and 1981) as quoted in Ladefoged and Maddieson (1996).

Table 30.1. Pharyngeal and epiglottal consonants

	Pharyngeal	**Epiglottal**	
voiceless		ʔ	stop
voiceless	ħ	ʜ	fricative
voiced	ʕ	ʢ	fricative

For pharyngeal fricatives, the active articulator is the TONGUE ROOT, approximating the back wall of the pharynx, coming close enough to produce audible turbulence. These sounds are sometimes described as approximants rather than fricatives, as they are often produced without friction in casual speech.

---

[77]A pharyngeal stop is reported to exist in one dialect of Syrian Arabic. We have no data and no specific citation concerning this claim. It may instead be the epiglottal stop. No symbol exists to represent a pharyngeal stop.

[78]For this reason, and for the sake of simplicity, epiglottal was intentionally omitted as a place of articulation in the introductory chapter of this book.

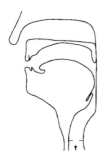

Figure 30.1 is a face diagram of a voiceless pharyngeal fricative, [ħ]. Notice that the tongue root is drawn very close to the back wall of the pharynx but not quite touching it.

The epiglottis functions as an independent articulator for the epiglottal consonants, interacting with the back wall of the pharynx. Figure 30.2 is a face diagram of a voiceless epiglottal fricative, [ʜ]. The tongue is not involved in articulation of epiglottal consonants, whose active articulator is even lower in the vocal mechanism than the tongue root.

Figure 30.1. [ħ]   Figure 30.2. [ʜ]

Production hints

It is helpful to use a mirror to check your production of these sounds: If you can hear noise deep in your throat but still see your uvula, then you must be at least very close to being in the correct articulator position for proper production of these sounds. Many people find it helpful to glide through a series of voiceless fricatives at progressively farther back places of articulation: palatal, velar, uvular, then finally "dropping off" to pharyngeal and epiglottal, that is, [ç x χ ħ ʜ]. Due to the increasing volume and length of the resonating cavity for the sounds, the perceived pitch of the turbulence heard will get lower as the tongue moves back.

Another approach to finding the pharyngeal place of articulation is to start from a lengthened [a] sound and continue voicing as you pull your tongue further and further back until your tongue root makes a constriction at the back wall of the pharynx that produces a fricative sound. This could be transcribed as [aː a̠ː ʕː].

It may be easier to start learning to produce a voiceless pharyngeal fricative, and then add voicing to it, than to start with the voiced fricative. The general tenseness of the pharynx may increase with the addition of voicing. The pitch of the voice during a voiced pharyngeal fricative will quite likely be very low.

In learning to pronounce a vowel following a pharyngeal fricative, it may be helpful to begin slowly, producing first the fricative followed by a vowel quite separate from it, and then gradually bringing the two together:
      ħ....a ħ...a ħ..a ħ.a ħa

Key concepts

pharyngeal fricative
epiglottal stop / fricative
tongue root
egressive pulmonic airstream

Oral exercise

1.   Practice reading aloud the following words.

    Columbian of British Columbia (Kinkade 1967:231–232.)

        ħamp   'fall off'
        tsiˈpaħː   'cloud of mosquitoes'
        snħtsħtsanaʔ   'earrings'

Arabic (Floyd 1981:93)

ˈħaːrab	'he fought'
ħaˈmiːr	'donkeys'
ħaˈriːr	'silk'
ˈʔaħmar	'red'
ħamː	'concern'
ʕamː	'paternal uncle'
ˈħəgərə	'he left me'
ħalˈla	'right away'
ʕˈʔala	'on'

Burkikhan Agul of Russia (S. Kodzasov, as cited in Ladefoged and Maddieson 1996:168)

muʕ	'bridge'	muʕar	'bridges'
muħ	'barn'	muħar	'barns'
mɛʜ	'whey'	mɛʜɛr	'wheys'
jaʡ	'center'	jaʡar	'centers'
sɛʡ	'measure'	sɛʡɛr	'measures'

Written exercise

Draw face diagrams of [ʕ] and [ʡ] and give the technical names for those sounds.

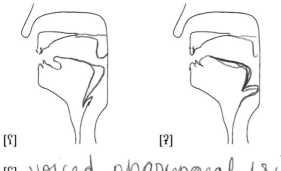

[ʕ]   [ʡ]

[ʕ] _Voiced pharyngeal fricitue_   wepa

[ʡ] _voiceles epiglottal stop_   wpa

31

Secondary Articulations

Goals

⌘ You will be able to define the terms *secondary articulation, palatalization, velarization, labialization, labial-velarization, labial-palatalization,* and *pharyngealization.*

⌘ You will control these six secondary articulations.

⌘ You will be able to give technical names for consonants involving any of the secondary articulations listed above, as well as being able to state what primary and secondary articulators are used in producing those consonants.

Up until now, the speech sounds that you have encountered in this book have involved just one primary active articulator, impeding, shaping, or directing a moving airstream. In this chapter, we introduce consonants with the PRIMARY ARTICULATORS doing the same things they were before, but with the addition of one or two other active articulators working simultaneously with the primary articulator, further affecting the shape of the airstream. These extra articulators are called SECONDARY ARTICULATORS, and their role in the production of speech sounds is called secondary articulation. Primary articulations involve great impedance of the airstream (like stops, fricatives, and nasals), whereas secondary articulations involve less impedance (more like approximants).

There are six main types of secondary articulation: PALATALIZATION, VELARIZATION, LABIALIZATION, LABIAL-VELARIZATION, LABIAL-PALATALIZATION, and PHARYNGEALIZATION. Each of these involves the lips and/or a part of the tongue articulating something similar to a nonsyllabic vowel at the same time the primary articulator is articulating the basic consonant sound, thus altering the sound of the primary articulation. For example, the [v] at the beginning of the English word "view" is palatalized, that is, the tongue blade or front humps up toward the hard palate at the same time that the labiodental articulation is occurring. There is a significant difference between the sounds of the labiodental fricatives in [vu] and [vʲu]. (The superscript "j" symbolizes palatalization.) Try saying "view" with and without palatalization on the [v].

palatal approximant (handwritten annotation)

Usually a secondary articulation is released after the primary articulation, resulting in a significant off-glide sound, as in the preceding [vʲu] or the word "schwa," [ʃʷa]. However, in some cases, both releases are simultaneous. Many speakers of English, for example, pronounce palato-alveolar sibilants with a secondary articulation called labialization (that is, lip rounding). Consider your own pronunciation of the word "shop." If you labialize these sibilants in English your lips are in the same position for the first consonant in "shop" as

161

they are for that in "schwa," but note that for "shop" there is a simultaneous coordinated release of both the sibilant and the rounding into the vowel. A delayed release of the labialization would result in "shwop."[79]

What follows is a discussion of six varieties of secondary articulation, and ways to symbolize them all, whether the secondary articulator's release is simultaneous to that of the primary articulator or slightly afterward. In general, secondary articulation with simultaneous release of the primary and secondary articulators is symbolized with a subscript symbol following the base consonant symbol, and secondary articulation with delayed release of the secondary articulator is symbolized by a superscript symbol following the base consonant symbol.

Palatalization   *palatalized*

Palatalization involves placing the tongue in position to articulate a [j] or [i] (that is, the front of the tongue humps up toward the hard palate) during another primary articulation. Typically, this secondary articulation involves delayed release, with a resultant [j] off-glide following the release of the primary articulators. Almost any consonant can be palatalized. The exceptions are probably consonants involving the pharyngeal place of articulation, whose primary articulation requires the whole body of the tongue to be so low in the mouth that the front portion of the tongue could not simultaneously be humped up toward the hard palate. Following are the two ways in which palatalization can be symbolized. The subscript notation was developed by Dr. Norris McKinney. Though not sanctioned by the IPA, it provides a useful means for differentiating between these timings on releases of the various secondary articulations.

- simultaneous release t_j
- off-glide t^j

The technical names and articulators of palatalized sounds are the same regardless of the relative timing of the releases. Both $[p_j]$ and $[p^j]$ are "voiceless bilabial palatalized stops;" their primary articulators are the lips and the secondary articulator the tongue blade or front. The face diagrams in figures 31.1 and 31.2 depict the contrast between [p] and $[p_j]$ or $[p^j]$.

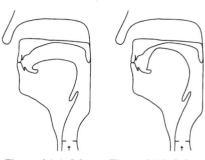

Figure 31.1. [p]   Figure 31.2. $[p_j]$ or $[p^j]$

Velarization

Velarization is a secondary articulation involving raising the tongue back toward the velum, as for the close back unrounded vowel [ɯ]. Only consonants whose primary articulators are toward the front part of the mouth can be velarized, because velar and uvular sounds already involve the tongue back as primary active articulator, and articulation of pharyngeal consonants requires the whole body of the tongue to be too low in the mouth to permit the tongue back to approach the velum.

Following are two ways the IPA symbolizes velarization.

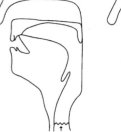

Figure 31.3. [d]   Figure 31.4. $[d_ɣ]$ or $[d^ɣ]$

- simultaneous release $t_ɣ$
- off-glide $t^ɣ$

The technical names and articulators of both $[d_ɣ]$ and $[d^ɣ]$ are "voiced alveolar velarized stops," and their articulators are the tongue tip (for the primary alveolar articulation) and the tongue back (for the secondary velarization articulation). Face diagrams in figures 31.3 and 31.4 depict the contrast between [d] and [d̪] or [dˠ].

It is helpful, in learning to velarize consonants without simultaneously labializing them, to try to say English words like the following, but without rounding your lips: swing, Dwight, twinkle, swear.

It should be noted in American English the lateral which occurs syllable-finally is velarized and is sometimes referred to as a "dark l". This stands in contrast to the non-velarized alveolar lateral (or "clear l") which occurs in other environments. Most English speakers have no problem producing those sounds in their "normal" English positions, but, as is the case with all sounds, it is necessary to learn to produce them anywhere in a word. *this is on the IPA chart*

$\begin{bmatrix} \sim \end{bmatrix}$
$\begin{bmatrix} ɫ \end{bmatrix}$

Labialization *Donald Trump lips*

Labialization involves rounding and sometimes protrusion of the lips during a primary articulation. Lip rounding creates a LABIAL RESONATING CAVITY (mentioned in passing in chapter 1); when sound resonates in the labial resonating cavity, resonation in the oral cavity is slightly altered as well. Any consonant, including a labial consonant such as [p] or [f], can be labialized simply by the addition of rounded lips. The lip rounding can stop at the same time that the primary articulation is released, or it can carry over briefly following that release. Both are called labialization, but they sound quite different.

- simultaneous release t_w
- off-glide t^w

Both [ʃ_w] and [ʃ^w] are "voiceless palato-alveolar labialized sibilants." The tongue blade and the lips are the primary and secondary articulators, respectively. Lip rounding is difficult to portray on a face diagram so we do not draw face diagrams for labialized consonants as distinct from those for nonlabialized consonants.

Labial-velarization

Labial-velarization involves the combination of two secondary articulations (labialization and velarization), that is, the lips are rounded and the tongue back is humped up toward the velum. Any consonant that can be velarized (see the preceding discussion) can also be labial-velarized. Labial-velarization typically involves nonsimultaneous release of the articulators, that is, there is typically a "w" off-glide.

Labial-velarization is symbolized in exactly the same way as labialization, with a superscript "w," [t^w]. It is unlikely for labial-velarization to be used contrastively with plain labialization. In fact, most people simply use the term "labialization" for both, not bothering to mention the addition of velarization. We recommend that you do this also, but try to be aware of whether or not the tongue back is also raised when native speakers produce these sounds; then make yours imitate theirs. Again, since lip rounding is difficult to portray on face diagrams, we do not draw special ones for labial-velarized consonants.

Labial-palatalization

The secondary articulation called labial-palatalization (which can alternatively be called palato-labialization) is a combination of palatalization and labialization, that is, the lips are rounded and the blade or front portion of the tongue is humped up toward the hard palate, all simultaneous with some other primary articulation. It may be helpful to think of producing a close front rounded vowel, [y], or a rounded palatal semivowel, [ɥ] simultaneously with the primary articulation.

Labial-palatalization typically involves delayed release, i.e., and off-glide, and is symbolized with a superscripted [ɥ], as in [t^ɥ].

[l^ɥ] is a "voiced alveolar labial-palatalized lateral approximant" with the tongue tip as the primary articulator and the lips and tongue blade or front as the secondary articulators. Any consonant that can be palatalized (see the foregoing discussion) can also be labial-palatalized. As usual, we do not attempt to portray lip rounding on face diagrams.

Pharyngealization

Pharyngealization is similar to velarization but occurs lower in the vocal mechanism, the tongue root being retracted toward the back wall of the pharynx as for a pharyngeal fricative. Again, only consonants whose primary articulation takes place fairly far forward in the mouth can be pharyngealized. Pharyngealization typically involves delayed release and is symbolized with a superscripted [ʕ], as in [$d^ʕ$].

The technical name of [$d^ʕ$] is "voiced alveolar pharyngealized stop." The tongue tip is the primary articulator, and the tongue root is the secondary articulator. The face diagrams in figures 31.5 and 31.6 depict the contrast between [d] and [$d^ʕ$].

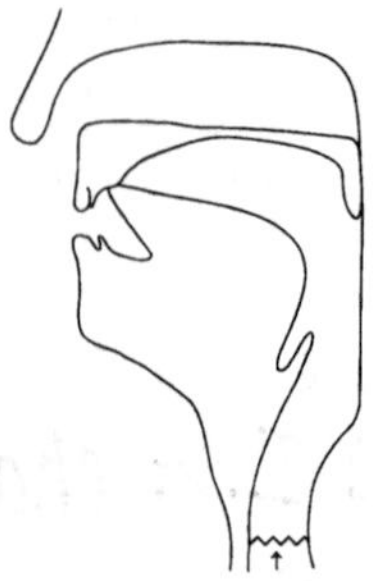

Figure 31.5. [d]

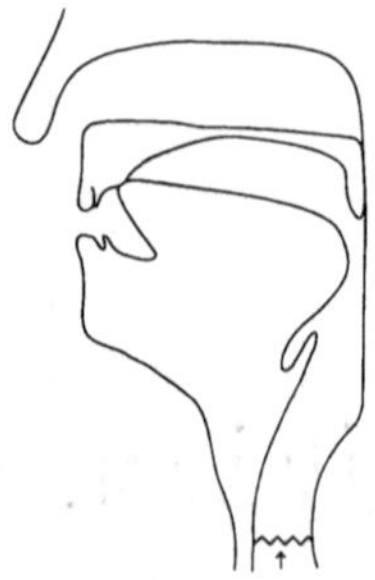

Figure 31.6. [$d^ʕ$]

Summary of secondary articulations and alternative transcriptions

Table 31.1 summarizes the six types of secondary articulations of consonants presented in this chapter. In the symbolization columns, standard IPA symbols are followed by common alternative symbols in parentheses.

Table 31.1. Summary of symbolizations of secondary articulations

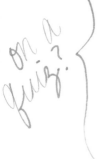

Secondary articulation	Description in terms of tongue and lip position	Symbolization: Simultaneous release	Symbolization: Off-glide
Palatalization	Tongue front humped up toward [i] or [j]	t_j ($\overset{y}{t}$)	t^j (t^y)
Velarization	Tongue back humped up toward [ɯ]	$t_ɣ$ (t̴)	$t^ɣ$ ($t^ï$)
Labialization	Lips rounded	t_w (t̫)	t^w
Labial-velarization	Lips rounded; tongue back humped up toward [w] or [u]	t_w (t̫)	t^w
Labial-palatalization	Lips rounded; tongue blade or front humped up toward [y]	none	$t^ɥ$ ($t^ü$)
Pharyngealization	Tongue root back toward pharynx wall as for [ʕ]	none	$t^ʕ$ ($t^ᴅ$)

Order of symbols in a series of superscripts and diacritics

Since secondary articulations can occur in combination with other qualities of consonants that are commonly symbolized by means of superscripts and diacritics, such as aspiration, glottalic airstream mechanism, etc., several superscript symbols can occur in a series. When this happens, the secondary articulation symbol is usually placed closest to the base consonant symbol, followed by whatever other symbol(s) is/are applicable, for example, [t^{wh}].

Key concepts

primary articulation / primary articulator
secondary articulation / secondary articulator
palatalization
velarization
labialization
labial-velarization
labial-palatalization
pharyngealization
order of symbols in a series
clear l / dark l

Oral exercise

Practice reading aloud the following words.

American English (final aspirations not present in all dialects)

ʃʷɪpʰ	'ship'
ɹʷætʰ	'rat'
kʷʰɪkʰ	'quick'
tʷʰɚlɣ	'twirl'
sʷap	'swap'
kʷʰoṵtʰ	'quote'

French (Marquita Klaver, personal communication)

mʷɛt	'sea gull'
mʲɛt	'crumb'
mᶣɛt	'mute (fem.)'
lʷi	'Louis'
lᶣi	'(to) him/her'
lʲe	'tied'

Columbian of British Columbia (Kinkade 1967:231–232)

ˈsχʷəʕʷχʷʕʷ	'fox'
ˈtsʼiʕʷən	'chip arrowheads'
ˈʔə́ħʷaʔ	'cough'

Russian (Floyd, field notes)

ˈlɣoᵊʃkə	'spoon'
lɣukʰ	'onion'
ˈlɣapa	'paw'

Jju of Nigeria (Carol McKinney, personal communication)

kʲʰaŋ	'thing'	tᶣʰej	'to sew'
tʲʰoŋ	'run'	sɾaŋ	'to be without'
ʃʲːa	'to find'	sɾ_waŋ	'to sit (sg.)'
nᶣon	'hen'	ɾan	'to be better than'
nʲat	'to hide'	ɾ_wan	'to be tired'
nᶣat	'guinea corn'	mʷi	'to smell'
kʷʰaŋ	'to grind'	mʲːi	'to lie'
tʷʰaŋ	'to count'		

Fante of Ghana (Floyd, field notes)

aʃᶣɪʃᶣɛ	'mirror'
atᶣʰɛ	'frog'
awɔtᶣʰɪ	'figure 8'
ndᶣom	'song'
adᶣɪdᶣɪ	'has come to rest'

Northern Tepehuan of Mexico (Burt Bascom, personal communication)

ˈsʲoɾoko	'tomorrow'
ˈid̪ʲi	'this'
ˈt̪ʲiːpu	'there isn't any'
ˈn̪ʲoki	'word'
aˈkit̪ʲa	'uncle'
ˈkiːd̪ʲi	'his house'
ˈgin̪ʲoβi	'my hand'

Written exercises

1. Give phonetic symbols for the following speech sounds (two symbols for each in cases in which there are different symbols for simultaneous release and off-glide timings).

    [   ] a voiced bilabial labial-palatalized nasal

    [   ] an alveolar labialized stop with egressive glottalic airstream

    [   ] a breathy velar palatalized stop

    [   ] a voiced alveolar velarized lateral approximant

    [   ] a voiceless labiodental pharyngealized fricative

    [   ] a voiceless palato-alveolar labial-velarized aspirated sibilant affricate

2.   Give a technical name for each of the speech sounds symbolized here.

[dʲ] _____

[nˠ] _____

[ʒʷ] _____

[gᶣ] _____

[ʃ̫ʷ] _____

[lˠ] _____

[mˤ] _____

32

Consonant Clusters, Vowel Clusters, and Vowel Glides

Goals

⌘ You will be able to define the term *consonant cluster* as a sequence of adjacent consonants and *vowel cluster* as a sequence of adjacent vowels.

⌘ You will gain facility in pronouncing data containing consonant and vowel clusters as well as a wide variety of glided vowels.

The term CLUSTER refers to a sequence of adjacent segments of the same category. Therefore, a CONSONANT CLUSTER is a sequence of adjacent consonants, and a VOWEL CLUSTER is a sequence of adjacent vowels.

In English, clusters of more than three consonants are quite rare, and word-initial clusters of more than two consonants do not occur unless the first consonant is an "s." While English contains many vowel glides, there are few clusters of syllabic vowels. In many other languages of the world, however, clusters of two or more consonants and three or more syllabic vowels occur frequently, for example, Seri and Kickapoo.

Seri of Mexico (Mary Moser, personal communication)

ptkamn	'lobster'
ʔɛ ˈkɛkt ˈktam	'father-in-law'

Kickapoo of Texas, Oklahoma, and Mexico (James Klumpp, personal communication)

waijeaˈwi	'it is round'
owinaˈki	'horns'
suːˈniahi	'money'
juːhi haiˈja	'he is here'
maːmaja	'early'
eːhˈpiaːni	'you come'

Sometimes a period is placed (on the line) between two segments to indicate a syllable break, for example, [la.ib], to indicate that the second vowel is a full vowel (a syllable peak) and should not be pronounced as a

169

glide off the preceding vowel. This should not be confused with the raised period (·), which is sometimes used as shorthand for the half length mark (ˑ) to indicate intermediate length on a segment.

As you pronounce the words involving consonant clusters, be careful not to insert any transitional elements such as aspiration or extra vowels between adjacent consonants unless the phonetic transcription so indicates. Likewise, be careful not to glide vowels in a vowel cluster (unless the phonetic transcription so indicates) such that you are breaking up the cluster with approximants such as "w" and "j," as English speakers do. Another temptation to avoid is inserting glottal stops between clustered vowels.

There are two kinds of vowel glides. When the less prominent vowel in a glide precedes the main vowel, the glide is called an ON-GLIDE. When the less prominent one follows the main vowel, the glide is called an OFF-GLIDE. In either case, a subscript arch is written beneath the less prominent vowel's symbol: [i̯u] or [ou̯]. Alternatively, the symbol for the less prominent vowel can be superscripted: [ⁱu], [oᵘ]. Central approximant symbols can also be used to represent the less prominent vowel: [ju] or [ow].

Key concepts

consonant cluster
vowel cluster
on-glide / off-glide

Oral exercises

1.   Read aloud the following vowel glides.

εu̯	(εw)	æi̯	(æj)	oə̯	ae̯
ou̯	(ow)	ai̯	(aj)	uə̯	oe̯
au̯	(aw)	əi̯	(əj)	æə̯	ie̯
æu̯	(æw)	ei̯	(ej)	iə̯	io̯
əu̯	(əw)	ɔi̯	(ɔj)	eə̯	eo̯
ɔu̯	(ɔw)	oi̯	(oj)	ɔə̯	æo̯
iu̯	(iw)	ui̯	(uj)		au̯
eu̯	(ew)				

2.   Practice reading aloud the following words.
   Chinook of Canada (Floyd 1981:76)

iɬˈtʃkʷa	'water'	ˈekʰtʰkʰ	'head'
ˈitʰkʷʰti	'house'	ˈektʃxam	'he sang'
ˈitʰkʰpʃ	'feet'	ˈetʃamxtʃ	'my heart'
iˈgeḻtʃutkʰ	'flint'	ˈnukstx	'smallness'
oˈʔolɛptʃkiç	'fire'	olˈxakxalpʰtʃʰkiç	'our fire'
tʰgakʰtʰkakʃ	'their heads'	aˈtʃokʰtsʰkʰtamit˺	'he roasts'
ʃˈtxaxamuks	'our dogs'	aˈklokʃtʰpʰtʃʰkʰ	'she carries it up
ˈokʃt˺	'louse'		from the beach'

Gogodala of Papua New Guinea (E. Pike 1978:64)

ˈga̠ɵbə	'tree'	ˈgæɵ	'angry'
ˈga̠u̠bə	'small kangaroo'	ˈga̠ɵ	'kind of coconut'
ˈbai̯.ə	'sago, food'	ˈbau̯	'kind of coconut'
ˈsæ.i̯ə	'boy's name'	ˈwa̠ɵ	'smoke'
ˈsæi̯.i̯ə	'fish trap'		

Zambali of Philippines (E. Pike 1978:66)

ta.ɨb	'a kind of wall'
ta.ˈiʔata.ɨ	'a grass'
hɨ.ˈhɨ.an	'to blame for something'
binaˈɨ.an	'to ripen'
kataˈo.an	'person'
kataˈwan	'God'
paʔamuˈkawan	'place of wild banana'
hiˈkajna	'you already'
hikaˈina	'we-exclusive already'
baˈba.i	'woman'
luˈbaj	'loincloth'
ˈta.inep	'dream'
ˈlajnet	'a bird'
kaˈta.o	'person'
kaˈtaw	'rafter'

Oaxaca Chontal of Mexico (E. Pike 1978:64)

ˈpojpa	'he went out'	lajˈw̥ax	'my hair'
ˈpoĵpa	'he cried out'	akḁĵˈmaʔ	'gourd bowl'
ˈpaxpa	'she washed it'	ɛlˈw̥iĵ	'the fiesta'
ˈpoʃpa	'he went on out'	ĵ̥ɛɣuj	'she is beating'
ˈxojpa	'now'	ˈw̥ɛðuj	'she wants it'
ˈxoĵpa	'it got used up'	hoˈlajʔuj	'he lives there'
ˈxoxpa	'he wept'		

33

Double Articulations

Goals

⌘ You will be able to define *double articulation* as articulation involving nearly simultaneous closures or releases of two sets of articulators in the mouth, those articulations matching in voicing and manner of articulation and contributing equally to the identity of the sound.

⌘ You will be able to explain the difference between double articulation, secondary articulation (see chapter 31), prenasalization (see chapter 21), and articulation of a series of separate consonants in a cluster (see chapter 32).

⌘ You will control *double stops* and *double nasals* involving the *labial-alveolar* and *labial-velar* places of articulation.

⌘ You will be able to read and draw face diagrams depicting doubly articulated speech sounds and to give technical names for each sound symbolized in this chapter.

Many languages have segments produced by means of two nearly simultaneous closures in the mouth, which match in voicing and manner of articulation. DOUBLE STOPS are common, and some languages also have DOUBLE NASALS.[80]

Either the initiations or the releases of the two closures are very nearly simultaneous in DOUBLE ARTICULATIONS. Languages differ as to the duration of the overlap of the two parts of the articulation.

Whenever two stops or nasals occur in sequence with close transition between them, the release of the first closure will at least slightly overlap the initiation of the second closure. The difference between double articulation of stops or nasals and this slight overlap due to close transition is that in close transition neither the initiations of the two closures nor their releases are simultaneous or even nearly simultaneous, whereas in a double stop either the initiations or the releases of the two closures are virtually simultaneous. The difference between double articulation and secondary articulation is that two manners of articulation involve different degrees of impedance (for example, the complete closure of a stop with a palatal approximant—[tʲ]), whereas in a double articulation both closures are complete. The phonetic phenomenon called PRENASALIZATION introduced in chapter 21 is quite different from double articulation in two ways: the place of articulation of the nasal usually matches that of the following stop or affricate, and, of course, the nasal and the stop or affricate do not match in manner of articulation.

---

[80]Aspirated double stops and double fricatives are so rare that we do not include them in this book. See Laver 1994:316–318 (Skåne Swedish, Urhobo of SE Nigeria, etc.) or Ladefoged and Maddieson 1996:330 (SePedi of Northern Sotho) for a description of these rare consonants.

The most common variety of double stop is the LABIAL-VELAR series (sometimes called *labiovelar*), involving bilabial and velar closures. Labial-velar double stops and/or nasals occur in various languages of Vietnam, Papua New Guinea, and Africa and in some Caribbean creoles. LABIAL-ALVEOLAR sounds (sometimes called *labioalveolars*) involving bilabial and alveolar closures occur in Yeletnye on Rossell Island and in several West African languages.[81]

Table 33.1. Symbols for double stops and nasals

	Labial-alveolar	Labial-velar	
voiceless	t͡p	k͡p	stop
voiced	d͡b	g͡b	
voiced	n͡m	ŋ͡m	nasal
voiceless		k͡ɓ̥	implosive
voiced	d͡ɓ	g͡ɓ	
passive articulators	upper lip, alveolar ridge	upper lip, velum	
active articulators	lower lip, tongue tip	lower lip, tongue back	

Note that in each case, the articulation further forward is listed first in the place of articulation label. However, it comes second in the symbol, perhaps because the further back articulation tends to be released before the further forward one. In the IPA system, the two symbols are placed side-by-side with a top ligature (often called a tie bar) drawn over the top of both to indicate that the two are functioning together as a unit, to distinguish the double articulation, for example, [g͡b], from a consonant cluster, for example, [gb].

Figure 331. shows face diagrams of the separately-articulated consonants [p] and [k] to show their contrast with the double stop [k͡p].

Production hints

Imitate a hen clucking:
[k͡pə k͡pə k͡pə k͡pə]. Then, by analogy, substitute other double articulations.

Say "pick, pick, pick," gradually lengthening the vowel and shifting the syllable border (that is, move the velar stop from the end of one

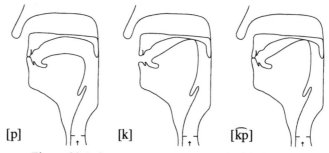

[p]   [k]   [k͡p]

Figure 33.1. Separate stops contrasted with double stop

syllable to the beginning of the next) until the two adjacent stops are articulated almost simultaneously. Do the same with sequences like "big, big, big," "man, man, man," etc.

Alternative transcription

Double articulations are often written using a superscripted symbol for the further-back articulation followed by a regular symbol for the further-front articulation, for example [ᵏp] and [ᵑm].

---

[81]Most of the information in this paragraph as well as throughout this chapter comes from Michael Cahill, personal communication.

Key concepts

double articulation
double stop
double nasal
prenasalization / prenasalized
labial-velar
labial-alveolar

Oral exercises

1. Practice the following sequences aloud, reading across the rows.

akpa	a͡kpa	k͡pa	pa
agba	a͡gba	g͡ba	ba
atpa	a͡tpa	t͡pa	pa
adba	a͡dba	d͡ba	ba
aŋma	a͡ŋma	ŋ͡ma	ma
anma	a͡nma	n͡ma	ma

2. Practice reading aloud the following words, noting that the Margi language data includes simple prenasalization and double articulations, as well as prenasalized double stops and affricates.

    Margi of Nigeria (Hoffman 1963:28–31; tone omitted)

t͡pəl	'chief'
t͡psat͡psa	'roasted'
t͡pʃat͡pa	'washed'
ⁿᵐt͡psaku	'to pick up'
ᵐpa	'to fight'
ⁿta	'to split'
ⁿtsaⁿtsa	'shouted'
ⁿtʃa	'to point at'
' t͡pət͡pɯ	'insufficient'
ɗ͡ɓəɗ͡ɓɯ	'chewed'
ɗ͡ɓənja	'to eat all'
n͡ma	'mouth'
ⁿᵐɗ͡ba	'to surpass'
ⁿᵐɗ͡bani	'to spoil'
ᵐba	'to tie'
ⁿdal	'to throw'
ⁿdʒa	'to open wide'
ɗ͡ɓia	'to chew'
ɗ͡ɓʒagɯ	'single woman's compound'

Igbo of Nigeria (Floyd 1981:113)

ák͡p̥ōk͡p̥ō	'bone'
ák͡p̥òròk͡p̥ò	'long'
ɔ́k͡p̥â:là	'peanuts'
ōk͡p̥ārà:	'grasshopper'
ᵐk͡p̥ōrōmk͡p̥ō	'short'
ūk͡p̥útáŋk͡p̥ō	'crooked'
ɛ̄k͡p̥érɛ̄	'prayer'

Bakwé of Côte d'Ivoire (Csaba and Lisa Leidenfrost, personal communication)

ìk͡pa	'salt'
ēk͡pā	'bug'
k͡pá	'peel'
èk͡po	'he goat'
sáŋbé:	'his father'
nʲàng͡bé:	'his mother'
ŋͫg͡bá:	'dog'

Written exercise

1. Draw face diagrams and write technical names for the following sounds.

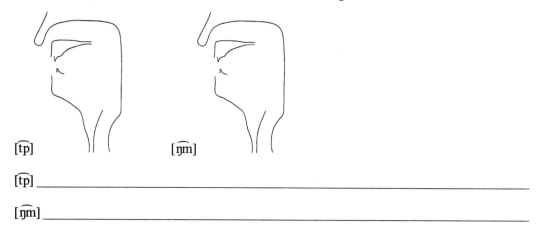

[t͡p]   [ŋ͡m]

[t͡p] _____

[ŋ͡m] _____

Transcription conversion exercises

Rewrite each of the following using only IPA symbols.

[ⁿmˈpsɑku]

[ᵹbˤənyɑ]

[ⁿmᵈbɑ]

[ᵹbžagï]

34

Tongue Root Placement and Vowels

Goals

⌘ You will be able to explain how tongue root placement relative to the pharyngeal walls, combined with raising or lowering of the larynx, affects the size of the *pharynx* and consequently the quality of vowels.

⌘ You will be able to define three terms expressing contrastive placements of the tongue root for vowels: *advanced, neutral,* and *retracted.*

⌘ You will control vowels displaying these three contrastive placements of the tongue root.

⌘ You will be able to give technical names for vowels displaying these three contrastive tongue root placements.

You have already encountered the tongue root and pharyngeal walls as active and passive articulators of pharyngeal consonants. The position of the tongue root with respect to the pharyngeal walls and the position of the larynx (raised or lowered) affect the size of the pharyngeal cavity, which may in turn result in particular vowel qualities that are contrastive in many African and Southeast Asian languages.

We distinguish three main tongue root positions, as depicted in figure 34.1.

Advanced tongue root

- position labeled (1) in figure 34.1
- articulated by moving the tongue root away from the back of the throat, making the pharyngeal cavity larger[82]
- often accompanied by lowering of the larynx
- makes vowels have a "hollow" quality to them
- may have a relatively lower pitch
- often accompanied by murmur (breathy voice)
- symbolized by writing [ˌ] (IPA) under the base vowel symbol
- sometimes called "muffled," "non-faucalized," "+ATR" (an abbreviation for "advanced tongue root"), "loose," "wide pharynx"

Figure 34.1.

Neutral tongue root position

- position labeled (2) in Figure 34.1
- produced with the tongue root in the "normal" position, that is, somewhere between the advanced and retracted positions; position varies depending on vowel
- the default tongue root position presumed if no diacritics are used with a base vowel symbol

Retracted tongue root

- position labeled (3) in Figure 34.1
- articulated by moving the tongue root toward the back of the throat, making the pharyngeal cavity smaller
- often accompanied by raising of the larynx
- makes vowels have a "choked" quality to them
- may have a relatively higher pitch
- often accompanied by creaky voice (laryngealization)
- symbolized by writing [ˌ] (IPA) under the base vowel symbol
- sometimes called "bright," "faucalized," "–ATR," "tight," "strident," "pharyngealized"

The technical name for one of these special vowels involves an insertion of the words "with advanced tongue root" or "with retracted tongue root" just after the word "vowel." If neither term is inserted in that slot, then it is assumed that the vowel involves neutral tongue root position. Although for phonetic purposes we distinguish three positions of the tongue root, most languages that contrast tongue root position have only a two-way contrast, +ATR versus –ATR. All vowels within one word tend to match in their tongue root placement, as in the Konni data on page 179.

Production hints

As an aid in advancing your tongue root, try anything that will help you think of making the pharyngeal cavity longer or wider, for example, speak while yawning, consciously lower your larynx or aim for a "woofy" sound. To aid in retracting your tongue root, try anything that will help you think of making the pharyngeal cavity shorter or narrower, for example, start from the tongue root position of a pharyngeal fricative and move it only very slightly away from the back wall of the pharynx, consciously raise the larynx or aim for a choked sound.

---

[82]It may be helpful to note that the advanced tongue root position is often recommended by voice teachers (though probably not by that name) to help their students maximize the size of the pharynx and thus provide the sung tone with a larger cavity in which to resonate.

Key concepts

pharynx
advanced tongue root position
neutral tongue root position
retracted tongue root position

Oral exercises

Practice saying the following words.

Igbo (Ladefoged and Maddieson 1996:301; unmarked vowels are mid tone)

ọ́bị̀	'heart'
ụ̀bị̀	'poverty of ability'
ịbụ́	'weight'
ọbụ̀	'it is'

Konni of Ghana (Cahill, personal communication)

[+ATR]		[−ATR]	
tígí-rí	'the house'	kʊ̀ʊ̀-rʊ́	'the hoe'
sìè-kú	'the path'	nɪ̀ɪ̀-kʊ́	'the rain'
kùm-bú	'the funeral'	nòm-bʊ́	'the meat'
yìsì-ké	'the antelope'	nánjʊ́-ká	'the fly'
dùn-é	'knees'	tàn-á	'stones'
dùn-é-hé	'the knees'	tàn-á-há	'stones'
tú-ò	'beans (sp.)'	nʊ́-à	'mouths'
tú-ó-hé	'the beans (sp.)'	nʊ́-á-há	'the mouths'
tókóró-sí-sí	'the windows'	nánjʊ́-sʊ́-sʊ́	'the flies'
yìsì-tí-tí	'the antelopes'	váá-tɪ́-tɪ́	'the leaves'
kùrì-yé	'has pounded'	pàsɪ̀-yá	'has peeled'
sùgùr-é	'is washing'	pògɪ̀l-á	'is holding'
tù-ó	'is digging'	kʊ̀-á	'is killing'
dígí-wó	'cooked'	gà-wá	'went'

Written exercise

Give technical names for the following vowels.

[ọ] _____

[ɔ] _____

[y] _____

[ẹ] _____

[ɪ] _____

35

Fortis and Lenis Consonants; Controlled and Ballistic Syllables

Goals

⌘ You will be able to explain the difference between *fortis* and *lenis consonants,* and between *controlled* and *ballistic syllables*.

⌘ You will control consonants and syllables with the above special characteristics.

The FORTIS / LENIS distinction does not refer to a novel kind of articulation but rather subsumes certain kinds of phonetic detail that you have already encountered into "macro categories" that facilitate phonological analysis.

Fortis and lenis consonants

If we whisper the English words "sap" and "zap," most English speakers can distinguish between the initial consonants "s" and "z," even though the voiced / voiceless contrast disappears in whispering. The contrast in the whispered words is manifested in a difference in intensity of the articulation of those initial consonants: the whispered "s" is stronger (which can be called fortis) and the whispered "z" is weaker (which can be called lenis). The terms fortis and lenis refer to a phonological contrast existing in some languages that is just as significant as the voiced / voiceless contrast.

Physiologically, the fortis / lenis distinction is achieved by varying the amount of build-up of respiratory pressure or adjusting the amount of airflow at the glottis and in the mouth during the articulation of a consonant. This results in varied amounts of voicing, length, or aspiration, and even in variation of the manner of articulation, for example, variation between stops and fricatives. Clearly, this fortis / lenis distinction is not reducible to a single parameter. Fortunately, it is rarely found in languages, and you should explore other explanations of contrast unless nothing else seems to explain the contrasts you find.

Korean voiceless stops and affricates have a three-way contrast, differing in the amount of aspiration present at their release. / t̤ / (fortis) is produced with tight closure of the tongue tip and no aspiration. / t̬ / (lenis) is produced with a slightly looser closure of the tongue tip which is released with a minimum amount of aspiration; it is much weaker than the fully aspirated /tʰ/.[83] These three types of consonants, called fortis, lenis, and aspirated, are demonstrated in the following data (Sang Nam Syn and Esther Kim, personal communication).

fortis (no aspiration)	t̬al	'daughter'	t͡ʃada	'salty'
lenis (slight aspiration)	t̩al	'moon'	t͡ʃada	'sleep'
aspirated (much aspiration)	tʰal	'mask'	t͡ʃʰada	'cold'

The terms fortis and lenis have been used to describe a bundle of phonetic features, particularly length and affrication, which work together to form a phonemic contrast in Jju of Nigeria (Norris and Carol McKinney). In the following Jju data, the forms in the left-hand column are phonemic representations, while those in the middle column are phonetic representations more like what you are used to seeing.

/g̩a/	[ga]	'may'
/g̩a/	[gɣa]	'to be quick'
/d̢ʒi/	[dʒi]	'(concord particle)'
/d̢ʒi/	[dʒːi]	'winged female termites'
/ji/	[ji]	'you (pl.)'
/j̩i/	[jːi]	'to steal'
/ɾ̩ak/	[ɾak]	'to refuse'
/ɾ̩ak/	[rak]	'to lick'
/b̩o/	[bvːo]	'again'
/b̩o/	[bvːʷo]	'to know, understand'

Table 35.1 (adapted from E. Pike 1978:131) outlines some tendencies for how the fortis / lenis distinction may manifest itself phonetically in languages.

Table 35.1. Phonetic tendencies of fortis and lenis consonants

	Fortis	**Lenis**
stops	aspirated voiceless long	unaspirated or weakly aspirated fluctuation between voiceless and weak voicing fluctuation between weak closure and continuant
fricatives	voiceless long	fluctuation between voiced and voiceless short
laterals / nasals	long	usually short

The reason why you might want to use diacritics under the consonant symbols, for example, / ̬ / for fortis and / ̩ / for lenis, rather than writing the exact phonetic detail, is that sometimes there is variation from one utterance to another as to which characteristic of the fortis / lenis distinction is manifested on that particular utterance. For example, a word-initial bilabial lenis stop may be said in three different ways on three successive utterances: once as [p], once as [b] (with weak voicing), and once as [β]. After you determine that the language has a fortis / lenis distinction, you can write all three of those bilabials as lenis /p̩/, rather than conclude that your ears have failed you and you are unable to transcribe data accurately.

---

[83]The notations given here for fortis and lenis segments come from the Americanist tradition. There do not seem to be any IPA symbols for this distinction.

The slanted lines around these segments, a notation borrowed from phonology, indicate that this is not phonetic transcription but instead a hypothesis regarding phonemes. An understanding of what defines a phoneme is beyond the scope of a phonetics course, so do not worry if this footnote is difficult to understand.

Controlled and ballistic syllables

The distinction between controlled and ballistic syllables[84] is more of a phonological concept than a phonetic one, but it is possible to specify some phonetic tendencies of the two types of syllables. The vowel in a BALLISTIC SYLLABLE tends to be short with a rapid decrescendo (decrease in volume), often terminating in a voiceless vowel. In contrast, the vowel in a CONTROLLED SYLLABLE tends to be longer and have either a slow decrescendo or a crescendo (increase in volume). It may be helpful to think of the difference between throwing a ball and carrying it to its destination, the thrown ball's motion being rapid (ballistic), and the carried ball's motion being steadier and slower (controlled).

Ballistic syllables are sometimes symbolized by placing a "decrescendo" symbol, borrowed from musical notation, above the vowel (and perhaps by adding a voiceless vowel symbol or an "h" after the voiced vowel, if that is phonetically what happens in the language): ['tŏǫ] or ['tŏh]. Controlled syllables are usually symbolized simply by placing a length symbol after the vowel: ['to:]. However, if there seems to be a contrastive difference between two types of controlled syllables, you may also want to indicate specifically, again by means of symbols borrowed from musical notation, whether the controlled syllable has a slow decrescendo, ['to:], or a crescendo, ['to:].[85]

Below are some words from Palantla Chinantec of Mexico (Alfred Anderson, personal communication), that demonstrate contrast between controlled and ballistic syllables.

Controlled		Ballistic	
li: ˥	'nut (sp.)'	lɪh ˥	'flower'
tʃiɛʔ ˥	'chicken'	tʃɪʔ ˥	'crab, padlock'
ʔma:ʔ ˥	'market, stall'	ʔmaʔ ˥	'mole'
mɯi ˧	'hawk'	mɯɛh ˧	'ball'
ʔmo: ˧	'sharp'	ʔmo ˥	'lukewarm'
		ʔmoʔ ˥	'expensive'
		buʔ ˥	'burro'

Key concepts

fortis / lenis consonants
controlled / ballistic syllables

Oral exercise

Read aloud the Korean, Jju, and Chinantec data presented in this chapter.

---

[84] This controlled versus ballistic syllable phenomenon has been attested only in a few dialects of Chinantec in Central Mexico and is somewhat controversial in nature, some linguists analyzing it as merely a difference between plain vowels (controlled) and a vowel-h (ballistic) sequence. Such analyses do not utilize the terms "controlled" and "ballistic" at all.

[85] Again, these symbols come from the Americanist tradition as there does not seem to be any IPA means of representing this controlled / ballistic distinction.

36

Clicks

Goals

⌘ You will be able to define the term *click* as a speech sound involving an *ingressive velaric airstream*.

⌘ You will control the clicks presented in this chapter.

⌘ You will be able to read and draw a face diagram and give the technical name for each click.

In chapter 1, we introduced the three airstream mechanisms used for speech sounds. You have already encountered speech sounds using the pulmonic and/or glottalic airstream mechanisms. We now focus on the third airstream mechanism, VELARIC, which is often called the "mouth air" mechanism. Unlike the glottalic airstream, which may be either egressive or ingressive, the velaric airstream is only ingressive. It may be used alone (for voiceless clicks) or in combination with egressive pulmonic airstream (for voiced clicks). Speech sounds involving an ingressive velaric airstream are called CLICKS.

English speakers use clicks when making a kissing noise, when trying to urge a horse to "giddy-up" and when showing pity (often written as "tsk, tsk, tsk"). However, these clicks in English do not occur in normal speech; they are used merely as special sound effects. In a few Bantu and Khoisan languages of Africa, clicks are used as contrastive consonants in normal speech.[86]

The velaric airstream mechanism is initiated by lowering or backing the body of the tongue while the tongue back is in closure against the velum. That is, the tongue back is in complete closure against the velum, as for a velar stop, while some other active articulator (the tongue tip or blade, or the lower lip) forms another closure with some other passive articulator (a point at or near the alveolar ridge, or the upper lip). Meanwhile, the body of the tongue lowers or moves back, creating a partial vacuum in the space in the mouth that is between the two articulators. When the forward articulation is released before the velar one, air rushes into that partial vacuum in the mouth, resulting in the click sound. Thus, for clicks the tongue back functions both as the further back active articulator of a double stop (see chapter 33) and as the initiator of a velaric airstream.

---

[86]Clicks were also reported to occur "contrastively" in a secret game language of Australia which was not a natural language (Ladefoged and Maddieson 1996:246).

Table 36.1. Click symbols

	Bilabial	**Dental**	**Alveolar**	**Retroflex**	**Palato-alveolar**		
voiceless	ʘ	|	!	!̣	ǂ		
voiced	g͡ʘ	g͡|	g͡!	g͡!̣	g͡ǂ		
voiced	ŋ͡ʘ	ŋ͡|	ŋ͡!	ŋ͡!̣	ŋ͡ǂ	nasal	
voiceless			‖			lateral	click
voiced			g͡‖				
voiced			ŋ͡‖			nasal lateral	

As usual, the technical name for a click is derived by reading the labels on the table clockwise. For example, [‖] is a voiceless dental click, and [ŋ͡‖] is a voiced alveolar nasal lateral click. The term "click" implies that the sound is made with "ingressive velaric airstream." Since an egressive pulmonic airstream is inherent within the term "voiced," it need not be specified overtly in the technical names of voiced clicks.

Figures 36.1 and 36.2 contain face diagrams depicting bilabial clicks. Note the velar closures. Figure 36.1, the voiced bilabial click, [g͡ʘ], looks exactly like that for the doubly articulated stop, [g͡b], except for the inward arrow drawn on the tongue back to indicate that the tongue back is the initiator of an ingressive velaric airstream. The upward arrow drawn below the larynx indicates that an egressive airstream is involved, as is the case for all voiced speech sounds, regardless of what other airstream mechanism is also used. Figure 36.2 depicts a voiceless bilabial click, [ʘ]. Notice that there is no arrow drawn below the larynx for this one because voiceless clicks do not involve a pulmonic airstream.

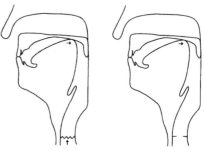

Figure 36.1. [g͡ʘ]   Figure 36.2. [ʘ]

Figure 36.3 is a face diagram of the voiced alveolar nasal click, [ŋ͡!].

Production hints

For most people, voiceless clicks are quite easy to produce in isolation. Try the clicks mentioned earlier in the chapter for urging a horse to "giddy-up" (a voiceless alveolar lateral click), expressing pity as in "'tsk, tsk, tsk" (a voiceless dental click), and a kissing sound (a voiceless bilabial click). The hard part is putting them into the context of other speech sounds, especially vowels. Try to produce a very slow vowel-click-glottal stop-vowel sequence, (for example,

Figure 36.3. [ŋ͡!]

[aʘʔa]), speeding it up until you can eliminate the glottal stop. Voiceless clicks usually release in one of six ways: directly into a vowel or into [h], [ʔ], [x], [k], or [q] before a succeeding vowel. Try each voiceless click with each of these release possibilities (see oral exercise 1).

To produce a nasal click, think of humming an [ŋ] while simultaneously producing a click. There is a natural tendency to maintain velic opening throughout the vowel following a nasal click, so focus your attention on not allowing nasalization to carry over onto the vowel.

The voiced non-nasal clicks are perhaps the most difficult to produce. Think of producing a [g] simultaneously with a voiceless click. Try producing a series of voiced velar stops with egressive pulmonic airstream, alternating with a repeated vowel, for example, [gagaga], then superimpose a click articulation on top of the [g], resulting in [gagag͡!a], etc. Some people find it helpful in the production of a voiced click to first produce a voiced nasal click and then consciously add velic closure. Voiced clicks, both oral and nasal, almost always release directly into a vowel.

Common alternative transcription

You may occasionally encounter a click transcribed with a left pointer following a symbol for a comparable segment produced with a pulmonic airstream. For example, [t[<]] represents a voiceless alveolar click, [b[<]] a voiced bilabial click, and [n̪[<]] a voiced dental nasal click.

Key concepts

velaric airstream
click
two airstream mechanisms used simultaneously

Oral exercises

1. Practice each voiceless click with each of the six most common releases, according to the table below. Also practice saying each voiceless click between two vowels.

	Bilabial	Dental	Alveolar	Alveolar lateral	Palato-alveolar	Retroflex
into a vowel	ʘa	ǀa	ǃa	ǁa	ǂa	ǃ̢a
into h	ʘha	ǀha	ǃha	ǁha	ǂha	ǃ̢ha
into ʔ	ʘʔa	ǀʔa	ǃʔa	ǁʔa	ǂʔa	ǃ̢ʔa
into x	ʘxa	ǀxa	ǃxa	ǁxa	ǂxa	ǃ̢xa
into k	ʘka	ǀka	ǃka	ǁka	ǂka	ǃ̢ka
into q	ʘqa	ǀqa	ǃqa	ǁqa	ǂqa	ǃ̢qa
between vowels	aʘa	aǀa	aǃa	aǁa	aǂa	aǃ̢a

2. Practice each voiced click (both the oral and nasal ones) with release into a vowel. Also practice saying each voiced click between two vowels.

Bilabial	Dental	Alveolar	Alveolar lateral	Retroflex	Palato-alveolar
ŋ͡ʘa	ŋ͡ǀa	ŋ͡ǃa	ŋ͡ǁa	ŋ͡ǃ̢a	ŋ͡ǂa
aŋ͡ʘa	aŋ͡ǀa	aŋ͡ǃa	aŋ͡ǁa	aŋ͡ǃ̢a	aŋ͡ǂa
ɡ͡ʘa	ɡ͡ǀa	ɡ͡ǃa	ɡ͡ǁa	ɡ͡ǃ̢a	ɡ͡ǂa
aɡ͡ʘa	aɡ͡ǀa	aɡ͡ǃa	aɡ͡ǁa	aɡ͡ǃ̢a	aɡ͡ǂa

3. Practice reading aloud these words containing clicks from Zulu of South Africa (Doke 1926:201).
    Voiceless clicks

ˈǀaːǀa	'to climb'
ˈǁoːǁa	'narrate, tell'
ũmˈǃaːla	'neck (usually of an animal)'
ˈǀhaːǀha	'to be evident'
ˈǀhaːza	'to explain'
ˈǁhoːsa	'Xhosa (language name)'
ũmˈǃeˈtʰuːga	'downhill slope'
ũmˈǃaːn̪sʔa	'uphill slope'

Nasal clicks

ɛliˈŋ͡ǀaːne	'little'
ikoloboˈloː ŋ͡ǀo	'seashell'
iˈŋ͡ǀʷiː ŋ͡ǀʷi	'honeybird'
kuˈŋ͡ǀoːno	'better'
ˈŋ͡ǃoːnga	'to pile up'
iˈŋ͡ǃoːla	'wagon, car'
ˈǁhoːn ŋ͡ǁʔa	'stab, jab'

4. Practice the following Zulu children's song (Smalley 1973:438), substituting a different click of your choice for each #.

#u-wa #a-wa   #u-wa #a   #u-wa #a-wa   #u-wa #a   #u-wa #a-wa

#i-pi-li #i   #o   #u-wa #a-wa   #i-pi-li #i   #o   #i   #u-li-əm #i

#u-li-əm #i   #u-li-əm #i   #o   #i   #u-li-əm #i   #u-li-əm #i

#u-li-əm #i   #o

Written exercises

1.   Write the symbol and technical name for the sound depicted in this face diagram.

[   ] _____

_____

2.   Draw face diagrams and give technical names for these sounds.

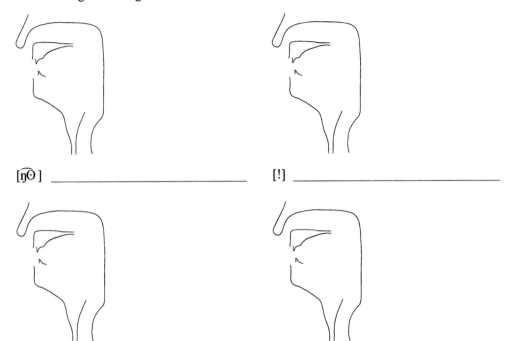

[ŋʘ] _____   [!] _____

[ɡǀ] _____   [ǂ] _____

Transcription conversion exercise

Rewrite each of the following, using only IPA symbols.

[ɑnˁɑ] _____

[itˁke] _____

[upˁʔo] _____

[lɑpˁku̥] _____

37

Palatography

Goals

⌘ You will be able to explain the purpose of *palatography* and what kinds of sounds can be investigated by means of this technique.

⌘ You will be able to choose a *test word* to facilitate research of an appropriate segment.

⌘ You will be able to make a *palatogram* and a *linguogram*.

⌘ You will become aware of reference materials concerning other procedures and equipment for doing experimental phonetics.

It is sometimes difficult to determine exactly what articulators and places of articulation are involved in the production of certain speech sounds. PALATOGRAPHY[87] is a technique for identifying the points of contact between the tongue and the roof of the mouth as a sound is articulated. Knowledge of the contact points makes possible deductions concerning probable variations in the shapes of the vocal cavities during an utterance.

Materials needed for field palatography

In order to do field palatography, the following materials are needed:

- olive oil, or any cooking oil
- activated charcoal powder, available from pharmacists, or instant cocoa powder
- inexpensive small, thick paintbrushes
- saucers for mixing oil and powder
- small mirrors, about 2 in. x 4 in. (5 cm x 15 cm), preferably with a narrow plastic frame or tape around it to dull the edges (it will be inserted into the speaker's mouth)
- a camera with close-up lens (optional, needed only if you want a permanent record of your palatogram)
- a removable artificial palate to fit into the mouth of the language speaker (optional)

Procedure for palatography

Step one: Choose a language speaker who has a sense of humor and is willing to try new things. Children, perhaps from ten to teenage, often work out well for making palatograms, as long as they are old enough to

---

[87]Most of the material in this chapter is drawn from Ladefoged 2003 and Cowan (no date).

pronounce words in an adult fashion. Adults are best but they may be more inhibited about trying what looks like a very weird procedure. Be sure to review all the steps with your language speaker before beginning the procedure, so he[88] can feel comfortable, knowing what will happen. It helps to demonstrate palatography using your own mouth before asking him to do it. He can thus see how simple and harmless a procedure it is. Be careful not to do anything that is culturally inappropriate around the mouth and head.

Step two: Determine what *one segment* you want to study by means of palatography. The segment of study needs to involve the tongue touching the roof of the mouth. Choose a natural word containing the segment, for example, [ʃɪp]. Be sure, however, that the test segment is the only segment in the word involving the tongue touching the teeth or the roof of the mouth. If such a word cannot be found, simply insert the segment into a vowel frame, for example, [aʃa]. The chosen word or frame is called the TEST WORD. It is vital that the language speaker know what test word to say before you go on to the next steps. If he needs to ask questions after step six, the experiment will be ruined, and you will need to start over.

Step three: In a saucer make a mixture of equal parts oil and powder. This mixture can stain clothes so drape some cloth around the speaker's neck to protect his clothing. Tell the language speaker what the black powder is, and that it is not harmful. If he wants to taste it, be sure he rinses his mouth with lemon water before you begin the actual test. Also, if you want to do palatography with more than one speaker, you should use different saucers, brushes, and mirrors for each speaker.

Step four: If photos are to be made, write the test word clearly in large print and place it where it will appear in the photo. Be sure your camera is properly focused and ready to take the picture without delay for adjustment. Aim it directly at the speaker's mouth along a line parallel to the plane of the teeth, as best as this can be determined.

Step five: Seat the language speaker so he is comfortable, with his head erect. Practice inserting the mirror into the speaker's mouth with the edge behind the upper back teeth. Then instruct the speaker to moisten his upper teeth and the entire roof of his mouth with saliva. He should swallow any extra saliva, as he cannot swallow from the time you start step six until you are finished. If an artificial palate is to be used, ask the speaker to insert it into his mouth and moisten it with his saliva.

Step six: Paint the oil / powder mixture onto the front half of the tongue. It is better to cover too much of the tongue than too little since you cannot be sure exactly which part will be used. Depending on the sound to be investigated, you may need to paint the top, sides, tip, blade, and even the underside of the tongue. From this point on, the language speaker must not swallow or say anything except the test word.

Step seven: Have him say the test word as naturally as possible, and then leave his mouth open.

Step eight: Ask the speaker to tilt his head back and open his mouth wide. Insert the mirror behind the top back teeth at a 45° angle so that the camera gets a picture of the roof of the mouth. This picture is called a PALATOGRAM. A flashlight can be used to avoid shadows while photographing in the mouth. The black mixture will have transferred to those parts of the palate with which the tongue came in contact, thus identifying the passive articulator. If an artificial palate has been used, this step is much simpler; the artificial palate can simply be removed and looked at and photographed outside of the speaker's mouth. The speaker may then speak, swallow, and rinse out his mouth.

Step nine: Palatograms focus on the passive articulator (part of the palate) of a segment. If, instead or in addition, you need to identify what active articulator (part of the tongue) is involved, you can reverse the above process by painting the roof of the mouth with the oil mixture. After saying the test word, the speaker can carefully rest his tongue on his lower teeth for a photograph called a LINGUOGRAM which shows the active articulator, now blackened where it came in contact with the painted palate.

Step ten: When you have carefully examined (and optionally photographed) all articulators, your palatography is finished. Finish up by carefully sterilizing all objects that might be used again.

---

[88]We refer to the speaker as "he" here for simplicity, but of course it could just as well be a woman.

Miscellaneous comments about palatography

The most satisfactory use of palatography is in the detailed study of the articulation of a single speaker. For example, by means of several palatograms and linguograms, you may want to compare one speaker's articulation of several similar segments or one speaker's articulation of the same segment in several different contexts. However, we do not recommend comparison of different speakers' articulations as this poses problems. Unfortunately, palatograms and linguograms of different speakers' production of the "same" sound can look quite different and palatograms of different speakers' production of "different" sounds can look quite similar. So, stick to one speaker as you do palatography.

A limitation of palatography is that it is two-dimensional and does not give an adequate impression of the depth of the palate, nor of the shape of the tongue at the time of contact. You can compensate for this by making a cast of the palate and drawing contour lines that can be correlated with photographs, and by painting the center of the tongue with a thin line of barium sulfate and taking x-ray photographs.

Many techniques are available for articulatory phonetics research besides palatography. We have chosen palatography for presentation in this book because it involves equipment that is easily portable to remote locations and does not necessitate electrical power. You may prefer to do acoustic research rather than articulatory research, in which case you would most likely use equipment such as Speech Analyzer.[89] See Ladefoged (1975 and 1982) and Johnson (1997) for fuller information concerning research procedures for acoustic phonetics. See Hardcastle and Laver (1999) for several excellent articles explaining various procedures and equipment to use in other kinds of experimental phonetics.

Key concepts

palatography / palatogram
test word
linguogram

Exercises

1. Evaluate each of the following utterances as a potential test word for palatography. If it would be a good choice, write "yes." If it would not be a good choice, write "no" and explain why not.

   [saʃa] _____

   [mila] _____

   [tʰ] _____

   [bufo] _____

   [iʒi] _____

2. Make palatograms and/or linguograms of segments of interest to you, being careful to choose appropriate test words.

---

[89]Speech Analyzer is available through SIL at www.ethnologue.com. We recommend that instructors using this book devote at least one class session to demonstrating Speech Analyzer or similar software available for phonetic research.

38

Miscellaneous Final Details

Goals

⌘ You will be able to explain what it means to *listen for contrast,* and you will be able to do so selectively and systematically.

⌘ You will be able to process (repeat and transcribe) utterances of longer than 3–4 syllables in an accurate fashion, using techniques for building up long utterances out of shorter, already-familiar data.

⌘ You will be able to fit some sounds not taught in this book into the existing tables of sounds and to propose reasonable ways of symbolizing them. You will also be able to make up technical names and figure out articulators and symbolizations for sounds that do not fit into the existing tables.

⌘ You will be able to explain why any phonetic transcription is simply a hypothesis and therefore subject to considerable revision

Congratulations on making it through a difficult course! We have presented you with a fairly comprehensive inventory of sounds and modifications of sounds. In this chapter we present some miscellaneous details that do not fit neatly into the other chapters and also a few items of advice that we think will be helpful to you as you undertake phonetic transcription in languages you have not previously studied.

Listening for contrast

Listening effectively for contrast involves more than just trying to pick out which segments of the vast inventory of sounds the vocal tract is capable of producing are actually used in your language of study. Several other major facts affect your listening.

- Sounds fall into categories, such that if you find one or two members of a category, it will be worthwhile to listen for others as well. There are often parallels between the inventories of two separate categories.
- Some differences between sounds are more significant than others.
- There can be confusing differences in pronunciation of a word standing alone as opposed to occurring within a context (a phrase or sentence).

Full details of such categories and contrasts are outside the scope of this book, instead belonging in a book on phonology, as they are the basis of most approaches to phonological analysis. For now, we will simply introduce the concept of significance of categories and provide some examples that should facilitate your transcription process.

Categories of sound: The sounds in this book were presented systematically according to the articulatory categories outlined in chapter 1. A basic grasp of the overall system, combined with an awareness of hierarchies of sounds that have been observed cross-linguistically (Greenberg 1966), serves to alert the investigator to the potential presence of as-yet-unencountered sounds within the phonological system of the language under investigation. Consider the voiced-voiceless opposition, for example. If you encounter a voiceless nasal, you will almost certainly also find its voiced counterpart, although the converse is not true. If you encounter voiced stops, expect to find voiceless ones as well. If you find breathy consonants, look for a parallel inventory of voiceless aspirates. The presence of even one click strongly suggests others in the larger phonemic inventory. The same is true of ejectives, and if you encounter implosives, it will probably be useful to search for parallels in the ejective category. See the checklist in figure 38.1 for ideas of general categories to consider in your investigation.

The effect of context on pronunciation: You are used to hearing short words said *in isolation*. The way that words are usually pronounced in this way, outside of any context, is called their CITATION FORM. Unfortunately, what seems to be an important contrast in citation form can be altered by the surrounding words or sounds so that some entirely different kind of contrast is important when words are used in context. Thus, it is important to listen for contrast rather than prejudicing yourself as to what contrast you expect to hear, that is, ask yourself "what is *different* between these two words?" rather than asking "which of these two words has quality x and which one has quality y?"[90]

It may be very helpful to make lists of words that you think share distinct qualities, for example, one list of words with the short vowel [i] and one list of words with the long vowel [iː]. Words that you have mistranscribed according to that criterion in citation form will stand out when read aloud in such a list (by a native speaker) and can then be transferred to the list where they belong. Secondly, you can place all the words in one list in a consistent context and focus on what quality they all share when in that context. Further discussion on the effects of context follow in the section on planning your elicitation sessions to build useful contexts and longer utterances.

Planning elicitation sessions to make transcription easier, more accurate, and more useful

In learning and analyzing languages, we are always concerned about getting data that is natural, that is, the way people would really say something, rather than a word by word translation of some English sentence. For this reason, it is best to ask for a natural sentence about a given topic rather than asking for a word by word translation of the English sentence. For example, try asking for "boy," "tree," and "climb," and then show a picture of a boy climbing a tree and ask what he is doing, rather than asking, "How do you say, 'The boy is climbing the tree'?" The difference is subtle, but the first method will almost certainly give you a natural sentence whereas the second method might yield a stilted translation of the English sentence, perhaps reflecting English word-order rather than that of the language.

So far, you may have transcribed mainly short words or sets of nonsense syllables, rarely containing more than three or four syllables. However, when you start eliciting real language data, you will be dealing with much longer utterances. This section provides you with some hints as to organizing your elicitation so that the data you get falls into familiar contexts and helps you notice significant patterns.
First, *plan* your data collection sessions. Never assume that you can think on your feet fast enough to collect useful data. You will want to request data in an order that will build on vocabulary you have already transcribed. For example, suppose you want to learn how to ask some questions about people's names. Begin by

---

[90]For example, there is a breathy-versus-voiced contrast on vowels in the citation form of words in a certain language of Nepal. However, when those same words are said in a context, the contrast is no longer breathy-versus-voiced but instead takes the following form: the vowel /i/ has two contrastive variants, one of which is "normal" and the other of which is tense, with the larynx raised. Likewise, the vowel /o/ has two variants, but this time the "non-normal" one has the larynx lowered. When the linguists working with this language stopped asking "which vowel is breathy?" and instead asked "what difference can I hear in a minimal pair involving some context?" they were able to sort out the phonetic differences. Likewise, the nature of contrast in Guerrero Náhuatl of Mexico differs depending on context. In isolation, there appears to be a contrast between long and short vowels. However, in context, the contrast is between controlled and ballistic syllables. Such considerations are outside the scope of an articulatory phonetics textbook; we include them here for those who have some interest in and understanding of phonological analysis.

asking for the word for "name," then perhaps "what is his name?" then "baby," "that baby," "what is the baby's name?," "what's that baby's name?" By planning ahead, you have set yourself up to succeed in writing down a fairly long utterance. Incidentally, building up data in this way, using small units whose meaning you know and whose phonetic form you have already written down at least approximately, will be very helpful in language learning and analysis as well as in facilitating accurate data collection. The more you know the language, the easier it is to transcribe its data.

A few words of caution are needed about building data from small units that you have previously transcribed, however. You may recall from the above discussion of listening for contrast that words often change somewhat in their phonetic form, depending on whether they are in isolation or in context. While first transcribing individual vocabulary words before building whole sentences from them is an extremely helpful and strongly recommended procedure, you cannot assume that those familiar words will appear *exactly* as you have transcribed their citation forms when they are used in context. For example, the vowel in the English word "that" changes quality, depending on whether it is in citation form or in context. In citation form, "that" is [ðætʰ], while in context, for example, "he told her that he liked chocolate," it is more typically [ðɪt]. Notice also that in the example sentence just given, the pronunciations of the two instances of "he" differ, the first one probably being [hi] and the second one just [i], and the stop at the end of "that" can become a voiced flap, resulting in "he told her [ðɪɾi] liked chocolate." Such phonetic variation between careful pronunciation of a word in isolation and in quick, casual pronunciation of words in context will be important to note. Both are equally important to make note of, as they will contribute about equally to your phonological analysis.

Here are a few examples of minor phonetic changes in Spanish words, depending on whether the words occur in citation form or in context:

[coṇ]	'with'
[coṇtiᶦjo]	'with you'
[com be]	'with a "b"'
[coŋ carṇe]	'with meat'
[ḷoṣ]	'the (plural, masculine)'
[ḷoṣ aḷtoṣ]	'the heights'
[ḷoṣ ṭreṇeṣ]	'the trains'
[ḷoẕ ðoṣ]	'the two (of them)'

In order for your data to reflect how the language actually works and the most natural pronunciation of those utterances, you must go beyond transcribing a "known" word such as [coṇ] or [ḷoṣ] in citation form and then simply inserting that form into each longer utterance containing the word. That citation form serves as a starting point for transcribing the word easily when it is plugged into longer utterances, but you must still recheck each word when it is used in context, to see whether the context has affected its phonetic form at all.

Such alteration in context is especially prevalent in tones. The following examples from Atatlahuca Mixtec of Mexico (Ruth Mary Alexander) illustrate great variation in the tones on the word meaning "egg," depending on what word precedes it. ([˥] indicates high tone, [˧] mid, [˩] low, and [꜌] extra low tone.)

[ⁿdɨ˧βɨ꜌]	'egg'
[ˈʔɨː˧ ⁿdɨ˧βɨ꜌]	'one egg'
[ˈʔɨ˧ᵑga˧ ⁿdɨ˧βɨ꜌]	'another egg'
[ˈtɑ꜌kɑ˥ ⁿdɨ˧βɨ꜌]	'each egg'
[ˈnu˧u꜌ ⁿdɨ˧βɨ˥]	'to the egg' (for example, add something to the egg)
[ˈʒu˧ku˧ ⁿdɨ˥βɨ˥]	'egg mountain' (place to get eggs)

Again, strict adherence to the transcription of the tones in the citation form of "egg" would have yielded faulty, misleading transcription.

To summarize, it is helpful to build large utterances from familiar, previously transcribed vocabulary. However, it is a mistake to assume that each word will remain phonetically constant, regardless of its context. Always check your transcription of each word, even though some are already at least basically familiar.

Transcription as a hypothesis

Even if you possess superb skills as a phonetician, it is highly unlikely that you will produce completely accurate transcriptions of your language of study, especially in the early months. It is vital to remain aware that *every phonetic transcription is simply a hypothesis* concerning what is occurring in the language. As is the practice in other sciences, you will refine your hypothesis many times, gradually making it more accurate, such that it more closely reflects realities of the sound system in the language. For example, if as your first hypothesis you strictly copy the tones of the citation form of the Mixtec word "egg" into all the various contexts presented in the preceding example, your initial analysis will be inaccurate and will evolve as your transcription becomes more inciteful.

However, even in your early months of transcription, it is important to write down as much as you can. It is far better to get *something* down on paper that is semi-accurate than to get nothing down at all simply because of fear that it will not be completely accurate. You will find that some parts of each utterance will be clear while others are muddy. Just write down the best hypothesis you can make at that time and plan to refine it.

Some preliminary transcription can be done effectively from audio or video tape or CD recordings since it is possible to adjust the playback speed and volume. Video technology is preferable as it provides a view of the speaker's mouth. An advantage of transcribing from recordings rather than from a live speaker is the flexibility of replaying each utterance over and over. As you listen repeatedly to an utterance, you can listen selectively, focusing on one aspect of the language at a time, rather than scrambling to try to hear all likely contrasts simultaneously.[91] However, remember that after transcribing from a "nonlive" source, it helps to verify your transcription in person when you can more clearly see a speaker's mouth.

You may find it helpful to use a checklist like the one provided in figure 38.1 (which is not exhaustive), listening clear through a paragraph or a list of words without transcribing anything at all on your first couple of passes through the recording. As you become aware of certain types of sounds, check off their categories on your list. If you do not find some of them, you can temporarily assume those are not relevant to that language or at least to that sample of the language; however, do not eliminate them as possibilities until you have checked with other people or published works in closely related languages and listened to many varied language samples.

It would be very helpful to become familiar with specific sound categories that are known to occur in the geographical area of your language of study. For example, if you are going to work in India, expect to find retroflexion, breathy consonants, and no tone. If your language of study is in West Africa, expect to find double articulations and tone.

____	nasalized vowels
____	creaky / breathy vowels
____	vowel glides
____	length
____	double articulations
____	aspiration
____	breathy consonants
____	clicks
____	ejectives
____	implosives
____	flaps / trills
____	retroflexion
____	secondary articulations
____	special tongue root placement
____	pharyngeal / epiglottal / glottal consonants

Figure 38.1.
Partial checklist of sound categories.

Dealing with sounds not taught in this book

Although you have encountered a fairly comprehensive inventory of the speech sounds used in the world's languages, a few have been omitted, either because they are very rare (for example, doubly articulated fricatives, Ladefoged and Maddieson 1996:330), or because linguists have not yet discovered them or reported

---

[91]We also introduced this idea in chapter 8, with regard to tracking. Repeated listening to recorded language material is highly effective in many aspects of language learning and linguistic study precisely because this makes you very familiar with the material and allows you to listen with selective focus.

their discovery (for example, flat alveolar fricatives or voiceless alveo-velar nasals). If you happen to uncover such a sound, be sure to let the linguistic world know about it.

Many of the tables in which the symbols for sounds are presented in this book contain empty boxes. Some of these boxes could be filled in (for example, interdental stops or voiceless retroflex alveolar nasal). If you encounter such a sound in a language that you study, it should be a fairly simple matter to figure out what articulators are involved in producing that sound, then make up a symbol and technical name consistent with those already in use for similar related sounds. Other boxes in the tables are empty because sounds that would fill them are either physically impossible to produce (for example, voiced ejectives or breathy glottal stop) or theoretically improbable (such as retroflex bilabials or flapped vowels). You need not worry about what to do about such sounds, as you will never encounter them.

You might encounter a few sounds that do not fit neatly into any of the tables given in the book. For example, Mura-Pirahã of Brazil has an unusual flap sound that begins with a brief bilabial closure followed by a lateral-type flap in which the tongue tip flaps past the center of the top lip and lands on the center of the bottom lip. You would need to make up a symbol and a technical name for it; for example, you might choose to write this flap as [ɺ̃], indicating that it is a lateral flap with the tongue hanging out, and calling it a "voiced interlabial lateral flap." Thus, the word for "milk" in Mura-Pirahã would be transcribed as [ɪʙoɺ̃ɛ] (Keren Everett, personal communication.

Key concepts

listening for contrast
citation form / isolation
in context
categories of sounds / parallel inventories

Written exercises

1. Think of at least two examples of words (or parts of words) in your native language whose phonetic forms change depending on whether they are used in isolation or in context. Write each form of the words in phonetic transcription. If possible, describe what the variation is (for example, vowel quality, voicing, length, etc.).

2. Following the example on page 197 concerning a baby's name, create a list of five utterances that build on each other, both at the beginning and end, starting with four syllables, and increasing to ten or so. Dictate your list to a fellow student.

39

Review Exercises and Tables(II)

Goals

Completing these exercises will facilitate your review of this textbook, especially the second half. These exercises are representative, not exhaustive, samples of the contents of this book. We suggest that you also read through the goals, key terms, and tables of symbols for each chapter.

1. In the following table, list fourteen places of articulation, from front to back in the mouth. Bracket together any places of articulation that involve the same active articulator. After each place of articulation, write at least one symbol representing a sound produced with that place of articulation.

Place of articulation	Symbol(s)

2. Which airstream mechanism(s) can involve an ingressive airstream (as used in real language)?

3.   Which airstream mechanism is always involved in producing voiced sounds?

4.   There are two classes of sounds that involve combinations of airstream mechanisms. Name these two classes, give the airstream mechanisms involved in each, and give at least two phonetic symbols representing sounds in each of these two classes.

5.   In ['ʔak'aɟamaʕ], how many syllables are there?

       What does the little vertical line under the [m] mean?

       What does the [ʔ] mean?

       What does the ['] mean?

       What does the [°] mean?

       What does the [ʕ] mean?

6.   Draw face diagrams for the following sounds.

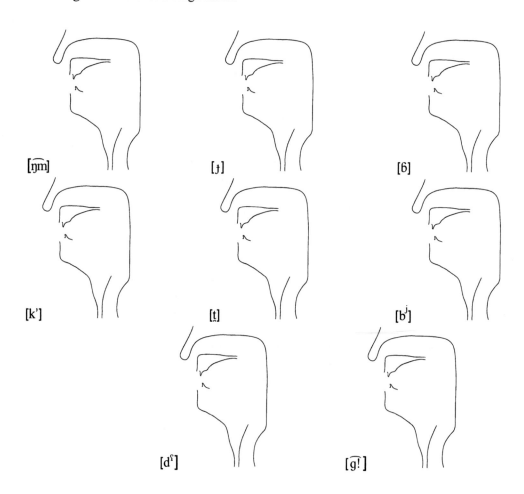

7.   Identify the sounds depicted in the following face diagrams.

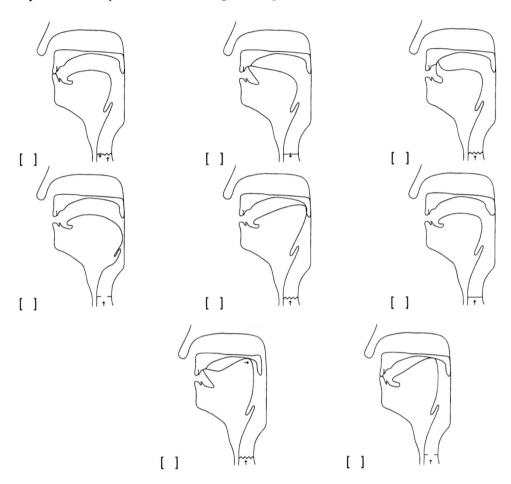

[ ]   [ ]   [ ]

[ ]   [ ]   [ ]

[ ]   [ ]

8.   List at least two likely combinations of speech styles.

9.   List at least two impossible (mutually exclusive) combinations of speech styles.

10. What (if anything) do the segments in each of the following sets of sounds have in common?

[ŋ͜! ŋ͡ʘ ɓ ɠ ɡ͜]

[ɡ k k͡p d͡b ɡ͈ ŋ͡ʘ]

[n͡m õ n̥ m ỹ ŋ͈]

[ɓ p m̥ o y dʷ õ ʃʷ w̥]

[θ ʼ t l̥ n̩ ! tʰ ɽ]

[z ŋ͡ʘ o̥ ḍ pʰ ʒ y ʃ æ̃ r]

11. Match each of the following terms with a symbol representing it. Write the number of the word beside the phonetic representation.

1	palatalized	[tʰ]
2	labial-palatalized	[tʷ]
3	velarized	[ⁿd]
4	labial-velarized	[ɖ̢]
5	labialized	[k͡p]
6	pharyngealized	[tᶣ]
7	prenasalized	[dˀ]
8	nasalized	[ẽ]
9	double articulation	[oṷ]
10	creaky	[e̜]
11	breathy vowel	[pʰtʰkʰ]
12	breathy consonant	[tˠ]
13	unreleased	[e̥]
14	aspirated	[ptk]
15	close transition	[g̊]
16	open transition	[b̥]
17	retroflexed	[kʲ]
18	glide	[g̰]
19	advanced tongue root	[e̩]
20	retracted tongue root	[e̙]
21	fortis	[tˤ]
22	lenis	[tᵥ]

12. Give the technical name for each of the following symbols.

[tɬ’]

[ɰ̢]

[cç]

[ɖ̢]

[nʷ]

[n͡m]

[e̞]

[pʲ]

13. What do palatograms and linguograms show, and why might they be useful?

14. Fill in a symbol representing a sound arrived at by making *only* the stated change. (Do not make any other changes in addition.)

Example: [t] becomes [d] by the addition of voicing.

[y]   becomes [   ] by changing the shape of the lips.

[z]   becomes [   ] by turning the tip of the tongue backward.

[k']   becomes [   ] by changing the direction of the airstream.

[l]   becomes [   ] by raising the tongue sides to complete closure.

[m]   becomes [   ] by adding velic closure.

[e]   becomes [   ] by partially opening the glottis adding breathiness.

[p]   becomes [   ] by raising the back of the tongue to closure at the velum.

[x]   becomes [   ] by increasing the amount of impedance of the airstream.

[g͡ʘ]   becomes [   ] by changing the airstream mechanism used.

[g]   becomes [   ] by releasing the stop into a fricative.

[s]   becomes [   ] by the addition of rounded lips.

[ʀ]   becomes [   ] by removing voicing.

[tʰ]   becomes [   ] by shifting the tongue tip forward toward the teeth.

15. Give symbols for any four sounds with the following articulatory qualifications.

[   ] [   ] [   ] [   ] voiced fricative

[   ] [   ] [   ] [   ] voiceless stop

[   ] [   ] [   ] [   ] central approximant

[   ] [   ] [   ] [   ] homorganic affricate

[   ] [   ] [   ] [   ] tongue back in closure at the velum

[   ] [   ] [   ] [   ] tongue tip curled back

[   ] [   ] [   ] [   ] tongue sides curled upward, resulting in a grooved articulator

[   ] [   ] [   ] [   ] back vowel

[   ] [   ] [   ] [   ] lip rounding added to a consonant

[   ] [   ] [   ] [   ] ingressive airstream

[   ] [   ] [   ] [   ] two airstream mechanisms used simultaneously

[   ] [   ] [   ] [   ] vowel with vocal folds apart and not vibrating

[   ] [   ] [   ] [   ] articulator in rapid, uncontrolled vibration in a moving airstream

[   ] [   ] [   ] [   ] tongue root toward back wall of pharynx

[   ] [   ] [   ] [   ] secondary articulation

[   ] [   ] [   ] [   ] double articulations

Table 39.1. Cumulative table of pulmonic consonants, chapters 1–38

	Bilabial	Labiodental	(Inter)dental	Dental	Alveolar	Retroflex alveolar	Fronted palato-alveolar	Palato-alveolar	Retroflex palato-alveolar	Palatal	Velar	Uvular	Pharyngeal	Epiglottal	Glottal	
vl.	pʰ			t̪ʰ	tʰ	ʈʰ		t̠ʰ		cʰ	kʰ	qʰ				aspirated
vl.	p			t̪	t	ʈ		t̠		c	k	q		ʡ	ʔ	stop
vd.	b			d̪	d	ɖ		d̠		ɟ	g	ɢ				
breathy	b̤			d̤	d̤	ɖ̤					g̈					
vl.	ɸ	f	θ							ç	x	χ	ħ	ʜ	h	fricative
vd.	β	v	ð							ʝ	ɣ	ʁ	ʕ	ʢ		
vl.				s̪	s	ʂ	ʃ̟	ʃ	ʃ̢							sibilant
vd.				z̪	z	ʐ	ʒ̟	ʒ	ʒ̢							
vl.					ɬ											lateral fricative
vd.					ɮ											
vl.					l̥						ʟ̥					lateral approx.
vd.				l̪	l	ɭ		l̠		ʎ	ʟ					
vl.	pɸ	pf	tθ							cç	kx	qχ				affricate
vd.	bβ	bv	dð							ɟʝ	gɣ	ɢʁ				
vl.				t̪sʰ	tsʰ	ʈʂʰ	tʃ̟ʰ	tʃʰ	ʈʃ̢ʰ							aspirated
vl.				t̪s	ts	ʈʂ	tʃ̟	tʃ	ʈʃ							affricate
vd.				d̪z	dz	ɖʐ	dʒ̟	dʒ	ɖʒ							
breathy								dʒ̤	ɖʒ̤							
vl.					tɬʰ						kʟ̥					aspirated
vl.					tɬ						gʟ					lateral affricate
vd.					dl											
vl.	m̥				n̥			ñ̥ / n̥̠			ŋ̊					nasal
vd.	m	ɱ		n̪	n	ɳ		ñ / n̠		ɲ	ŋ	ɴ				
					ɹ	ɻ										approximant
vl.		f̌			ɾ̥	ɽ̥										flap
vd.	b̆	ⱱ			ɾ	ɽ										
vd.	m̆				n̆	ṇ̆										nasal flap
vd.					ɺ	ɺ̢										lateral flap
vl.	ʙ̥			r̥	r̥							ʀ̥				trill
vd.	ʙ			r̪	r							ʀ				

Table 39.2. Cumulative table of consonants involving nonpulmonic air mechanisms, chapters 25 (ejectives), 28 (implosives) and 36 (clicks)

	Bilabial	Labiodental	Dental	Alveolar	Retroflex (alveolar)	Palato-alveolar	Palatal	Velar	Uvular	
	p'			t'	ʈ'		c'	k'	q'	ejective stop
		f'	θ'	s'		ʃ'	ç'	x'	χ'	ejective fricative
(vl.)		pf'	tθ'	ts'	ʈʂ'	tʃ'	cç'	kx'	qχ'	ejective affricate
				ɬ'						ejective lateral fricative
				tɬ'						ejective lateral affricate
vl.	ɓ̥			ɗ̥				ɠ̊	ʛ̥	implosive stop
vd.	ɓ			ɗ			ʄ	ɠ	ʛ	
vd.						d͡ʒ				implosive affricate
vl.	ʘ		ǀ	!	ǃ	ǂ				click
vd.	g͡ʘ		g͡ǀ	g͡!	g͡ǃ	g͡ǂ				
vd.	ŋ͡ʘ		ŋ͡ǀ	ŋ͡!	ŋ͡ǃ	ŋ͡ǂ				nasal click
vl.				ǁ						lateral click
vd.				g͡ǁ						
vd.				ŋ͡ǁ						nasal lateral click

Table 39.3. Consonants involving double articulations

	Labial-alveolar	Labial-velar	
voiceless	t͡p	k͡p	stop
voiced	d͡b	g͡b	
voiced	n͡m	ŋ͡m	nasal
voiceless		k͡ɓ̥	implosive
voiced	d͡ɓ	g͡ɓ	

Table 39.4. Vowels

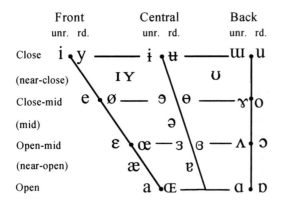

Table 39.5. Modifications of vowels

nasalized	ẽ
voiceless	e̥
breathy	e̤
creaky	ḛ
length added	eˑ or eː
advanced (fronted)	e̟
retracted (backed)	e̠
raised	e̝
lowered	e̞
with advanced tongue root (+ATR)	e̘
with retracted tongue root (−ATR)	e̙

Table 39.6. Central approximants (nonsyllabic vowels)

	Labiodental	Alveolar	Retroflex alveolar	Palatal	Labial-palatal	Labial-velar	Velar	
vl.	ʋ̥	ɹ̥		j̊	ɥ̊	ẘ	ɰ̊	approximant
vd.	ʋ	ɹ	ɻ	j	ɥ	w	ɰ	

References

Beach, D. M. 1938. *The phonetics of the Hottentot language.* Cambridge: Cambridge University Press.

Cahill, Michael. 1996. ATR harmony in Kɔnni. In David Dowty and Rebecca Herman, and others (eds.), *Papers in phonology*, 13–30. Ohio State Working Papers in Linguistics 48. Columbus: Ohio State University.

Cahill, Michael. 1999. *Aspects of the morphology and phonology of Konni.* Ph.D. dissertation, Ohio State University.

Catford, J. C. 1977. *Fundamental problems in phonetics.* Edinburgh: Edinburgh University Press.

Cowan, George. no date. Unpublished review of Ladefoged 1957.

Crystal, David. 2003. *A dictionary of linguistics and phonetics*, 5th edition. Oxford: Blackwell Publishing.

Delattre, Pierre C., Alvin M. Lieberman, and Franklin Cooper. 1955. Acoustic loci and transitional cues for consonants. Republished in Ilse Lehiste (ed.), *Readings in acoustic phonetics,* 283–287.

Denes, Peter B., and Elliot N. Pinson. 1993. *The speech chain: The physics and biology of spoken language.* 2nd ed. New York: W. H. Freeman and Company.

Dixon, R. M. W. 1980. *The languages of Australia.* Cambridge: Cambridge University Press.

Doke, C. M. 1926. *The phonetics of Zulu.* Witwatersrand.

Floyd, Rick, compiler. 1981. *A manual for articulatory phonetics.* Dallas: Summer Institute of Linguistics.

Floyd, Rick, compiler. 1986. *A manual for articulatory phonetics.* 2nd revised edition. Dallas: Summer Institute of Linguistics.

Greenberg, Joseph H., ed. 1966. *Universals of language,* 2nd edition. Cambridge, Mass.: MIT Press.

Gregerson, Kenneth J. 1976. Tongue-root and register in Mon-Khmer. *Oceanic Linguistics Special Publications* 13:323–369.

Handbook of the International Phonetic Association: A guide to the use of the International Phonetic Alphabet. 1999. Cambridge: Cambridge University Press.

Hardcastle, William J., and John Laver. 1999. *The handbook of phonetic sciences.* Oxford: Blackwell Publishers.

Hoffmann, Carl. 1963. *A grammar of the Margi language.* London: International African Institute, Oxford University Press.

International Phonetic Association. 2005. Approval of the new IPA sound: The labiodental flap. *Journal of the International Phonetic Association* 25(2):261.

Jacobson, Leon. 1977. Phonetic aspects of DhoLuo vowels. *Studies in African Linguistics*, Supp. 7:127–155.

Jockers, Heinz. 1991. *Studien zur Sprecht der Tiv in Nigeria.* Europäische Hochschulshriften Reihe XXI, Series Linguistic BD 94. Frankfurt am Main.

Johnson, Keith. 1997. *Acoustic and auditory phonetics.* Cambridge, Mass.: Blackwell Publishing.

Jones, Daniel. 1962. *An outline of English phonetics,* 9th edition. Cambridge: Heffer.

Kagaya, Ryohei. 1974. A fibroscopic and acoustic study of the Korean stops, affricates and fricatives. *Journal of Phonetics* 2:161–180.

Kaiser, L., ed. 1957. *Manual of phonetics*. Amsterdam: North Holland.

Kinkade, M. Dale. 1967. Uvular-pharyngeal resonants in Interior Salish. *International Journal of American Linguistics* 33:228–234.

Ladefoged, Peter. 1957. Use of palatography. *Journal of Speech and Hearing Disorders* 22:764–774.

Ladefoged, Peter. 1968. A *phonetic study of West African languages*. Cambridge: Cambridge University Press.

Ladefoged, Peter. 1971. *Preliminaries to linguistic phonetics*. Chicago: University of Chicago Press.

Ladefoged, Peter. 1972. The three glottal features. *Working Papers in Phonetics* 22:95–101.

Ladefoged, Peter. 1976. The phonetic specification of the languages of the world. *Working Papers in Phonetics* 31.

Ladefoged, Peter. 1982. *A course in phonetics,* 2rd edition. New York: Harcourt Brace Jovanovich.

Ladefoged, Peter. 1993. *A course in phonetics,* 3rd edition. New York: Harcourt Brace Jovanovich.

Ladefoged, Peter. 1996. *Elements of acoustic phonetics,* 2nd edition. Chicago: University of Chicago Press.

Ladefoged, Peter. 2001. *Vowels and consonants: An introduction to the sounds of language.* Malden, Mass.: Blackwell Publishers.

Ladefoged, Peter. 2003. *Phonetic data analysis: An introduction to fieldwork and instrumental techniques.* Malden, Mass.: Blackwell Publishers.

Ladefoged, Peter, Anne Cochran, and Sandra Disner. 1977. Laterals and trills. *Journal of the International Phonetic Association* 7:46–54.

Ladefoged, Peter, Joseph DeClerk, Mona Lindau, and George Papçun. 1972. An auditory-motor theory of speech production. *Working Papers in Phonetics* 22:48–75.

Ladefoged, Peter, and Ian Maddieson. 1996. *The sounds of the world's languages.* Oxford: Blackwell Publishers.

Laufer, Asher, and I. D. Condax. 1979. The epiglottis as an articulator. *Journal of the International Phonetics Association* 9:50–56.

Laver, John. 1994. *Principles of phonetics.* Cambridge: Cambridge University Press.

Lehiste, Ilse, ed. 1967. *Readings in acoustic phonetics.* Cambridge, Mass.: MIT Press.

Lehiste, Ilse. 1970. *Suprasegmentals.* Cambridge, Mass.: MIT Press.

Lehiste, Ilse, and Gordon E. Peterson. 1959. "Transition, glides and diphthongs." Republished in Ilse Lehiste (ed.), *Readings in acoustic phonetics,* 228–237.

Li, Fang Kuei. 1948. The distribution of initials and tones in the Sui language. *Language* 24:160–167.

Lindau, Mona. 1975. Features for vowels. *Working Papers in Phonetics* 30.

McKinney, Carol, and Norris McKinney. 1978. Instrumental phonetics: An aid with orthography problems. *Notes on Literacy* 23:15–16.

McKinney, Norris P. 1984. The fortis feature in Jju (Kaje): An initial study. *Studies in African Linguistics* 15:177–188.

McKinney, Norris P. 1990. Temporal characteristics of fortis stops and affricates in Tyap and Jju. *Journal of Phonetics* 18:255–266.

Merrifield, William. 1963. Palantla Chinantec syllable types. *Anthropological Linguistics* 5(5):1–16.

Nemoy, Elizabeth, and Serena Foley Davis. 1937. *The correction of defective consonant sounds.* Boston: Expression Co.

O'Connor, J. D. 1973. *Phonetics.* Harmondsworth, England: Penguin Books.

Olson, Kenneth S., and John Hajek. 2003. Crosslinguistic insights on the labial flap. *Linguistic Typology* 7:157–186.

Peterson, Gordon. 1957. Laryngeal vibrations. In L. Kaiser (ed.), *Manual of phonetics*, 149–155.

Pike, Eunice V. 1974. A multiple stress system versus a tone system. *International Journal of American Linguistics* 40:169–175.

Pike, Eunice V. 1978. *Dictation exercises in phonetics,* 3rd printing. Huntington Beach, Calif.: Summer Institute of Linguistics.

Pike, Kenneth L. 1942. *An intensive course in English for Latin-American students, I: Pronunciation.* Ann Arbor: University of Michigan.

Pike, Kenneth L. 1943. *Phonetics: A critical analysis of phonetic theory and a technic for the practical description of sounds.* Ann Arbor: University of Michigan Press.

Pike, Kenneth L. 1947. *Phonemics.* Ann Arbor: University of Michigan Press.

Pike, Kenneth L. 1948. *Tone languages.* Ann Arbor: University of Michigan Press.

Pike, Kenneth L. 1953. Intonational analysis of a Rumanian sentence. *Cahiers Sextil Puscariu* 2:59–60.

Pike, Kenneth L. 1967. Tongue-root position in practical phonetics. *Phonetica* 17:129–140.

Pike, Kenneth L., Ralph P. Barret, and Burt Bascom. 1959. Instrumental collaboration on a Tepehuan (Uto-Aztecan) pitch problem. *Phonetica* 3:1–22.

Pullum, Geoffrey K., and William A. Ladusaw. 1996. *Phonetic symbol guide*, 2nd edition. Chicago: University of Chicago Press.

Skinner, Leo. 1962. Usila Chinantec syllable structure. *International Journal of American Linguistics* 28:251–255.

Smalley, William A. 1973. *Manual of articulatory phonetics*, rev. ed. Pasadena, Calif.: William Carey Library.

Stockwell, Robert, and J. Donald Bowen. 1965. *The sounds of English and Spanish.* Chicago: University of Chicago Press.

Tucker, A. N. 1940. *The Eastern Sudanic languages*, 1. London: Oxford University Press.

Tucker, A. N., and M. A. Bryan. 1956. *The non-Bantu languages of North-Eastern Africa.* Handbook of African Languages, Part III. London: International African Institute, Oxford University Press.

Tucker, A. N., and M. A. Bryan. 1966. *Linguistic analyses: The non-Bantu languages of North-Eastern Africa.* London: International African Institute, Oxford University Press.

Unpublished lesson plans from the courses in articulatory phonetics as taught by the Summer Institute of Linguistics.

Westermann, D., and I. C. Ward. 1933. *Practical phonetics for students of African languages.* London: Oxford University Press.

Index of Languages

Subject Index

ERRATA TO TEXT

Bickford, Anita C. 2006. Articulatory phonetics: Tools for analyzing the world's languages. 4ᵗʰ ed. Dallas: SIL International.

pg	item
6	Tbl. 1.2: number 6 – change "palato-alveolar" to "postalveolar"
	NOTE: Make the change of "palato-alveolar" to "postalveolar" throughout the book, in text, tables and figures. Subsequent instances will not be included on this list of errata.
6	Tbl. 1.2: number 10 – change Passive Articulator to "back of pharyngeal wall"
6	Tbl. 1.2: insert new number 11 – POA "epiglottal" AA "epiglottis" PA "back of pharyngeal wall"
6	Tbl. 1.2: number 11 "glottal" – change to number 12
6	Tbl. 1.3: add entry – AA "epiglottis" POA "epiglottal"
36	Fig. 5.7: move [ɒ] from unrounded to rounded column (see Fig. 7.2, p. 50)
65	Tbl. 10.1: correct symbols in "Contours" column: the symbol for "low" should be [a̖] and the symbol for "extra low" should be [a̠] (but with more space between the "a" and the "_".
82	add colon ":" to end of last sentence on page.
106	Qn. 13, last item: change "mid open" to "open-mid".
108	Fig. 19.2: for "length" add " or ĕ "
121	second entry for "dead dog" should read "[dɛdᵊˈdɔg]"
129	Goals, second bullet: change "palato-alveolar" to "postalveolar" (three places); <u>do not change in third bullet</u>; change in text (six places)
131	Tbl. 24.1: Add symbols with underbox in Fronted postalveolar column, e.g., [t̪ʰ], etc.
159	Arabic wordlist, last item should be [ʕɑlɑ].
203	qn. 10: second set, [d͡b] should be [g͡b].
203	qn. 10, next to last set, apostrophe should be [ǁ] „vl. alveolar lateral click'.
206	Tbl. 39.1: correct symbol for „vl. alveolar lateral approximant' is [l̥].
206	Tbl. 39.1: Add symbols with underbox in Fronted postalveolar column, e.g., [t̪ʰ], etc.

9 781556 711657